A Winter's Snake

A WINTER'S SNAKE

Dramatic Form in the
Tragedies of
JOHN WEBSTER

CHRISTINA LUCKYJ

The University of Georgia Press
Athens and London

© 1989 by the University of Georgia Press
Athens, Georgia 30602
All rights reserved
Designed by Debby Jay
Set in Linotron Janson
The paper in this book meets the guidelines for permanence and
durability of the Committee on Production Guidelines for Book
Longevity of the Council on Library Resources.

Printed in the United States of America
93 92 91 90 89   5 4 3 2 1
Library of Congress Cataloging in Publication Data

Luckyj, Christina, 1956–
    A winter's snake: dramatic form in the tragedies of John Webster /
    Christina Luckyj.
        p.   cm.
    Bibliography: p.
    Includes index.
    ISBN 0-8203-1144-8 (alk. paper)
        1. Webster, John, 1580?–1625?—Technique. 2. Tragedy. I. Title.
PR3188.I4L83   1989
822'.3—dc19   88-38689
                                                                CIP

British Library Cataloging in Publication Data available

For George and Moira Luckyj

to aspire some mountain's top,
The way ascends not straight, but imitates
The subtle foldings of a winter's snake
The White Devil I.ii.350–52

CONTENTS

~~~~~~

Preface   xi

Introduction: WEBSTER AND THE ART OF
                        REPETITION   xiii

Chapter One: WINDING AND INDIRECT:
                   Nonlinear Development   1

Chapter Two: AN EXCELLENT PICTURE-MAKER:
                   Opening Parallels and Contrasts   29

Chapter Three: WOMEN OF PLEASURE AND MEN
                        OF CONSCIENCE:
                   Subplots and Final Acts   51

Chapter Four: CONCENTRIC DESIGN   105

Conclusion   148

Notes   155

Works Cited   165

Index   177

PREFACE

THE image of "a winter's snake" in Flamineo's soliloquy at the end of the first act of *The White Devil* suggestively captures important qualities of Webster's drama. Like a snake, his drama "runneth and glideth and wrigleth with wrinkles, corcels and draughts of the body" (John Russell Brown 3 1n); it moves with muscular energy, not in simple forward thrust, but in rhythmic, repetitive undulation. Like "a winter's snake" that "putteth out himselfe in cold" (John Russell Brown 3 1n), Webster seems to invite exclusion from the company of other Renaissance playwrights because of his resistance to conventional formal analysis. This study is an attempt to restore him to that company by illuminating his reliance on inherited dramatic strategies such as repetition. By focusing attention on Webster's two great plays, I hope to highlight the unique brilliance of his tragic vision by examining its careful formal articulation.

I have relied on John Russell Brown's editions of *The White Devil* and *The Duchess of Malfi* as the most accessible and authoritative currently available, although I have retained Q's spelling of "Brachiano." Full references for theatrical reviews mentioned in the text are given in a special section in the list of Works Cited. Where no acknowledgment is made of promptbook sources, I have relied on my own impressions of productions I was able to see: the 1983 York Graduate Theatre Company *White Devil* and the 1985 National Theatre *Duchess of Malfi*.

I am grateful to the Social Sciences and Humanities Research Council of Canada for doctoral fellowships which allowed me to write this book. My thanks are also due to the Associates of the University of Toronto for a travel grant which enabled me to research the stage history of Webster's plays in England. An Izaak

Preface

Walton Killam Postdoctoral Fellowship at Dalhousie University permitted some final touches. For giving me generous access to prompt-books and theatrical reviews in their possession, I am grateful to the publicity managers of the Greenwich, Royal Exchange, and National theatres, as well as to the librarians at the Victoria and Albert Theatre Museum, the Nuffield Library of the Shakespeare Birthplace Trust, and the Stratford, Ontario, archives. I thank David Carnegie for helping me to locate stage history materials.

The second part of chapter 3 is a revised version of an essay which first appeared in *Studies in English Literature, 1500–1900* 27 (1987) as "'Great Women of Pleasure': Main Plot and Subplot in *The Duchess of Malfi*." I am grateful for permission to use this material.

For inspiration in writing this book, I must first thank the critics mentioned in it, all of whose notions about Webster and about Shakespeare stimulated and shaped my own. I must also thank the many theatre reviewers on whose sensitivity and experience I so often relied for guidance. I owe more immediate gratitude to those with whom I discussed my work in detail. In offering criticism, Jill Levenson was enthusiastic and scrupulous, and Charles Forker rigorous and thorough; to both I am grateful. Sandy Leggatt introduced me to Webster, encouraged me and shared many fine insights with me. My greatest debt is to Sheldon Zitner, my thesis supervisor, whose influence on this study is profound and incalculable. Whatever strengths it possesses are due to his patient direction; its weaknesses I acknowledge mine. My parents, George and Moira Luckyj, have supported me in every way possible. And to my husband, Keith Lawson, and my daughter, Julia Lawson, I owe all love and gratitude.

INTRODUCTION

〰〰〰〰〰〰〰〰〰〰〰〰〰〰〰〰〰〰〰〰〰〰〰

WEBSTER AND THE ART OF REPETITION

〰〰〰〰〰〰〰〰〰〰〰〰〰〰〰〰〰〰〰〰〰〰〰

REPETITION is a universal principle of art, a way in which a work announces that it has form. Repetition appeals to the "innate forms of the mind," writes Kenneth Burke, to our "feeling for such arrangements of subject-matter as produce crescendo, contrast, comparison, balance, repetition, disclosure, reversal, contraction, expansion, magnification, series, and so on" (46). For I. A. Richards, "rhythm and its specialised form, metre, depend upon repetition, and expectancy" (134); for E. M. Forster "rhythm" in fiction is "repetition plus variation" (148–49). The organization of parts into an organic whole, the "rhythm" of a work, is based on repetition. Suzanne Langer extends the implications of aesthetic repetition through a discussion of the function of repetition in music: "Repetition is another structural principle—deeply involved with rhythm, as all basic principles are with each other—that gives musical composition the appearance of vital growth. For what we receive, in the passage of sound, with a sense of recognition, i.e. as a recurrence, is oftentimes a fairly free variant of what came before, a mere analogy, and only logically a repetition; but it is just the sort of play on a basic pattern, especially the reflection of the over-all plan in the structure of each part, that is characteristic of organic forms" (129). Later, Langer asserts that her discussion of rhythm in music "may be applied without distortion or strain to the organization of elements in any play that achieves 'living' form" (355). It is clear that all literary artists, like all musicians, rely on the principle of repetition to give their works rhythmic form and organic unity.

For Renaissance rhetoric the principle of repetition was particularly important. In *The Arte of English Poesie* (1589), George Puttenham praises it: "And first of all others your figure that worketh by iteration or repetition of one word or clause doth much alter and affect the eare and also the mynde of the hearer, and therefore is counted a very brave figure both with the Poets and rhetoriciens" (198). Erasmus's popular text in rhetoric, *De duplici copia verborum et rerum* (1511) set out to teach every student "to vary a theme by constant practice: first once, then twice, then thrice, then oftener, until finally he can vary it a hundred or even two hundred times" (Doran 48). The Renaissance love of copiousness and variety often amounted, in literature, to saying the same thing in as many different ways as possible. Madeleine Doran points out, "When we know that writers had such training [in rhetoric], we should not wonder at the punning changes played on words, at the constant synonymous variation of phrases, at the heaping up of detail, at the multiplication of epithets, at the elaborateness of descriptive pictures, at the fondness for figures of iteration, of analysis, of analogy or illustration, or any feast of languages to which we may be treated" (49). The Renaissance ideal of eloquence, expressed in a preference for figures of amplification such as repetition, allowed a point to be made in several different ways not only for delight but also for emphasis. Puttenham remarks, "For like as one or two drops of water pierce not the flint stone, but many and often droppings do: so cannot a few words (be they never so pithy or sententious) in all cases and to all manner of minds, make so deep an impression, as a more multitude of words discreetly and without superfluity uttered" (197). "Sometimes wordes twice spoken, make the matter appeare greater," wrote Thomas Wilson in 1560 in *The Arte of Rhetorique* (114). For both these critics, the repetition and variation of material are intended for more than mere ornamentation, just as the study of rhetoric is intended for more than the simple pleasures of verbosity. Rhetoric is designed for persuasion, and repetition is for emphasis, intensification, and comparison. All these can contribute to the excellence of a work of art.

Renaissance drama owes much to the interest in rhetoric. Doran points out, "English renaissance drama is rhetorical from first to last. . . . Exuberance rather than economy remains characteristic of the plays of Jonson, Chapman, Marston, Webster, and Shakespeare" (51). This exuberance, moreover, manifests itself not only in the language but also in the structure of the plays, which are characterized not by economy or compression but by copiousness and multiplicity. "The English dramatists retained a very large portion of a given story," writes Bernard Beckerman. "They arranged but did not eliminate. In fact, they frequently supplied additional events. . . . This multiplicity of events is a prime characteristic of this drama. To the Lear story Shakespeare adds the tale of Gloucester, to that of Helena and Bertram the story of Parolles" (30). In order to organize these many events, the dramatists used devices such as repetition. They selected events which would mirror or contrast with other events, repeating and varying their material, as did the rhetoricians. Instead of attempting to create a linear, causally connected narrative proceeding logically like a lawyer's brief from point to point, they built a broadly analogical framework for the action. Furthermore, their use of repetition was not only a way of mirroring, and thus connecting, different parts of the play, but also a way of emphasizing and intensifying the development of the tragic action. Mark Rose remarks, "Frequently Shakespeare will give us two or three scenes in close succession designed upon similar patterns in order to produce an effect of intensification through repetition" (72). This kind of strategy moves the drama forward, not through a conventional emphasis on the logical progression of the "story," but through a heightening of its underlying dynamics. Repetition proved a flexible device for English Renaissance dramatists, establishing the analogies, contrasts and emphases so important for their particular kind of dramatic construction.

Until recently, studies of Shakespeare's use of repetition were confined either to patterns of imagery or to situations repeated in different plays.[1] Neither approach is useful in understanding the pattern of events of an individual play. More recent critics have drawn attention to the importance of repetition as a means of effecting thematic and structural connections between different parts of an individual Shakespearean play, and binding them into a unified whole.[2] Because these critics go beyond the primarily verbal aspect of themes and images to explore the dramatic construction of Shakespeare's plays, their studies signal a new direction in Shakespearean criticism.

These new studies of Shakespeare's construction owe much to the recent redefinition of the term as it applies to Shakespeare and his contemporaries. For criticism earlier in this century, and indeed for much of eighteenth- and nineteenth-century criticism, dramatic construction implied only the conventional expectations of cause-effect, linear plot development, typical of classical drama. Recent critics have to some extent succeeded in freeing Elizabethan drama from those expectations, in part by emphasizing the significance of traditional English forms in shaping the drama. Along with Beckerman, Maynard Mack is among the earliest critics to give voice to a dissatisfaction with conventional ways of describing Shakespeare's dramatic construction, and to suggest the influence of a strong native dramatic tradition on Shakespeare's form. After acknowledging the significance of A. C. Bradley's contribution to our understanding of Shakespeare's construction, Mack goes on to say:

> Still, it is impossible not to feel that Bradley missed something—that there is another kind of construction in Shakespeare's tragedies than the one he designates, more inward, more difficult to define, but not less significant. This other structure is not, like his, generated entirely by the interplay of plot and character. Nor is it, on the other hand, though it is fashionable nowadays to suppose so, ultimately a verbal matter. It is poetic, but it goes well beyond what in certain quarters today is called (with something like a lump in the throat) 'the poetry'. Some of its elements arise from the playwright's visualizing imagination, the consciousness of groupings, gestures, entrances, exits. Others may even be prior to language, in the sense that they appear to belong to a paradigm of tragic 'form' that was consciously or unconsciously part of Shakespeare's inheritance and intuition as he worked. (12)

Mack's sense of Shakespeare's "more inward" structure emphasizes both the playwright's visual imagination and his dependence on inherited dramatic forms. Similarly, Beckerman asserts that the rather haphazard conditions of the Elizabethan theatre, combined with the demands of the repertory system, led not to chaotic composition but to "pragmatic dramatization," defined as "the development of drama in response not to abstract theory but to the deeply ingrained artistic practices of the age" (27). Like his fellow dramatists, Shakespeare relied on the theatrical tradition he had grown up with as well as on his own keen dramatic instinct.

Repetition was one of the dramatic devices inherited by the Elizabethans. In his study of late medieval drama, David Bevington remarks: "One cannot account for these plays by aesthetic laws of unity, correspondence, subordination, and the like, because they were not composed with such ideas in mind. If some contemporary had had occasion to speak for the critically inarticulate authors of these plays, and had extracted a pattern or series of patterns from their work, he might have spoken quite differently of repetitive effect, multiplicity, episode, progressive theme" (3). Clearly, Shakespeare and his contemporaries continued to exploit such devices, among them repetition. Moreover, the late medieval drama that provided Renaissance dramatists with a structure also suggested ways in which that structure might be reinforced visually. Alan Dessen claims that "one answer to the problem of sequential form [was] provided by the late morality dramatists—the use of analogues for the viewer's eye to link disparate moments in the dramatic action" (50). Visual analogues allowed structural patterns of repetition and modulation to be apprehended instantly by an audience in the theatre.

Although recent studies of Shakespeare's dramatic construction have presented him as a careful craftsman working in an established tradition of repetition and multiplicity, their conclusions have rarely been extended to Shakespeare's contemporaries. Critics "would do well to extend more generously [their] inferences about Shakespeare to the Jacobean playwrights as a group," notes Mack (40). This is particularly appropriate in the case of Webster, whose dramatic construction has long been misunderstood. It has become almost a commonplace to claim that Webster's plays are loose and haphazard and that the brilliance of individual scenes and speeches is achieved at the expense of his overall construction. Whether Charles Lamb's fashionable strategy in his *Specimens* of displaying gems out of their setting reflected or encouraged nineteenth-century tendencies to separate poet from playwright,[3] it soon set the predominant view of Webster. A. W. Ward's attitude is typical: "What Webster in general reproduces with inimitable force, is a succession of situations of overpowering effect; in construction he is far from strong" (3:65). Later critics are similarly divided: Rupert Brooke shows enthusiasm for Webster's "supreme dramatic moments" and contempt for the "childishnesses and blunders" of his dramaturgy (96, 136); F. L.

Lucas praises Webster's dramatic intensity, and bemoans "things ill-connected and ill-constructed, things crude and gross and merely puerile" (1:21, 17); T. S. Eliot admires Webster's tragic seriousness and "acute sense of the theatre," yet complains about "the inconsequential nature of the plot and the inconsistency of people's behaviour" ("Duchess" 826, 825). More recently, Roma Gill applauds "the experimental stagecraft" of *The White Devil*, with its multiple perspectives, yet condemns Webster's "dangerous tendency to focus his attention on the smaller unit instead of and sometimes at the expense of the larger" (59, 42). Similar criticisms of Shakespeare drew from Coleridge the impassioned query: "Are the plays of Shakspeare works of rude uncultivated genius, in which the splendor of the parts compensates . . . for the barbarous shapelessness and irregularity of the whole?" (4:53). His eloquent response was that Shakespeare, unlike the ancients, constructed his plays "by blending materials and fusing the parts together" (4:58). Critics both recognized and admired Webster's episodic intensification as the source of his dramatic power, but were unwilling to concede that it could be a principle of construction. The intense tragic vision they praised depended on a dramatic organization they recognized only as a failure. In his preface to *The White Devil* Webster confesses, "If it be objected that this is no true dramatic poem . . . willingly, and not ignorantly, in this kind I have faulted" (25). The structure of Webster's plays may emerge because of, rather than in spite of, their theatrical brilliance and their strong emphasis on the individual scene. Like Shakespeare's, Webster's may be a drama of "multiple unity"[4] which relates parts to one another and to the whole through analogy and repetition. This is a far cry from the classical drama, which is "compressive and retrospective" rather than extensive and multiple (Beckerman 31). "For th[e] advantage of multiplicity of implication the Elizabethan sacrificed concentration of effect," observes Beckerman. "Unable to grasp this shift in emphasis, many critics have treated the lack of concentration in Shakespearean structure as evidence that the poet did not know how to construct plays" (47). What Beckerman says here of Shakespeare could well be said of Webster.

In recent criticism, aesthetic objections to Webster's drama have become fused with moral ones, indicating perhaps what Richard Levin calls a "compensatory zeitgeist" that values moral definition more highly in an age of ambiguity (*New Readings* 45). Modern critics find fault with Webster's multiplicity because it does not allow for a clear, progressive development of a moral view. One might trace the modern emphasis on morality in drama to Matthew Arnold's pervasive influence on criticism and education. In the preface to his 1853 edition of *Poems*, Arnold connected the austere, linear form of Greek drama with its "unity and profoundness of moral impression," contrasting it implicitly with the morally inferior multiplicity of Shakespeare, who lacked "the severe and scrupulous self-restraint of the ancients" (12, 11). Following Arnold's example, many modern critics continue to judge dramatic form by its efficiency as a moral conductor. Madeleine Doran, for example, complains of "the emphasis put on the single scene for immediate striking effect even at the expense of the total design" of Webster's drama because it results in "both ambiguity of ethical implication and disjointedness of form." Yet she praises this drama as "endlessly arresting—for its intensity of passion and gesture, its richness of poetic texture, its flashes of profound insight into human feeling and human dilemma" (354–55). The familiar divided response to Webster is repeated by Clifford Leech in his assessment of *The Duchess of Malfi* as both a "moving exploration of the human mind" and "a collection of brilliant scenes, whose statements do not ultimately cohere" (*John Webster* 65). Similarly, Harold Jenkins objects to Webster's inversion of the moral polarities of the traditional revenge plot in *The White Devil*, but admires the play's "imaginative rhythm" (51). His view is repeated by Robert Ornstein, who finds no "moral emphasis and focus" in the design of *The White Devil* and thus concludes that it is "artistically unpurposed"; Webster is more interested in "the supreme moments of agony and duress that lay bare the soul" (129, 133). These "moral" critics share several assumptions. The nineteenth century's rejection of the "horrors" of *The Duchess of Malfi*[5] has been replaced by a modern dislike for the "vision of evil" in *The White Devil*. Though the dramaturgy of both plays is similar, it is praised in *The Duchess of Malfi* because of its apparent moral clarity and condemned in *The White Devil* because of its moral complexity. This subordination of aesthetic features to moral issues does not advance our understanding of Webster's construction. All these critics assert that Webster's tendency to write for brilliant effect in individual scenes is the source of both his moral weakness and his tragic vision. Yet, while they seek without success "a coherent moral attitude . . . which enables us to integrate or organize . . . discontinuities of action and character" (Kirsch 104), the "moving exploration of the human mind" (Leech, *John Webster* 65) they admire seems inextricable from its resistance to a single moral view. The oversimplification of Shakespeare that frequently accompanies moral attacks on Webster illuminates the shortcomings of these approaches. Doran and Ornstein contrast *The White Devil* with *King Lear*, in which there seems to be a clear "moral judgment" (Doran 356), and a strong, unifying "moral emphasis and focus" (Ornstein 129). Jenkins compares it with *Hamlet*, which, in his view, observes the strict moral polarities of the conventional revenge plot by presenting us with a "good" revenger and an "evil" object of revenge (47–49).[6] Yet Hamlet the "good" revenger murders Polonius and casually sends Rosencrantz and Guildenstern to their deaths; King Lear, like Vittoria or Brachiano, glimpses and loses sight of some larger vision and finally transcends any notion of moral judgment. Conventional categories of virtuous and vicious human nature apply no more to Shakespeare than to Webster. Furthermore, it is Webster's aesthetic design, rather than a single moral focus, which allows us to organize the apparent "discontinuities" in his plays. His dramaturgy is founded on juxtapositions, parallels and repetitions which resist reduction to a single moral belief, yet need not lead to a chaotic vision of human experience.[7]

There have of course been many attempts to defend Webster's dramaturgy. One modern response to those who find Webster's plays morally and aesthetically confusing is to claim that the confusion is deliberate, and that Webster is an Old Testament prophet for the Theatre of the Absurd. J. R. Mulryne, for example, connects Webster with Beckett, Genet and Ionesco in their common use of an "anti-construction" with which to express the irreconcilable perspectives of tragedy and comedy ("Tragicomedy" 152, 141). Normand Berlin claims that *The Duchess of Malfi* has affinities with modern absurdist theatre (361). Similarly, Jacqueline Pearson portrays Webster as a tragicomic ironist whose construction is designed "to express significant contrasts and discontinuities" in an attempt to go beyond the "tragic absolutes" and embrace "the Whole Truth" (2, 55). John McElroy maintains that Webster deliberately disorients his audience in order to frustrate their conventional judgments

(301), and John Russell Brown suggests that Webster's discontinuities of speech and characterization force his audience to become "aware of the unspoken thoughts and feelings underneath" (*White Devil* liii). The strength of this recent approach is its insistence on the disturbing vitality of Webster's constantly shifting perspectives; its weakness is its almost total reliance on audience response—often difficult to characterize—at the expense of ignoring Webster's selection and disposition of materials. The argument for generic heterogeneity would justify any dramatic discontinuity and welcome any superfluity in the interest of "imitative form," the dramatist's attempt to subject his audience to the experience he is dramatizing. Since this approach does not impose, but rather excludes, structure, it cannot really offer an aesthetic defense of Webster. As Arthur Kirsch points out, "even in representing chaos a play itself must offer a coherent experience" (105).[8]

If the critics of imitative form concern themselves solely with the experience of the spectator and neglect the artist's shaping of material, critics of theme and image completely ignore the realities of stage performance. Hereward Price, for example, reduces the action and characters of both Webster's plays to "symbols of one idea," the deceptive nature of appearances (194). Apart from its inadequacy in explaining specific events like *The White Devil*'s trial scene, whose dramatic power resides in its rejection of any simple dichotomy between appearance and reality, Price's approach fails to account for Webster's choice of specific events. Similarly, by claiming Webster as a "baroque" artist, Ralph Berry contends that his characters and actions are subordinated to a more abstract conceptual unity of theme and image patterns. Berry confesses the problems of his own approach, however, when he writes, "the play structure contains much more than the ideas that may be abstracted. The characters of a Webster play obstinately maintain a life of their own; they assert it against the very text" (81). A text that is at odds with the dramatic life of the play is indeed problematic.

The dramatic life of Webster's plays has received the attention of some modern critics. Inga-Stina Ewbank, for example, finds that Webster achieves a complex tragic clarity in his plays by juxtaposing different perspectives in the aesthetic design.[9] Lois Potter and Roger Warren stress the importance of these opposed perspectives for stage performance: Potter draws attention to the juxtaposition of the worlds of Malfi and Rome in *The Duchess of Malfi*, and Warren reminds us that the play's madness and horror are balanced in performance by the elegant, civilized world of the court. Michael Best emphasizes symmetries and oppositions among various characters in *The Duchess of Malfi*, while Charles Forker treats both plays as fusions of romantic and revenge tragedy. Similarly, B. J. Layman and Larry Champion find patterns of contrast in the structure of *The White Devil*. All these critics attempt to discover what Una Ellis-Fermor calls "the real underlying form" of Webster's plays, describing them as "a two-dimensional map of moods and personalities in their relations to each other rather than as a single-dimensional line of progression from event to event" (30). Unlike earlier critics, they do not expect Webster's plays to adhere either to a classical, linear model of construction or to a reductive moral view in which good and evil are clearly distinguished. Unlike most of Webster's defenders, these critics neither deny patterns of order in the plays nor do they rely solely on verbal elements to assert their aesthetic unity. Perhaps most important, they explain the divided response of earlier critics by showing that the alleged "incongruities" of Webster's plays are vital tensions that impart great strength to his dramatic writing. Criticism, however, has yet to treat in detail important aspects of Webster's construction or to account fully for the progressive unfolding of the plays on the stage. Though Elizabethan plays are not linear in the classical sense, they too are bound by the duration of stage performance and the nature of audience attention. Furthermore, because defensive criticism has been chiefly intent on justifying Webster's peculiarities, it overlooks the dramatic strategies he shares with his contemporaries. While Webster's vision is clearly unique, his dramaturgy is based on inherited formal strategies of scene and play construction. Webster, like Shakespeare, relied heavily on "the deeply ingrained artistic practices of the age" (Beckerman 27), exploiting the basic rhetorical strategy of repetition in episodes, scenes, and groups of scenes.

Critics have often noted various kinds of repetition and variation in Webster's plays. First, as Robert Dent has demonstrated, Webster continually repeats and modifies the material of other writers. Second, Webster uses the same themes and characters in all his plays, repeating and varying his own verbal and nonverbal structures. John Russell Brown remarks that "Webster had a persistent and brooding mind, and for him creation often involved repetition; he worked in series, like a painter who re-aligns the elements of one composition in his next to suggest less obvious inter-relations, new astringencies, or sudden simplifications of form. Within Webster's plays, scenes echo each other, and his two great tragedies, both set at court and with a central heroine, are in important ways two versions of a single subject" (*Duchess* xxx).[10] Third, apart from repeating himself and others, Webster frequently repeats situations within his own plays. Pearson points out that "Webster was a notoriously slow worker: one reason for this is the extraordinary richness of the plays and his meticulousness in providing this elaborate web of cause and effect, of echo, repetition, parody and allusion" (60). Forker notes, "As in *The White Devil*, so in *The Duchess of Malfi* Webster imposes a kind of artistic coherence upon the fragmentary and inconclusive universe of the play through a pattern of verbal and visual parallels that, individually considered, might seem almost fortuitous" (357). Potter notes that Webster's "fascination with the idea of repetition, whether for ritual, irony, or parody, ha[s] resulted in an element in the play which no conceivable performance can fully exploit" (180). Evidence of Webster's delight in repetition and variation is plentiful. Scenes like *The White Devil* II.i, in which Isabella replays Brachiano's rejection of her by reproducing his exact words and gestures, illuminate Webster's self-conscious use of repetition. Visual analogues, like the poisonings of Isabella and Brachiano, reflect a deliberate attempt to connect different parts of the play through repetition.[11] Yet the very abundance of repetition in Webster's plays has resulted in confusion as to its function. Some critics confine their attention to recurring verbal images, while others treat the repeated dramatic situations and stage images as evidence to support their own view of the plays' parodic structure. Still others, like Potter, remain uncertain as to the purpose of such repetition, and dubious about its realization in the theatre.

Although the frequency of repetition in Webster's plays has often been noted, little critical attention has been devoted to its contribution to the plays' rhythm and overall dramatic structure, or to its role as a powerful unifying force on the stage. The underlying formal structures adopted by both Shakespeare and Webster survived precisely because they served stage performance, and so it is no accident that reviews of actual performances can provide valuable clues to Webster's original design. As fresh impressions recorded by an experienced and sensitive member of the audience, theatrical reviews can often help to illuminate, not elaborate verbal echoes or image links, but the broad rhythms of repetition that can be grasped—consciously or unconsciously—by an audience in the theatre. Although reviews are subjective, fallible and sometimes contradictory, they frequently unsettle conventionally accepted readings of a play and suggest connections and patterns that are not otherwise apparent. Used in conjunction with promptbooks, for example, reviews may reveal that alteration of Webster's text has distorted or obscured his design, or that a particular stage interpretation has enhanced or suppressed significant features of the play. Used as a corrective to traditional criticism, reviews may show us that what have long been considered faults in the study are actually beauties on the stage. Because both reviews and promptbooks spring directly from the theatre—the medium for which Webster wrote—they can usefully guide the judgment of the armchair critic, who is inevitably at one remove from the full life of the play. Of course, modern productions of Webster's plays are a long way from the original productions, and neither the professional theatre nor the professional theatre critic is always reliable. Because the postwar Elizabethan revival tends to reflect a modern "suspicion of all institutions and all sources of value," it may emphasize the "uncertain equilibrium" and jarring incongruities of Webster's plays at the expense of his underlying order (Jensen 233, 231). Furthermore, the enormous influence of Shakespeare on the theatrical tradition may result in some distortion of Webster's plays. Peter Thomson observes that "the conditions under which the British theatre generally rehearses and stages its productions are better suited to discovering what Webster has in common with Shakespeare than what is uniquely his" (26). By the same token, however, the Shakespearean bias of the theatre may help us to rediscover the formal principles that underlie Webster's dazzling and quixotic style. For both structure and surface, dramatic intention and theatrical realization— where these are separable—contribute to an audience's experience of a play in the theatre. Webster's aesthetic control in his great tragedies is not limited to local effects, but extends to larger dramatic structures, some of which may not be immediately obvious to a theatre audience. Yet by studying carefully the impressions registered by an audience—by considering the evidence of unsuccessful performances as well as a range of possible successful ones—the critic may be able to discern some of the formal structures from which they emerge. As Michael Goldman puts it, "There will always be a significant connection between the small figures of acting—the local, repeated patterns of process by which the actor keeps his projection of the character alive and interesting—and the larger action of the play, just as there is a connection between the brushstroke of a painter and the felt significance of his design" (13). I hope to make explicit such a connection between the theatrical experience of Webster's plays and their dramatic construction. For this reason the evidence for Webster's dramatic skill is culled from both the plays' texts and their stage histories. From this evidence emerges the importance of repetition as a strategy of construction, not only inherited from earlier drama and exploited by Webster's contemporaries, but utilized uniquely and effectively by Webster himself. The following chapters will explore Webster's use of repetition to relate the passages and scenes of his plays through parallel, contrast, intensification, recapitulation, and reversal. In each case, the repetition and modulation of material will be examined for their contribution to the development and clarification of Webster's moral vision.

CHAPTER ONE

~~~~~~

WINDING AND INDIRECT:
Nonlinear Development

~~~~~~

BECKERMAN points out that the "climax" of a Shakespearean play is usually a sustained sequence of repeated, intensified episodes; in *Coriolanus*, for example, Coriolanus's struggle with the tribunes occurs not once but twice (42). In *Othello*, the triumph of Othello and Desdemona over the obstacle of parental opposition in the first act is replayed in their survival of the storm in the second act. The basic pattern of the first two acts is then repeated in the third act: twice Iago and Roderigo rouse the citizens with the bell; twice Othello is confronted with an important challenge. The first time, Othello and Desdemona stand united against an angry and jealous father; the second time, however, distrust and suspicion grow not between parent and child but between husband and wife. Shakespeare repeats and modifies such large sequences of dramatic material in order to clarify the underlying shape of the tragedy. According to Beckerman, in Shakespeare's plays, "the impulse to dilate upon the story achieves maximum expansion in the center of the play" (40). Like Shakespeare, Webster is less concerned with developing a causally linked narrative than with exploring and emphasizing the different aspects of a central experience. Like Shakespeare, Webster uses repetitive form, de-emphasizing the play's linear progression for the advantage of reworking and expanding his basic material. In the central acts of both his major tragedies, Webster repeats and modulates large dramatic sequences of events to clarify and intensify the direction of his play.

1

THE WHITE DEVIL

Jenkins maintains that there is "some confusion about what is being avenged" in *The White Devil*.

> For Camillo's murder Vittoria is apprehended, but though the play
> . . . has stressed her culpability in advance, the murder is never
> brought home to her and she is sentenced as a whore. The murder of
> Isabella is not even discovered till after Vittoria has been sentenced,
> when the play is already half over. Yet it is *this* murder which at length
> gives the revengers their chance to set to work. . . . It is as though his
> sources, with the murder of Camillo as well as Isabella, and the re-
> venge tradition, with its ghosts and poisonings and mad scenes, have
> supplied him with too much material, which his imagination cannot
> effectively control. (50–51)

In his criticism of the structure of *The White Devil*, Jenkins isolates an important feature of its overall design. The two murders that are speedily dispatched in the dumb shows of the second act provide separate revenge motives which lead first to the arraignment and then to the final deaths of the protagonists. Webster's suppression of knowledge of the murder of Isabella, like his suppression of knowl-edge of the Duchess's marriage in *The Duchess of Malfi*, allows him to draw out his action. In *The White Devil*, the murders are discovered sequentially; in *The Duchess of Malfi*, information about the Duchess's marriage is gleaned by degrees. After the climactic trial of the third act of *The White Devil*, a new revenge motive is introduced and a new "plot" unfolds. Far from betraying a confusing overabundance of source material, or a slavish regard for the chronological sequence of events (Boklund, *White Devil* 145), Webster's split structure in *The White Devil* is his own. Boklund points out that, "in marked contrast to what has so far been believed, Webster had a notably succinct story on which to base his tragedy." Confusing and tenuous as much of the source material may be, it clearly indicates a simple cause/ effect relation between the double murder and the joint revenge (Boklund, *White Devil* 135–36). Boklund observes that "the trial scene . . . is independent of any source," and Vittoria, after her capture, was simply imprisoned in a "monasterie of Nunnes," whence she was freed by Brachiano (112, 110). Webster, on the other hand, deliberately brings one action to a climactic stalemate in the trial scene, entirely suppressing the other murder so that he can introduce a new revenge action halfway through the play and move the action toward a denouement. The divided focus that results gives Webster opportunities for repetition and variation that he later exploits for a similar purpose in *The Duchess of Malfi*.

In an attempt to impose neoclassical form on *The White Devil*, Greg tries to locate the climax or turning-point in the play. He hesitates between the arraignment scene (III.ii) and the scene in the house of convertites (IV.ii). In his view, both scenes are important: "The scene in which Vittoria and the duke quarrel divides with the 'arraignment' the honours of the play." In his view, IV.ii contains "the subtlest and most complex delineation of character to be met with in Webster" (119). Though he admits that "the climax, the point of culmination of the plot . . . should obviously possess a dramatic value corresponding to its architectonic importance," he finally concludes that the arraignment, the obvious choice, comes too early in the play to serve as its climax. He argues instead for the scene in the house of convertites as the climactic turning-point because "it is on the scene in the house of convertites rather than on the trial that the plot turns. . . . The scene of Brachiano's jealousy . . . leads up to the culminating point of the play, in which Vittoria attains momentarily to the height of her ambition. This point is likewise the turn of fortune, for by the very move by which the guilty couple think to triumph they step into the net woven for them by Francisco" (124). Greg's argument is clearly inadequate. The "culminating point" at the end of IV.ii is shrouded in the ambiguity of Vittoria's silence and dramatically undermined by Flamineo's long-winded tale. Brachiano's plan for their escape occupies an insignificant portion of the scene, which is dominated by the dramatic confrontation between the lovers. That their escape is really a trap set by Francisco does not become clear until the following scene. In the play's overall construction, the arraignment is obviously dominant. Yet Greg's sense of the importance of IV.ii to the play's movement and direction is confirmed in a review of the 1976 Old Vic production by Irving Wardle, theatre critic for the *Times*, who called the scene "a fine piece of feminine derision, and the most passionate passage in the production" ("Old Vic"). Its position in the play's construction is curious. Coming as it does so soon after the arraignment (usually considered the set-piece of any performance[1]), and repeating some of the same material in a different context, the scene appears to be a redundancy hardly justified by its contribution to the plot. The split structure of *The White Devil*, which generates both the trial and the quarrel, appears only to slow the pace of the action and to overload it with redundancies. Yet the dramatic impact of both scenes is clearly important to the play's overall shape.

In an early essay, T. S. Eliot maintains that "a certain apparent irrelevance" in drama may be the clue to "an under-pattern, less manifest than the theatrical one" ("Marston" 229). This is certainly true of *The Duchess of Malfi*, where, as we shall see, Bosola's futility in the second act allows Webster to intensify his tragedy through repetition in the third act. The fourth act of *The White Devil* is riddled with apparent irrelevancies—Francisco's adoption and subsequent rejection of a succession of revenge strategies (IV.i), Flamineo's parable of the crocodile (IV.ii), and the papal election scene (IV.iii), to name a few. While the first revenge action culminates in the trial, the second revenge action does not really get under way until the final act. Yet in the intervening act, from a mere hint in his sources (Boklund, *White Devil* 110), Webster develops a complex scene that mirrors his invented trial and allows for full structural repetition.

As in *The Duchess of Malfi*, structural repetition in *The White Devil* is followed by a highly visual scene which represents iconographically the inevitable defeat of the protagonists and ends any uncertainty about the outcome of the plot. The banishment scene of *The Duchess of Malfi* and the papal election scene of *The White Devil* both consolidate the final direction, but only after the underlying dynamics of the tragedy have been emphasized through repetition. In his review of the 1960 Royal Shakespeare Company production of *The Duchess of Malfi*, Martin Holmes protests that "neither here nor at the Haymarket were we given that turning-point in the middle of the play," the banishment scene. He goes on to link the banishment scene with the papal election scene in their common use of ceremony to achieve a precise dramatic impact. "As with the papal election scene in *The White Devil*, Webster knew what an effect could be created, and how much information conveyed, by an impressive piece of pageantry, and it is a matter for regret that he has not, of late years, been given a chance of showing it" (450–51). The banishment scene was a high point of the 1971 production of *The Duchess of*

Malfi at Stratford, Ontario, as the review in the *Times* testified (Wardle, "Beardsley Garden"). Afterwards, the audience watches, not for what will happen, but for what must happen. Through repetition, Webster de-emphasizes the force and immediacy of "story" in preparation for the inevitable outcome. At the same time, repetition enables him to define the real direction of his tragedy, its "under-pattern."

The first movements of both *The Duchess of Malfi* and *The White Devil* end on a high note. An intense confrontation is left unresolved, and the emotion generated is barely controlled. At the end of the third act of *The White Devil*, the sudden explosion of Flamineo leaves Lodovico trembling with rage:

> I learnt it of no fencer to shake thus;
> Come I'll forget him, and go drink some wine.
> (III.iii.135–36)

The violent confrontation between the two men is left unresolved dramatically, for the following scene disappoints expectation. A similar point of tension is reached at the end of the second act of *The Duchess of Malfi*. Ferdinand's violent threats against the Duchess are more ominous because held in check:

> In, in; I'll go sleep—
> Till I know who leaps my sister, I'll not stir:
> That known, I'll find scorpions to string my whips,
> And fix her in a general eclipse.
> (II.v.76–79)

The third act of *The Duchess of Malfi* then dissipates the play's momentum by changing its tone and direction. Similarly, the fourth act of *The White Devil* suspends, rather than extends, the expectations aroused by the previous action. Monticelso advises Francisco:

> Bear your wrongs conceal'd
> And, patient as the tortoise, let this camel
> Stalk o'er your back unbruis'd: sleep with the lion,
> And let this brood of secure foolish mice
> Play with your nostrils, till the time be ripe
> For th' bloody audit, and the fatal gripe.
> (IV.i.14–19)

This passage anticipates Antonio's description of Ferdinand at the beginning of the third act of *The Duchess of Malfi*:

> He is so quiet, that he seems to sleep
> The tempest out, as dormice do in winter:
> Those houses that are haunted are most still,
> Till the devil be up.
>
> (III.i.21–24)

As Ferdinand is suddenly "weary" (III.i.39), so Francisco is unexpectedly "turn'd all marble" (IV.i.4). For the second movement of each play, the pace of the action is slowed and the causal structure weakened. The muted, softened force of the antagonists in both plays signals a change in focus. By introducing a kind of dramatic paralysis, Webster again diverts attention from the linear narrative and engages our attention for a different end. In *The Duchess of Malfi*, Act I with its powerful wooing scene is balanced against Act II with Bosola's dominant satiric perspective; the third act must decide the final direction. In *The White Devil*, the crimes of the protagonists in Act II are balanced against their heroic defense in Act III; the fourth act is designed to clarify the issues.

In the fourth act of *The White Devil*, the immediacy of the confrontation between Lodovico and Flamineo at the end of Act III gives way to the lengthy, deliberate speeches of Francisco and Monticelso. The expectation of revenge, invoked in Monticelso's opening reminder to Francisco that their "sister's poisoned" (IV.i.3) is immediately undercut by Francisco's reply:

> Far be it from my thoughts
> To seek revenge.
>
> (IV.i.3–4)

As the scene continues, Francisco's refusal to pursue revenge is undercut in its turn by his expressed desire to see Monticelso's "black book" (IV.i.33), containing the names of "notorious offenders" (IV.i.31), "agents for any villainy" (IV.i.90). In the 1983 York Graduate Theatre Company production in Toronto, Francisco's verbal refusal to undertake revenge was undercut by his stage gesture. Francisco knelt before Monticelso upon the lines:

I know there's thunder yonder: and I'll stand,
Like a safe valley, which low bends the knee
To some aspiring mountain.

(IV.i.23–25)

His movement visually suggested that Francisco expected his brother to carry out the revenge. Yet these are hardly conventional revengers—as soon as the usual properties of revenge are introduced, they are dismissed. The "black book" is considered more as a social document than as a tool for revenge in the lengthy speeches of Francisco and Monticelso (IV.i.45–87). When Francisco finally recalls his purpose, he decides he must approach his revenge "more seriously" (IV.i.98). He then conjures up the ghost of Isabella, another conventional property of the avenger. Yet once again Francisco dismisses it:

remove this object—
Out of my brain with't: what have I to do
With tombs, or death-beds, funerals, or tears,
That have to meditate upon revenge?

(IV.i.112–15)

Finally, after numerous attempts to attend "seriously" to "this weighty business" of revenge, Francisco changes his tone and calls for "idle mirth" while he composes a love letter to Vittoria (IV.i.118–19). The scene presents a succession of attitudes to the revenge convention and undercuts each one in turn. These are desultory avengers, whose self-conscious trying-on of attitudes undermines the play's revenge structure at a point when it threatens to determine the play's shape.

Webster's design in undermining the revenge convention in the fourth act is strengthened by repetition. The brothers have vowed revenge in the past. In Act II, before any real crime has been committed by the protagonists, Monticelso declares,

It may be objected I am dishonourable,
To play thus with my kinsman, but I answer,
For my revenge I'd stake a brother's life,
That being wrong'd durst not avenge himself.

(II.i.391–94)

Francisco replies, "Come to observe this strumpet" (395), elliptically anticipating the arraignment before the murders have been committed. The murders seem almost an irrelevance to the revenge plot— the trial is designed to expose Vittoria's "black lust" (III.i.7) rather than to investigate Camillo's murder, and in IV.i Francisco dismisses Isabella's ghost to focus once again on Vittoria's sexuality. The new revenge motive in Act IV is actually a replay of the old one. Webster's divided focus—with the murder of Camillo inciting the first revenge, the murder of Isabella the second—allows for the reduplication of the revenge motive even as it undermines it.

The repetition of the revenge motive in *The White Devil* fulfills two important functions in the play's construction. First, such repetition, combined with the emergence of a new, vital, Machiavellian revenger in Francisco, signals the inevitable defeat of the protagonists. Second, and somewhat paradoxically, the talk of revenge, undercut and disconnected from its immediate stimulus by the sequence of events, loses its significance as a causal agent. Through this kind of structural repetition Webster mitigates the tendencies of his tragedy toward either cautionary tale or melodrama. Since there is no direct linear narrative connecting the protagonists' crimes with their punishment, it is (or ought to be) difficult to see the latter as a direct or a necessary result of the former. Although the play's events strictly speaking lead to the destruction of the protagonists by the avengers, Webster so fragments and undercuts this simple cause/effect relation that quite a different structure emerges, as we shall see. This point is missed by critics who maintain that Francisco is the "pivotal figure in a play whose structure is largely determined by his action" (Boklund, *White Devil* 150). The structure of events undermines even as it asserts Francisco's control.

As his control is undermined, Francisco gains an attractive new identity by appropriating Flamineo's voice. Imitating even Flamineo's social criticism, Francisco now offers the perspective on the protagonists that belonged to Flamineo in the play's first half.[2] In the first act, Flamineo remarked, "what an ignorant ass or flattering knave might he be counted, that should write sonnets to her eyes, or call her brow the snow of Ida, or ivory of Corinth" (I.ii.115–18). Francisco adopts a similar scornful, satiric pose when he pens his letter to Vittoria. As a result, in the following scene Flamineo is freed from his limited function as the lovers' foil because of Francisco's appropriation of his role, and he can take on another more complex function, as we shall see later.

In *The White Devil*, Webster minimizes the pull of generic expectations while exploiting their structural usefulness. His play is articulated through the revenge-plot structure, yet it manipulates that structure for its own ends. When, in the fourth act, it becomes clear that the avengers will triumph in the "plot," Webster at the same time works quickly to clarify the important issues. He does so by means of repetition, recalling and reworking past scenes in a major effort to redefine the nature and direction of his tragedy.

The second, repeated sequence of events in *The White Devil* that begins in Act IV greatly abbreviates and transforms the first sequence. The first two scenes of Act IV are set side by side in an intense compression of the play's first half, as villain-revengers are compared with villain-heroes. The two scenes reflect Webster's different interest in the two groups: the first is episodic, the second dramatic; the first avoids open confrontation, the second erupts into passionate conflict; the first isolates the villain-revengers from one another, the second creates a composite stage image of union from disunion. The rhythm of IV.i is desultory and digressive; the rhythm of IV.ii is intensely dynamic, driving toward a point of climax and reversal. The first scene is primarily "reactive," showing a succession of responses to a previous crisis, Isabella's murder; the second scene is primarily "active," showing, despite the initial reaction to the stimulus provided by Francisco, a movement toward a visible transformation on the stage. The distinctly different rhythms of the two scenes are important to a consideration of their dramatic effect in the play's overall shape.[3]

The scene in the house of convertites—so important on the stage—is largely irrelevant to the plot. Brachiano's decision to help Vittoria to escape and then to marry her occupies only 15 of the scene's 247 lines and thus fails to justify its length in narrative terms. The scene is above all, Bliss points out, rich in "allusive parallels to earlier scenes" (121). The confrontation between Brachiano and Vittoria recalls most vividly the arraignment scene, as Brachiano takes the place of the accusers while Vittoria again defends herself.[4] Yet it also replays the bitter rejection scene between Brachiano and Isabella (II.i), in which Brachiano's rejection of Isabella was followed by Isabella's rejection of Brachiano in turn. Finally, the scene sends us back to the lovers' first meeting in I.ii, as it reduplicates the staging of the earlier scene with Flamineo as observer and commentator. At this important point in the play, Webster chooses to redefine his protagonists by means of a complex web of echoes and associations.

The scene—which should be examined in some detail—begins with a replay of Camillo's comic jealousy in the first act. Flamineo's comic treatment of the cuckold resurfaces.

> Jealousy is worser, her fits present to a man, like so many bubbles in a basin of water, twenty several crabbed faces,—many times makes his own shadow his cuckold-maker. (I.ii.110–13)

The stage business between Brachiano and Flamineo, as Francisco's letter is rapidly tossed back and forth, reduces Brachiano's fury to absurdly mechanical gestures. As in the first act, Flamineo undercuts Brachiano's "rival" with clever puns:

> "Who prefer blossoms before fruit that's mellow?"
> Rotten on my knowledge with lying too long i' th' bed-straw.
> (IV.ii.36–37)

While Flamineo treats Francisco's threat to Brachiano precisely as he had treated Camillo's earlier, Brachiano himself adopts Camillo's former role as outraged husband. Flamineo's attempts to defuse Francisco's threat and to expose Brachiano as a comic cuckold are only partly successful, however. Brachiano's fury at Vittoria, though triggered by Francisco's stratagem and thus without foundation, powerfully reactivates the play's major issues. Whereas Camillo's well-founded suspicions were treated earlier by Flamineo as mere illusions, Brachiano's ill-founded ones reanimate the questions left unresolved by the trial and transcend Flamineo's attempts to contain them. The power that Flamineo wielded over Brachiano throughout the first half is suddenly reversed when Brachiano asks threateningly, "Do you know me?" (IV.ii.56), and Flamineo is forced to reassert their hierarchical positions: "You're a great duke; I your poor secretary" (IV.ii.60).

When Vittoria enters, Brachiano calls her a "stately and advanced whore" (IV.ii.76) and quite deliberately recalls the trial scene:

> Thy loose thoughts
> Scatter like quicksilver, I was bewitch'd;
> For all the world speaks ill of thee.
>   (IV.ii.100–102)

The rhetoric of Monticelso and Francisco is reapplied and reex-amined in the first part of this scene. The perspective of the "world" is no longer imposed on Vittoria by her enemies in public, but is articulated by her lover in an intimate context. And, while Vittoria suffers from Brachiano what she endured on his behalf in the trial scene, Brachiano must accept from Vittoria the rejection he gave Isabella in the second act. The two voices of accusation and counter-accusation that have been heard so often throughout the play are raised again in this scene. Yet the overtones of role-playing that contaminated Isabella's rejection of Brachiano and Vittoria's self-defense at her trial are diminished here. Brachiano's anger imi-tates Monticelso's, yet is based on fabrications; Vittoria's self-righteousness is less a public performance than a justified outcry at her lover's betrayal, and both these distinctions contribute to the scene's dramatic conviction. In contrast to the scene with Isabella, Brachiano's rejection of Vittoria is motivated not by weariness and disgust, but by passion; Vittoria's rejection of Brachiano proclaims not her own innocence—for she admits she has been his "whore" (IV.ii.145)—but the masculine hypocrisy of which she has been a victim.

> Is this your palace? did not the judge style it
> A house of penitent whores? who sent me to it?
> Who hath the honour to advance Vittoria
> To this incontinent college? is't not you?
> Is't not your high preferment? Go, go brag
> How many ladies you have undone, like me.
>   (IV.ii.114–19)

The impact of the scene is strengthened by its visual resemblance to the early courtship scene of the first act. There, because of multiple commentaries and a highly public context (with Flamineo, Zanche, and Cornelia all present as observers), our judgment of the lovers was hampered. Here we are given more of the material we need on which to base a judgment because the scene explores the love relationship fully in a more private context.

Webster's most effective scenes in the theatre—scenes that, according to one theatre critic, determine the play's overall shape—are "jagged scenes of transfigured incident" (Coveney review), and this scene is no exception. In the first half, the paradigms of senseless accusation and rejection are played out by Brachiano, while Vittoria replays her own past roles with new force. Yet halfway through the scene the theatrical pattern changes abruptly. Brachiano's furious accusations suddenly melt into unconditional acceptance when Vittoria's defiance becomes despair, as she "throws herself upon a bed" (IV.ii.128 s.d.) face down and weeps. The tears which Brachiano before viewed as "dissembling" (IV.ii.95) now proceed from "matchless eyes" (IV.ii.133); the same "cursed hand" (IV.ii.98) is now desired in a gesture of reconciliation (IV.ii.169). The moment recalls Shakespeare's *Coriolanus*, when Volumnia's furious rejection of her son finally prompts him to yield and he "holds her by the hand, silent." Shakespeare's moment is rich in the same ambiguity as Webster's—human weakness and human greatness are confounded in a single gesture. Brachiano, like Coriolanus (and like Antony), is at his most heroic when he is most vulnerable. Likewise Vittoria, like Volumnia (and like Cleopatra), remains richly ambiguous. After the women achieve their desire, their subsequent silence leaves open a range of stage interpretations. Vittoria's silence may be quiet triumph, wordless contempt, or private devastation. Critical views of the scene range from one critic's contention that "there is revealed a tenacity of attachment and devotion that transcends mere lust" (Seiden 98), to another critic's view that "characters whose previous actions had meaning for them (or Cornelia) as free moral choices now suffer a reduced stature" (Bliss 122). Whether in fact "Brachiano is mastered by Vittoria" (Waage 93), or the lovers' reconciliation is a genuine act of mutual love and forgiveness, is not resolved by Webster. The scene is more complex dramatically than any other in the play, demanding as it does a mixed and full response from its director, actors, and audience alike. Thus, although it refuses to resolve the complex relationship of the protagonists into a simple moral formula, it does confirm the author's commitment and invite the audience's commitment to that complexity.

Webster does not flinch in this scene from showing Brachiano and Vittoria locked in a union that is both physically and emotionally intense. The scene recalls the first wooing in that little seems to have changed—Brachiano is still "lost" in Vittoria's charms, Vittoria is still powerful and ambiguous, Flamineo still "cold, itchy, filthily knowing" (Brooke 140). Yet from the multiple, fragmented perspectives of the first act, Webster has shifted to a composite tableau of which the following interchange is an example:

> *Vittoria*   O ye dissembling men!
> *Flamineo*   We sucked that, sister,
>   From women's breasts, in our first infancy.
> *Vittoria*   To add misery to misery.
> *Brachiano*   Sweetest.
> *Vittoria*   Am I not low enough?
>   Ay, ay, your good heart gathers like a snowball
>   Now your affection's cold.
> *Flamineo*   Ud's foot, it shall melt
>   To a heart again, or all the wine in Rome
>   Shall run o' th' lees for't.
>   (IV.ii.182–89)

The three voices intermingle in a shared rhythm, not of real conflict, but of underlying assent. Vittoria's gentle protests are absorbed by the humorous rejoinders of Flamineo and the loving protestations of Brachiano. Critics are divided on Flamineo's function in the scene—some contend that "even Flamineo's obscene comments fail to leave their smudge on Brachiano and Vittoria's love" (Seiden 97), while others maintain that "Flamineo's smutty devaluation and self-interested coaching dominate the final accord, as they did not in I.ii" (Bliss 121). Flamineo's incessant participation in the scene undercuts the lovers' potential status as romantic heroes, while illuminating their human vulnerability. Flamineo acts as a kind of screen onto which the negative aspects of the relationship are projected and transferred. He mitigates these negative overtones by appropriating and exaggerating them, while at the same time providing a human perspective on the lovers. Webster's use of Bosola in Act II of *The Duchess of Malfi* is similar; his obscene distortions of the

Duchess's pregnancy nonetheless serve to convey her new humanity and vulnerability. Indeed, Bosola's observation that "the like passions" (II.i.104) hold sway over princes and commoners underlies Webster's design in portraying the Duchess as a fertile woman with ordinary domestic desires. Like Bosola's, Flamineo's language here is broad and analogical; he generalizes and reduces the lovers so they become not individuals but examples of general instinctive human behavior: "O we curl'd-hair'd men / Are still most kind to women" (IV.ii.195–96). He is allowed to participate in the scene because of Webster's need to balance the dramatic power of the potentially heroic reconciliation with a more comprehensive human perspective. In this scene, Brachiano and Vittoria move beyond the simple heroic defiance of their trial scenes (II.i and III.ii) and the crude Machiavellianism of their murders. While he distances and generalizes the lovers through Flamineo, Webster at the same time brings into focus the combination of guilty desire and heroic self-will that motivated them. Forker points out, "In the grotesque and terror-ridden universe the pair must inhabit . . . grandeur and pettiness, devotion and selfishness, nobility and crime are somehow compatible" (261). In the fourth act, their mixture of guilt and innocence is no longer hopelessly ambiguous, but intensely, recognizably human, even comic.

At the end of the scene, Flamineo delivers a tale that has frequently been criticized as an irrelevance. Flamineo himself suggests one interpretation of the tale, while Brachiano adopts another— critics have found still others.[5] Yet the tale's precise meaning is less important than the general paradox of love and pain that it explores. The crocodile in the tale enjoys the "present remedy" and "ease" provided by the bird, yet attempts to swallow it; the bird, while it eases the "extreme anguish" caused the crocodile by the worm, yet pricks and wounds the crocodile in order to escape (IV.ii.222–35). The three protagonists of *The White Devil* are bound together in a similar symbiosis; their self-interest and their painful manipulation of one another somehow coexist with their mutual desire and even love. The play's final scene, in which Vittoria and Flamineo turn on one another, only to die side by side a few moments later, illuminates the same complex vision. Flamineo's tale encapsulates the paradox as it begins to emerge strongly in the play. As it redirects our attention to the interplay of energies in the scene, Flamineo's parable also slows down the forward momentum of Brachiano's plan for Vittoria's escape. By taking the audience backward into the scene with its complex triangle of relationships suggested by crocodile, worm and bird, rather than forward into the linear narrative, the tale reemphasizes the scene's dramatic importance as separate from its function in the plot.

With Flamineo in IV.ii, Webster mitigates both the generic pull of melodrama and the sweeping momentum of the plot. In this way he clarifies oppositions central to his tragedy. The crude satire of Francisco is contrasted, not with the lovers' romantic heroism, but with their vulnerable error-prone humanity.[6] Their new humanity compensates for the loss of their "heroic" stature and for their replacement by Francisco as stage-managers of the action.

In the second movement of *The White Devil*, as a theatre critic has pointed out, "as the cast thins, the pace slackens. The richness of the word begins to penetrate—'and now I'll go weeping to heaven on crutches'" (Donaldson review). In both tragedies, Webster slows the pace by means of repetition in order to achieve such intensification. A new clarity and lucidity emerge in the language of IV.ii, in speeches like Brachiano's:

> Your beauty! O, ten thousand curses on't.
> How long have I beheld the devil in crystal?
> Thou hast led me, like an heathen sacrifice,
> With music, and with fatal yokes of flowers
> To my eternal ruin. Woman to man
> Is either a god or a wolf.
>
> (IV.ii.88–92)

In *The Duchess of Malfi* III.ii, the powerful, sweeping lines belong to Ferdinand:

> The howling of a wolf
> Is music to thee, screech-owl, prithee peace!
>
> . . . .
>
> If thou do wish thy lecher may grow old
> In thy embracements, I would have thee build
> Such a room for him as our anchorites
> To holier use inhabit: let not the sun
> Shine on him, till he's dead.
>
> (III.ii.88–89, 100–104)

15

In the intimate confrontation between Vittoria and Brachiano in *The White Devil*, and between the Duchess and Ferdinand in *The Duchess of Malfi*, the plays' central dialectic of opposed perspectives is clearly presented. In *The White Devil*, Brachiano changes his perspective when his fury at Vittoria suddenly shifts to unconditional, loving acceptance of her. In *The Duchess of Malfi*, Ferdinand's crazed wrath is juxtaposed with the Duchess's quiet domestic desires, highlighted in her previous loving interview with Antonio. At a similar point in the development of both plays, Webster chooses to contrast the mysterious, irrational perspective of lovers with the equally power- ful and irrational perspective that threatens their love. In *The White Devil*, Brachiano himself illustrates both attitudes. And in both plays the finest rhetoric belongs, not to the lovers, but to their en- emies. By contrast, the world of the lovers is conveyed not through language but through gesture: in *The White Devil*, through the clasp- ing of hands and the physical embraces of the reconciliation scene, and in *The Duchess of Malfi*, through the intimate disrobing and play- ful banter of the bedroom scene. Thus Webster pits the linguistic against the verbal resources of his art in order to heighten the central conflict of each play.

The fourth act of *The White Devil* shows the development of inti- macy and humanity in the central love relationship. At the same time, all three protagonists in *The White Devil* remain both manip- ulators and victims—as Flamineo implies in his tale—and Vittoria's ambiguity is confirmed rather than removed. While he captures dra- matic interest in his protagonists with this scene, Webster maintains a complex perspective on them. Their complexity is illuminated by contrast with the simplicity of the antagonists by whom they are framed. Although Francisco sends the love letter that provokes Brachiano's jealousy, the rest of the scene quickly surpasses his ini- tial provocation. Only later does Francisco claim, "'twas this / I only laboured. I did send the letter / T'instruct him what to do" (IV.iii.52–54). His device originally appears designed to create a rift between the lovers, in which he does not succeed. At any rate, the grip on the protagonists that Francisco later appears to tighten is not strong enough to match the dramatic intensity of the previous scene. Since Francisco's clarification of his plan comes after the scene in the house of convertites, in retrospect it is impossible to agree that his "god-like perspective frames and distances all the reversals and manoeuvrings" or that "in Francisco's diabolic plan they are all actors meekly responding on cue" (Bliss 122). The love letter both undermines the revenge structure and sets in motion the echoes and repetitions of the following scene. Francisco's control over the narrative line is confirmed only when it has been effectively transcended.[7]

In Act IV of *The White Devil* Webster rephrases the revenge motive and generates a new sequence of events that repeats earlier material from a new perspective. As a result, the play's linear progression is undercut for the greater advantage of clarifying its final direction. The repetition of the revengers' scheming in IV.i allowed by Webster's split structure confirms their control over the action but at the same time undercuts the significance of that control in the play's dramaturgy. More important is the complex, dynamic exploration of human love and pain in IV.ii that is emphasized by the surrounding scenes. The lovers' scene in turn repeats earlier scenes—the wooing of Act I, the rejection of Act II, the trial of Act III. The second movement of the play makes the final direction clear even as it de-emphasizes causality and plot progression. The villains will gain their ends, but the nature, not the fate, of the protagonists will be the real focus of interest. The same strategy of structural repetition that reduces the villains brings the protagonists into intimate focus.[8]

The kind of construction suggested here may explain how Webster's intense tragic vision of "the progress of passionate life through its fulfilment to its inevitable destruction" (Jenkins 51) can be articulated through a pattern of events that appears "disjointed" (Gill 42) and discontinuous. Though *The White Devil* seems to rush headlong to its conclusion, its structure is, as John Russell Brown points out, "a gothic aggregation rather than a steady exposition and development towards a single consummation" (xliv). Forker notes, "Webster gives us a plot structure commensurate to a world of labyrinthine deceit, 'winding and indirect'" (289). Yet it is in Act IV of *The White Devil* that the multiplicity and "discontinuousness" for which Webster has been alternately praised and criticized become instruments of the intensification of his tragic vision. In Act IV, as we have seen, he both uses and transcends his own revenge plot structure and, by delaying the forward movement of the linear narrative, he actually advances the course of his tragedy. Webster's protagonists may be, as Ornstein calls them, "heroic characters who escape the restrictive bonds and illusions of mortality only to be swept to disaster by the irresistible tide of their desires" (137), but Webster articulates this vision by means of careful and deliberate dramatic construction.

THE DUCHESS OF MALFI

Academic and theatrical critics alike have pointed to the slow development of the tragic action over a span of several years in the second and third acts of *The Duchess of Malfi*. Abraham Wright, a Caroline clergyman and Webster's earliest critic, maintained: "And which is against the laws of the scene, the business was two years a-doing, as may be perceived by the beginning of the third act where Antonio has three children by the Duchess, when in the first act he had but one [sic]" (35). Three hundred years later, Leech attributes the notorious "delay" to a conflict between Webster's regard for his sources and his own dramatic instincts: "Ferdinand's strange patience during the long interval between Acts II and III is a . . . serious matter, throwing a haze of improbability over his character and this part of the action. Doubtless Webster could not resist introducing Bosola's immediate discovery of the birth of the first child, but then proceeded to follow Bandello's story by keeping the marriage secret for a long period" (*John Webster* 68). Similarly, Doran criticizes the play for "excessive looseness of time and place" (361). A recent theatre critic, in answer to the question, "Why is it that Bosola, that baffling spy, cannot discover what is going on in the Duchess' household after three years?" ingeniously declares that "to shorten the play would cheat Webster of the time he needs to exhibit virtuosity in evil" (Whittaker review). Early in the century, William Archer criticized Bosola's role as an imperceptive spy as utterly improbable and the consequent extension of the action as apparently purposeless. In his opinion, "the catastrophe should have followed like a thunder-clap" (*Nineteenth Century* 96). In fact, the first three acts repeat a similar sequence of events twice over, so that the "thunder-clap" of a catastrophe appears to be muted deliberately.

The first and the third acts begin in much the same way, with Antonio and Delio appearing on the stage to greet one another. The beginning of Act III is obviously designed to recall the beginning of

Act I. Whereas in Act I Delio greeted Antonio with, "You are welcome to your country, dear Antonio" (I.i.1), in Act III their positions are reversed, and Antonio greets Delio with, "Our noble
friend, my most beloved Delio!" (III.i.1). Delio's speech to Antonio
in III.i quite explicitly recalls the earlier scene:

> Methinks 'twas yesterday: let me but wink,
> And not behold your face, which to mine eye
> Is somewhat leaner, verily I should dream
> It were within this half-hour.
>
> (III.i.8–11)

Webster here makes a humorous, self-conscious reference to his violation of the unity of time between the second and third acts, having
allowed several years to elapse in the story, while maintaining dramatic tension in the theatre. Dramatic convention is thus exposed,
while the change in Antonio's position since Act I is emphasized.
Antonio's reply illuminates this change:

> You have not been in law, friend Delio,
> Nor in prison, nor a suitor at the court,
> Nor begg'd the reversion of some great man's place,
> Nor troubled with an old wife, which doth make
> Your time so insensibly hasten.
>
> (III.i.12–16)

The world in which time passes quickly and easily—the world of
the theatre—is not the world of those who experience profound
difficulty and pain. The deep changes wrought in the lovers between the second and third acts cannot be compassed by theatrical
time, Antonio implies. At this point in the play, Webster appears to
be drawing the audience's attention to the theatrical artifice for a
particular reason. By slowing the pace of his action and at the same
time violating theatrical illusion, Webster exposes the structural
principles of his play to the audience. The deliberate recreation of
the staging of the beginning of the play calls attention to itself as the
beginning of a second phase or new cycle in the action. We are back
at the beginning—this second cycle repeats the substance of the first
in order to illuminate the progress of the tragedy.

Both sequences begin with this encounter between Antonio and

Delio as servants or courtiers in attendance at Malfi. The next major move is to a court scene, which is oddly abbreviated or interrupted. In the first scene of the play, a departure is the first real topic when the princes gather together. Ferdinand begins the court scene by announcing, "Here's the Lord Silvio, is come to take his leave" (I.i.151). In the first scene of the third act, as soon as Ferdinand enters, Delio announces that "The Lord Ferdinand / Is going to bed" (III.i.37–38). The court scenes arouse expectations only to disappoint them.[9] In the first court scene, the ceremonial encounter of the Duchess and her brothers is undercut by Antonio's verbal commentary; in the second court scene, Ferdinand's public speech of forgiveness to the Duchess is rapidly undermined by the private disclosure of his suspicions. Both court scenes are then followed by a conspiratorial conference between Ferdinand and Bosola, during which a key is probably exchanged.[10] The wooing scene of Act I is then clearly recalled by the first half of III.ii, as a private and delightful interview between Antonio and the Duchess again takes center stage, though again menaced by what has preceded it. The menace is then fulfilled by an antagonist whose vision is at odds with that of the Duchess—in III.ii, the vision of Ferdinand; in II.i, that of Bosola. Bosola's disgust with human sexuality and its origin in "a rotten and dead body" (II.i.57) follows immediately upon the frank sensuality of the wooing scene; Ferdinand's view of the Duchess as "unquenchable wild-fire" (III.ii.116) and of Antonio as her "lecher" (III.ii.100) is juxtaposed with the playful intimacy of the bedroom scene. Then a similar pattern of evasion and pursuit is dramatized. In II.i and ii, panic and confusion reign as the Duchess goes into labour, and Antonio invents a number of excuses, among them the following:

> We have lost much plate you know; and but this evening
> Jewels, to the value of four thousand ducats
> Are missing in the duchess' cabinet.
>
> (II.ii.52–54)

In III.ii, "more earthquakes" (III.ii.155) threaten to ruin the lovers, and the stage again reflects the chaos with a confusing number of exits and entrances. The Duchess invents a "noble lie" (III.ii.180) which she hopes will save them:

Antonio, the master of our household,
Hath dealt so falsely with me, in's accounts:
My brother stood engag'd with me for money
Ta'en up of certain Neapolitan Jews,
And Antonio lets the bonds be forfeit.

(III.ii.166–70)

In both scenes, thefts are invented by the Duchess and Antonio, officers are assembled, and finally the game is given away, in Act II by Antonio (with his dropping of the horoscope), and in Act III by the Duchess (with her trusting admission to Bosola). As the earlier sequence was marked by Bosola's discovery of a key piece of "intelligence"—the birth of the Duchess's child (in II.iii)—so the later sequence comes to a head with Bosola's discovery of the identity of the father of that child (in III.ii). The consequent rage of Ferdinand, and his determination to act, is the dramatic climax of both sequences. The scene that begins, "I have this night digg'd up a mandrake" (II.v.1) is later echoed in the stage action of III.iii where Ferdinand is described as "a deadly cannon / That lightens ere it smokes" (54–55). In both scenes, Ferdinand is tuned to a hysterical pitch.

It is clear that the first two acts trace a sequence of events that is largely repeated in the third act. The general outline of both sequences is strikingly similar, and the visual repetition in performance can be even more evident. Given such clear evidence of deliberate structure in the play, it becomes difficult to accept critical commonplaces about Webster's haphazard dramatic construction. We may agree that in watching *The Duchess of Malfi*, "we find ourselves watching a monster—cold, slow, writhing, a boa constrictor riveting us with its unplotted undulations" (Whittaker review) but we can hardly accept that this riveting tension is entirely "unplotted."

The repetition of similar structures in Webster's drama reflects something more than simply "episodic" or "discontinuous" playwrighting, as some critics claim. According to Doran, "episodic structure is essentially serial, a stringing together of events in mere temporal succession; each complication is solved as it arises, and a new one succeeds it" (295). She connects this episodic structure with Webster and other Jacobeans: "The tendency to organize events around several episodic centers, with the connections falling slack between them, curses such otherwise fine plays as those of Chapman, Tourneur, Webster, and Ford" (298). Doran's criticism, however, applies more aptly to Webster's source than to his play. In the story of the Duchess translated from Belleforest in Painter's *Palace of Pleasure*, repeated events, like the renewed exhortations to the reader to avoid the Duchess's well-deserved fate, do not succeed in unifying an essentially episodic linear narrative. In Painter, the initial discovery of the Duchess's actions (made after the birth of her second child), is carried to the ears of her brothers by rumor alone; their reactions, "swelling wyth despite, and rapt with furie" (190), are quickly passed over in a few sentences. The arousal of their suspicions prompts them to plant spies in the Duchess's court; this, in turn, forces the lovers to separate and finally to give themselves up when they are reunited at Ancona (191–98). After the lovers' public confession, the brothers vent their spleens at length, and finally force the lovers to separate a second time. In Painter's story, repeated actions are woven unemphatically into the chain of causally connected events so that they do not draw attention to themselves or illuminate significant contrasts or changes in the shape of the narrative. In Webster's play, the antagonism of the brothers and Bosola toward the lovers is developed fully in the first two acts to allow full structural repetition in the third act. Though Painter's version is logical and sequential in a way that Webster's is not, it remains mere narrative, a chronological chain of episodes. Webster's play, with its rough transitions and deliberate violation of strict linear causality, elaborates and thus emphasizes the repetitions that are almost buried in its source.

In the first two acts of *The Duchess of Malfi*, Webster builds his action to a point of extreme tension that he then deliberately leaves dramatically unresolved. George Rylands, who directed the successful 1945 production of the play, confirmed that "the first movement [that] ends after Act II" achieves its climax in "Ferdinand's revelation to the Cardinal of their sister's shame and disobedience" (vii–ix). The third act does not follow as an immediate consequence of the preceding action, but rephrases the same sequence of events in an altered form. Its "climax" (in III.iii) is more muted because the sustained intensity of the death scene is still to come. The end of the second, intensified and abbreviated, "movement" of the play is sig-

nalled by the ceremonial banishment scene, which confirms visually
the Duchess's inevitable defeat at the hands of her brothers. Her
defeat, however, is finalized only after her control and transcendence of her circumstances have been emphasized through repetition. The repetitive construction of the first three acts has a number
of important consequences for the play.

Coleridge gives first place in his list of Shakespeare's "characteristics" to the dramatist's arousal of "expectation in preference to surprise." He goes on to describe this important quality: "As the feeling with which we startle at a shooting star compared with that of
watching the sunrise at the pre-established moment, such and so
low is surprise compared with expectation" (4:61). A great many of
Webster's dramaturgical techniques can be understood in similar
aesthetic terms. In writing a play, his problem is to maintain dramatic tension while minimizing suspense. He must redirect the attention of the audience from "story" to the dynamic interplay of
energies and responses. As Beckerman says of Elizabethan drama:
"The poets sought to project multiple aspects of a situation" because
"interest was not in the conflict leading to a decision, but the effect
of the decision itself" (29, 33). This combined stress on effect rather
than cause, and on multiple effects rather than on one single effect,
may well have led to the dramatists' use of repetitive form. Repeated
scenes or groups of scenes not only emphasize multiplicity of effect
but also de-emphasize the narrative line, for the advantage of "expectation" over "surprise." Webster combines repetitive form with
interruptive form, giving his work the appearance of "discontinuity"
complained of by critics, but gaining distinct advantages for his play
on the stage.

Repetitive form is one way of de-emphasizing causation in drama.
Because there is no single, direct linear narrative proceeding from
the Duchess's wooing of Antonio to her death, it is dramatically
impossible to see the latter as a result of the former—though some
commentators have tried to force the play into this pattern. The
play is not a cautionary tale. Nor is it a melodrama, in which the
Duchess is simply victimized by the crazed fury of her brothers.
The play is constructed so that the two worlds, of the Duchess and
Antonio, and of the Arragonian brothers, remain irreconcilable and
separate. Their causal relation is less important than their essential
qualities. Ferdinand's anger, for example, as it becomes increasingly

familiar on the stage, appears more and more automatic and irrational, disconnected from any discernible impetus or motive. The domestic calm of the Duchess and Antonio, on the other hand, is equally groundless and "irrational," menaced on all sides. The reassertion of both these dispositions in the replay of the third act clarifies their mutual independence and incompatibility. Ferdinand's fury is more distant and seemingly mechanical at the end of the third act (in III.iii) than at the end of the second. The fate of the Duchess is entirely predictable and inevitable, since the machinery of the play has twice put her through the same motions. Her fate is finally sealed in III.iv, the banishment scene, and the whole focus of the audience's interest is now not on what will happen, but on what must happen. The play's dramatic construction has aroused expectation rather than laying the basis for surprise. This is particularly important in preparation for the death scene, which should unfold not with shocking horror but with quiet inevitability.

Another important advantage of repetitive construction is its invitation to comparison. An action that is repeated allows the audience to measure the distance it has travelled since its first encounter with that action. In the first scene of the play, for example, it is clear that Ferdinand gathers his courtiers around him to await the arrival of the Duchess in her own court. When she enters, accompanied by ladies-in-waiting, Ferdinand's first words to her are deferential, as he presents one of his courtiers: "Here's the Lord Silvio, is come to take his leave" (I.i.151). It is the Duchess who holds the central authority, and gives the commands. In the first scene of Act III, however, the situation has changed. The Duchess enters without attendants, and the first announcement, made by Delio (now Ferdinand's servant), assumes Ferdinand is the central authority: "The Lord Ferdinand / Is going to bed" (III.i.37–38). It is Ferdinand, finally, who orders the Duchess to leave at the end of their brief interchange, then summons his own spy in her court. The parallelism between the two court scenes emphasizes their differences. Not only has Ferdinand assumed greater control, but the Duchess has also willingly surrendered political authority for domestic peace. The first scene of Act II in fact makes it quite clear that the Duchess doesn't desire formal authority as the head and center of a court; her real authority as a prince emerges chiefly in the death scene. Just as Ferdinand's control over the court at Malfi has increased in the third act, so has the domestic security of the Duchess and Antonio grown. Unlike the wooing scene, whose rhythm some critics have found nervous and "jerky" (Pearson review), the second scene of Act III shows the Duchess and Antonio as relaxed, open and secure. Their new intimacy is frequently emphasized by the staging as the Duchess undresses before Antonio, removing jewellery, gown and all the symbols of her station. In the 1960 Royal Shakespeare Company production, for example, the Duchess removed her own rings, earrings and bracelets while Antonio removed her necklace (an eerie anticipation of the strangling?); in the 1971 RSC production, the Duchess was "undressed by Cariola"; in the 1980 Royal Exchange production, the Duchess took off her gown.[11] The love of Antonio and the Duchess seems to grow in proportion to the menace that surrounds them.

After the scene of increased intimacy between the lovers, the second cycle shows a corresponding intensification in the attack that follows. Ferdinand's confrontation with the Duchess in III.ii is a more direct and passionate threat than Bosola's general cynicism and comic "apricocks" ruse to ferret out proof of her pregnancy in the second act. Yet the Duchess's resistance is strengthened in this second cycle. In the first cycle, the Duchess is forced off the stage while Antonio remains to invent excuses and make mistakes; in the second cycle, Antonio flees from Malfi while the Duchess remains a strong stage presence throughout the act. The Duchess's firmer control in the intensified replay of Act III is emphasized by contrast with Ferdinand's subsequent anger which, unlike his outburst of II.v, is distanced and muted by the commentary of III.iii. Thus it is clear that, even as the Arragonian brothers gain control in the plot, they lose ground in the play's world, and the Duchess assumes a more prominent role. In the first cycle, Act I was weighed against Act II, the lovers' vision against that of their enemies. Act III, the second cycle, recapitulates the opposition in order not only to intensify it but also to resolve it in the Duchess's favor.[12]

The intensification achieved by the repetition of material in the first three acts of *The Duchess of Malfi* is heightened by the extended time lapses between each act. Webster's violation of the unities has attracted considerable critical censure despite Samuel Johnson, who pointed out long ago that "time is, of all modes of existence, most obsequious to the imagination" (78). Stage productions of the play, ranging from the earliest to the most recent, have often attempted to minimize the "improbable" time gaps. In Poel's 1892 production, Acts II and III were conflated to eliminate repetition and time lapses, necessitating substantive changes in the text. A much more recent production of the play at the National Theatre in 1985 followed Poel's lead in attempting to maintain temporal unity.[13] The child born in the second act remained an infant throughout, and the "two children more" (III.i.7), born between the second and third acts, were entirely omitted. During the banishment and separation scenes (III.iv, v), the Duchess held a wailing infant in her arms. As a result, the pathos of the Duchess's situation was heightened. The brothers' fury appeared more monstrous, the Duchess's transgression less extreme. Yet by suggesting an expanse of time in the play Webster's intention was to give full and equal weight to the opposing groups.[14] A third stage production, at the Royal Exchange in 1980, exploited Webster's original time frame fully. The boy and girl for whom the Duchess shows concern before her death (IV.ii.203–5) appeared throughout the third act, in the bedroom scene (III.ii) and in the separation scene (III.v).[15] The domestic, familial context allowed Helen Mirren as the Duchess to play out fully on the stage the world she created and must leave. As the reviewer for the *Stage* put it, "Helen Mirren admirably blends nobility and humanity in the title part with the warmth of her scenes with Antonio and the children contrasting with the almost contemptuous coolness with which she confronts her executioners later on" (Review, "Manchester"). The reviewer for the *Sunday Times* remarked that the play's contracted time frame emphasized the Duchess's "speed and daring," as she "has no sooner brought Antonio to her bed than she's had his child, and no sooner had his child than she's had three children by him" (Review, "Is Murder Really Necessary?"). Boklund comments, "The silent part played by the children in *The Duchess of Malfi* turns what was merely a tragic love story into a family tragedy, with all the additional pathos and increased scope that this implies" (*Duchess* 96). By using repetitive sequences, reinforced by an extended time frame, Webster is able to give equal weight to the opposed worlds of his tragedy, and to intensify their opposition.

The opposing principles of familial love and psychotic rage that dominate the play are embodied in the dynamic confrontation between Ferdinand and the Duchess in the second scene of the third

act. Again, because of the repetitive construction of the first three
acts, the attention of the audience is drawn not merely to the story
of a Duchess destroyed by her brothers—which has in fact been
suggested from the beginning—but to the dramatic intensity of two
powerful forces meeting on the stage. This emphasis is particularly
important because the "story" is only part of the dramatic experience. The play is not only about the Duchess's destruction at the
hands of her brothers, but also about human destructiveness and
human resilience, pain and joy—the fit objects of tragedy. In diverting attention from the linear narrative, by using repetitive form,
analogical probability, and ceremonial dumb show to minimize the
primacy of "story," Webster is in fact directing our attention to what
the play is really about.

Webster's original design in the second and third acts of *The
Duchess of Malfi* can be further illuminated by comparison with
William Poel's attempt to revise it for his 1892 production.[16] In order to maintain the unities as far as possible, Poel eliminates the first
three scenes of Act II (including the "apricocks" plot), and sub-
stitutes a complex piece of stage business to account for Bosola's
discovery of the horoscope. Antonio does not drop the horoscope,
but carefully locks it away in a cupboard, whence it is retrieved by
the vigilant Bosola in a delicately orchestrated sequence of movements unhappily reminiscent of Restoration comedy. Ferdinand and
the Cardinal are present at Malfi from the beginning of the second
act, and their actions are clearly motivated by their desire to marry
the Duchess to Count Malateste. Entire passages from III.i and
III.iii are interpolated early in the second act to establish the
brothers' suspicions regarding the Duchess's secret marriage. The
last scene of Act II (II.v) elides effortlessly into the first scene of Act
III, and no time lapse is implied. When compared to Poel's version,
the deliberate repetitions of Webster's structure in the first three acts
become evident. Poel is forced to make extensive transpositions and
cuts in Webster's text in order to construct a logical, causally connected, linear narrative leading from Bosola's scheming to Ferdinand's revenge. Yet Poel's conflation of the second and third acts
gains compression at the expense of tragic expansion. In Poel, the
Duchess becomes merely a victim of an elaborate plot mechanism;
in Webster, opposing passions fully articulate their natures and play
themselves out in slow motion. In Poel, when all the action is

causally connected and visible on the stage without shifts in time or place, it becomes strictly *dependent* on time and place; in Webster, the irreconcilable passions cannot be contained, as it were, in the time frame of the play itself. The expanded time of the play suggests the vast size and endurance of its opposed forces. Poel's revision of *The Duchess of Malfi* illuminates by contrast the complementary functions of temporal expansion and structural repetition in Webster's play.

Kenneth Burke points out that, through the use of repetitive form, "by a varying number of details, the reader is led to feel more or less consciously the principle underlying them" (125). If there is an underlying principle that is reinforced through structural repetition in the play, it is surely the self-sufficient integrity of the love scenes that are framed by the distorted menace around them. Because in each case the menace precedes as well as follows the love scene, our sense of the inevitability of disaster is heightened while narrative causality is undercut. The repetition of the same pattern assures clarity in the aesthetic design.

CHAPTER TWO

~~~~~~

AN EXCELLENT PICTURE-MAKER: *Opening Parallels and Contrasts*

~~~~~~

IN the opening scenes of a play, a dramatist must define the limits of his play's world and place his protagonists in relation to it. In Elizabethan drama, Beckerman observes, "the first scenes perform a vital function. They establish the premises upon which the action will be built" (33). In the opening scenes of his major tragedies, Webster first attempts to provide a context—other than the conventional biases one brings to the theatre—within which acts are to be judged. By repeating and varying stage images in the opening sequence of scenes, Webster then places his protagonists in relation to that context. Each scene or episode modifies as it repeats the one before it; in this way Webster establishes complex, cumulative parallels and contrasts among different characters. In his use of this strategy Webster is by no means unique. Rose points out that "Shakespeare's usual practice in relating scene to scene is to select and dispose his material so that each scene comments upon the one preceding" (74). One thinks, for example, of the opening scenes of *King Lear*, in which one parent-child relationship is implicitly compared with another, or of the beginning of *Twelfth Night*, which contrasts the lovesick Orsino with a grieved but buoyant Viola. A close examination of the opening scenes of *The White Devil* and *The Duchess of Malfi* reveals Webster, like Shakespeare, to be a conscious artist, making use of inherited structures of repetition and modulation and exploiting the resources of the stage in order to create a complex, controlled dramatic world.

THE WHITE DEVIL

In the historical sources for *The White Devil*, Lodovico Orsini, a distant kinsman of Brachiano's, appears only at the end of the story as the murderer of Vittoria (Boklund, *White Devil* 18). Webster integrates Lodovico into the rest of the play, and uses him to open the play as well as to bring it to a close. The first scene of *The White Devil* presents an encounter between Lodovico and his friends, Gasparo and Antonelli, as they react to news of his banishment. Gasparo and Antonelli pay mechanical lip-service to notions of social justice, while Lodovico drives himself into an anarchic frenzy in response to their platitudes and warns:

> I'll make Italian cut-works in their guts
> If ever I return.
>
> (I.i.52–53)

The curious artifice of Lodovico's image only heightens the viciousness of his threat. His explosion in these lines marks the climactic moment of the scene, which then returns to its opening tone of bitter resignation. The construction of the scene is circular: it does not so much present two opposed perspectives as delineate a common movement toward release. In his review of the 1976 production at the Old Vic, Irving Wardle commented on "the art of shared rhythm (such as the *prestissimo* opening), from which the action can rise to a fiery atmospheric plateau where single, down-to-earth lines can generate the most extraordinary emotional response" ("Old Vic"). This shared rhythm is, in Wardle's view, the key to playing such scenes on the stage. *The Duchess of Malfi*'s most obvious example of a scene like this one is II.v, where the apparently opposed voices of the Cardinal and Ferdinand don't really communicate, but propel the scene forward at a feverish pace. Together, they generate enough energy not only to sustain the scene's tension but also to push it toward a climax that is even more intense than its highly charged opening. Like the first scene of *The White Devil*, the voice of restraint and the voice of release are carefully counterpointed so that a rhythm of gradually escalating emotion is achieved. The purpose of this scene is not to present a real conflict, but to delineate a move-

ment of the will as it struggles with impediments, finally issues in
violent desire, and then subsides again into ironic acceptance of its
own limitations. The first scene of *The White Devil* traces in microcosm a larger movement in the play as a whole. Jenkins points out
that the imaginative rhythm of *The White Devil* lies, not in its
revenge-plot structure, but in "the progress of passionate life
through its fulfilment to its inevitable destruction" (51). The protagonists' defiance leads them to a heroic, though fallible and human, assertion of their greatness, until finally they must confront
the greater power of death, of which the revengers seem merely
agents. The conflict upon which the plot appears to turn is thus a
catalyst for the protagonists' tragic experience. The opening scene
prepares an audience for the play's peculiar rhythm, which is a collective rather than an individual one, based not on the revenge structure but on the independent triumph and final defeat of the will.
This rhythm is repeated not once but many times in the course of
the play.

Lodovico's appearance at the beginning of the play, like a theme in
music, gives in simplified form the play's primary idea. Apart from
suggesting a shared rhythm that anticipates the play's total movement, it presents a very clear, static stage picture. In it, a single,
isolated man confronts society's judgment upon him in the chorus of
Antonelli and Gasparo. The individual will and its violent, anarchic
potential are highlighted in contrast to the conventional commonplaces voiced by the social group. The perfunctoriness of the
real struggle between them only emphasizes their symbolic differences. Mack points out that "the one pervasive Jacobean theme tends
to be the undertaking and working out of acts of will" (41). Webster
highlights the individual will by placing it in the context of social
disapproval; this is to be his theme repeatedly in the following
scenes, as first Cornelia, then Monticelso and Francisco, attack
Brachiano's illicit desire in conventional terms. Here, the discussion
among Lodovico and his friends both highlights questions of social
justice and at the same time limits the range of moral alternatives
available to decide such questions. Gasparo and Antonelli are
spokesmen for the ideal of social justice:

The law doth sometimes mediate, thinks it good
Not ever to steep violent sins in blood,—

> This gentle penance may both end your crimes,
> And in the example better these bad times.
>
> (I.i.34–37)

Yet the ideal is withdrawn even as it is advanced; as James Smith declares, "Gasparo's and Antonelli's parade of the word justice, it seems clear, is mere hypocrisy" (120). Any credible notion of justice fades when it becomes obvious that the "law" (I.i.34) that banished Lodovico was simply a mechanical, irrational act of rejection by his equally corrupt followers.

> Your followers
> Have swallowed you like mummia, and being sick
> With such unnatural and horrid physic
> Vomit you up i' th' kennel.
>
> (I.i.15–18)

In the opening scene, Webster directs the attention of the audience to moral issues while he deliberately complicates and neutralizes the conventional view of them. Lodovico's obsessive violence is set against the unconvincing conventionality of his friends, which makes a simple moral interpretation of Lodovico impossible. As Lodovico in the first scene sounds a note of criminal defiance that will later be echoed by the protagonists, Antonelli and Gasparo are outlines for the figures of Cornelia, Marcello, and Isabella. The conflict that is visually and verbally evoked in the first scene is reworked and elaborated in the rest of the play. In a general sense, the trial that is implied when the play opens is reanimated later, in Brachiano's informal trial by Francisco and Monticelso in II.i; in Vittoria's arraignment in III.ii; in the private "trial" of Vittoria by Brachiano in IV.ii; and finally in the justice administered by Giovanni at the end of the play. In fact, the play begins and ends with the punishment of Lodovico, and passes through a series of trials, both private and public. The repetition of this dramatic situation at key points in the linear progression of the play lends it a certain unity in performance. More immediately, the two scenes that follow the first scene are specifically designed as significant variations on the basic theme that is presented initially.

The opening scene prepares the audience for the intensity of Brachiano's passion for Vittoria in the following scene. Lodovico's violent destructiveness, aimed at Brachiano in the first scene, is an emotional equivalent on the stage to the passion with which Brachiano is gripped when he first appears. Brachiano's opening line, "Quite lost Flamineo" (I.ii.3), becomes a credible cry in the midst of a world that the audience has seen as dangerous and anarchic, a world that Flamineo's banter can never quite eclipse. What Lodovico says and how he behaves in the first scene give Brachiano the dramatic impact he needs in the second. When Jenkins complains that Webster undermines the revenge structure of his play with this first scene, in which "the shadow is cast before the deed is committed" (54), he ignores Webster's aesthetic purpose in executing this conventional stroke of dramaturgy. The threat of inevitable doom and destruction that Lodovico represents from the beginning is fulfilled, not in the revenge of the second act, but in the more immediate passionate despair of the first. Lodovico's "revenge" precedes Brachiano's "crime" in the linear dramatic narrative; violent emotional upheaval precedes the desperation of passion in the dramatic rhythm. The first scene builds Brachiano's world on the stage; James Smith comments that "its function . . . is to prepare the background against which, during the second scene, the principal characters are to appear. To use a common metaphor, the atmosphere is to be created in which they breathe" (122).

The first scene also prepares us for Webster's strategy of repetition. Lodovico refers to Brachiano as his own analogue—another "great man" who seeks to ruin others with his own debauchery and who also deserves banishment for his crimes (I.i.38–42). Several critics have noted the similar entrances of Lodovico in I.i and Brachiano in I.ii. Lucas describes the dramatic rhythm of the first two scenes:

> "Banished!"—no work in English begins more vividly than *The White Devil* with this angry cry of the bitter Lodovico, the destined deathsman of the play, who is to close the tragedy as he opens it, when at last, his vengeance accomplished and his hot blood cooled, he goes to rack and torment as a weary man to his bed. This headlong opening is followed by a scene of swift gibe and counter-gibe between Lodovico and his half-mocking comforters; it ends; the stage is hidden in torch-

lit darkness, and then comes the second lightning-flash—"Quite lost
Flamineo!" (1:21–22)

The striking similarity in the explosive self-descriptions Brachiano
and Lodovico utter in response to an offstage event establishes an
immediate connection between them on the stage. The connection
emphasizes Brachiano's isolation and powerlessness, and suggests
his potential for violence. Yet the analogy, important as it is in defining Brachiano's basic situation, is designed to show more than simply "different aspects of the same theme—the workings of evil
which, though among the same people, must vary indefinitely"
(James Smith 130). That is Lodovico's version of the analogy, which
the evidence of performance casts into doubt. Parallels in the dramatic treatment of the two characters serve chiefly to illuminate important differences between them.

Lodovico provides a backdrop for Brachiano against which he can
be differentiated. Although Lodovico himself points to their common situation, at the end of the scene he emphasizes his position as a
victim of "great men" like Brachiano:

Great men sell sheep, thus to be cut in pieces,
When first they have shorn them bare and sold their fleeces.
(I.i.62–63)

The following scene begins with the pomp of a torchlit procession,
fulfilling Lodovico's image of his triumphant opponents and contrasting with Lodovico's solitary exit to his banishment. Lodovico
prepares the audience to see a "great man" whose sins remain un-
punished, and the initial stage image confirms that impression. Yet
the ceremonial grandeur is immediately undermined by Brachiano's
desperate cry that he is "Quite lost" (I.ii.3). The torches are ordered
off the stage by Flamineo, and the theatre itself begins to reflect the
inner darkness of Brachiano's despair, a despair that is heightened
by contrast with Flamineo's crude banter. The outward dissimilar-
ity between Lodovico and Brachiano suddenly collapses into an unexpected similarity which in turn suggests crucial differences.

Of course, directors have chosen to interpret Brachiano in a number of ways. In the 1984 Greenwich production, as Irving Wardle
tells it, "Gerald Murphy's Brachiano first appears spreadeagled

against a wall and vomiting over the dinner table before groping his way into Vittoria's favours" (Review, "Greenwich"). This was a clear misrepresentation of Webster's intention, as was, at the opposite extreme, the 1925 Renaissance Theatre production that, according to Lucas's review, portrayed Brachiano as "a rather insignificant-looking young Lothario, shorter than most of the characters on the stage, particularly his own Duchess." These are crude exaggerations of Brachiano's tendencies toward desperate recklessness on the one hand, and fatal weakness on the other; both are outside the range of acceptable stage interpretations of the text, as the reactions of theatre critics testify. Webster chooses first to emphasize Brachiano's frightened vulnerability in contrast to Lodovico's ruthless violence, and second, once this contrast has been firmly established, to highlight Brachiano's defiant strength in his confrontation with the brothers. The second scene of the play fulfills expectations aroused in the first scene in an unexpected form. Like Lodovico, Brachiano is a lost and desperate man who acts out of that desperation; unlike Lodovico, a murderer and hardened villain, Brachiano is a lover. After neutralizing the impact of conventional moral judgments on both men, Webster can develop finer dramatic distinctions between them. Though both Brachiano and Lodovico are condemned by the standards of conventional morality, they are very different on the stage, and it is there that they are judged.

In the first scene, Gasparo and Antonelli appear to be Lodovico's social inferiors and dependents. They address him as "my lord" (I.i.12,33) and emphasize his loss of the "noblest earldom" (I.i.15).[1] His banishment, however, makes him dependent on them, inverting the normal social hierarchy. He is forced to listen to their platitudinous condemnation of him, and finally gives them some money (I.i.61) to help them repeal his banishment. Lodovico himself draws attention to his relation with them; money given to them is like a bribe given to the "knave hangman" (56), though he must at the same time be "ever bound" (60) to them. There is a similar inversion of the balance of power in the following scene between Brachiano and Flamineo. Brachiano's position as a social superior is emphasized at the beginning of the scene, with "my lord" uttered three times in the first five lines, "duke" twice, and "noble" once. The verbal reinforcement of Brachiano's elevated social rank heightens by contrast his vulnerable emotional situation. As the scene progresses, Flamineo's initial obsequiousness changes to a jocular tone of masculine equality with Brachiano. The change is an abrupt one, occurring immediately after the departure of attendants, and marked by Flamineo's shift from verse to prose as he begins to "talk freely" (I.ii.17). Like Gasparo and Antonelli, Flamineo increasingly takes advantage of Brachiano's dependence in order to impose his own vision on him. While Brachiano, with his halting interjections, immersed in his immediate obsession with Vittoria, appears to be almost oblivious of Flamineo, Flamineo carries on a lively monologue in which love is degraded to the level of mere lust. As James Smith points out, Flamineo "has to encourage the passion, and at the same time to degrade it" (125). In both scenes the vulnerability of the "great man" permits the servant or social inferior to hold sway over him.

The White Devil's first two scenes both appear to present two visions of the world in conflict; the social vision of accommodation is pitted against the anarchic vision of the individual. Again, however, repetition serves the purpose of contrast. In the first scene, the social vision of Gasparo and Antonelli is, like Lodovico's, not one of collective justice, but one of continual power struggles among corrupt individuals. Just as there seems to be little difference between Lodovico and the "great men" who vindictively banish him, there is little distinction between Lodovico and his companions. In the violent world described by Antonelli and Gasparo, Lodovico's murders seem of minor importance; Lodovico himself dismisses them as mere "flea-bitings" (I.i.32). His silence throughout most of the scene indicates his assent to their descriptions of his acts, as well as his impatience with their platitudes. The situation is far more complex in the second scene, whose construction allows Brachiano to transcend Flamineo's restricted vision. Brachiano's silence during Flamineo's diatribes conveys his separateness from them; Flamineo, though he begins and ends the scene, is quite eclipsed by Brachiano at its center. He makes repeated attempts to describe Brachiano's passionate urgency with elaborate metaphor: first, Vittoria is compared to a "buttery-hatch at court," Brachiano to "passionate crowding . . . hot suit after the beverage" (I.ii.23–25); second, Vittoria is "just like a summer birdcage in a garden," Brachiano is like one of the "birds that are without [that] despair to get in" (I.ii.43–45). Yet neither of these descriptions adequately conveys the silent intensity of the man on the stage. Flamineo's metaphors, with which he attempts to control Brachiano, are plural and impersonal observations that are contradicted visually by Brachiano's singular, isolated, and human stage presence. Although in the opening scene there is direct confrontation between Lodovico and his friends, on a deeper level there is agreement. In the second scene the reverse is true; Flamineo and Brachiano appear to pursue the same end, but are implicitly at odds with one another. In each case the central figure is vulnerable because of his situation and dependent on his social inferiors. Yet ultimately Lodovico's vulnerability is due to his crimes; Brachiano's, to his love for Vittoria. This is an important distinction with which to launch the play's main action.

When the play begins, Lodovico is a caricature of the criminal that Brachiano will become later in the play—banished for his crimes by his enemies, "great men" who are not just but vengeful and irrational. It is the play's construction itself that illuminates the essential differences between Lodovico, the caricatured criminal, and Brachiano. Lodovico's crimes are history when the play begins, rooted in mysterious, wanton evil; Brachiano's crimes and their genesis, his love for Vittoria, are the action of *The White Devil*. Lodovico is the villain-hero of another play which is almost over when this one begins; Brachiano is the villain-hero of this play, and carries with him its beginning, middle, and end. By presenting Lodovico in the first scene as a caricature of Brachiano, Webster is able both to emphasize the broad outlines of his play in little and to suggest by analogy finer distinctions in the body of the play.

The first scene of Act II measures the contrast established in the first two scenes between Lodovico and Brachiano by duplicating exactly the stage image of the first scene. Productions that choose to alter the blocking of either scene obscure the symmetry and clarity of Webster's design. According to Wardle's review in the *Times*, Antonelli was cut from the opening scene in the 1976 production at the Old Vic, an omission which would have made the visual analogy with the first scene of the second act impossible ("Old Vic"). As Antonelli and Gasparo had joined forces against Lodovico, like a "well . . . with two buckets" (I.i.29), so Francisco and Monticelso confront Brachiano. The creation of a parallel stage picture is conspicuous and deliberate in II.i; the stage is filled with servants and attendants only to be emptied immediately (II.i.19 Brown's s.d.), leaving the three men alone on the stage. Monticelso attacks Brachiano first.

> O my lord,
> The drunkard after all his lavish cups,
> Is dry, and then is sober, so at length,
> When you awake from this lascivious dream,
> Repentance then will follow.
>
> (II.i.32–36)

The metaphor with which he chooses to castigate Brachiano echoes the real charges made against Lodovico by the similarly self-righteous Antonelli.

> All the damnable degrees
> Of drinkings have you stagger'd through.
>
> (I.i.18–19)

Antonelli's alliteration is almost comic in its mechanical overemphasis, and draws attention to the speaker's exaggeration rather than to the crime of which he speaks. Similarly, Monticelso's elaborate metaphor draws attention to his ingenious connections of thought and language rather than to Brachiano's action. The tone and rhythm of the two scenes are as similar as their substance. In both interviews, Lodovico and Brachiano at first remain silent before the accusations against them; then both burst out impatiently and finally grow to an uneasy reconciliation with their interlocutors. Again, the repetition of the same situation on the stage illuminates a central difference between them. Though the shocked, hypocritical tone of Antonelli's and Gasparo's accusations undermines their credibility for the audience, the information they provide about Lodovico's crimes is entirely reliable. Francisco and Monticelso, on the other hand, give a version of Brachiano's crime that misrepresents the evidence of the preceding scene.

> Some eagles that should gaze upon the sun
> Seldom soar high, but take their lustful ease,
> Since they from dunghill birds their prey can seize.
>
> (II.i.49–51)

In this case, the audience knows more than do the brothers. Brachiano's desperate passion can hardly be described as "lustful ease"; this trivializing of the relation between Brachiano and Vittoria heightens our memory of their strong mutual commitment in the previous scene. Moreover, the brothers' moralizing tone is contaminated by an element of crude enjoyment, present, for example, in the speech above and reminiscent of Flamineo, even in its reference to birds. Their attacks tell us more about them than about Brachiano, since we have already seen on stage what they describe. Webster restages the dramatic situation of I.i in order to show the audience how far it has travelled in the interim. Brachiano is not the mercenary criminal that Lodovico is, however the brothers would have it; the repeated stage image makes this clear. His "crime" is love, not gluttony or murder. Although Webster's construction in the first three scenes of *The White Devil* is designed to inhibit conventional moral judgments by putting them in the mouths of villains, he nonetheless draws fine moral and dramatic distinctions.

In *The White Devil*, the contrasts and parallels between the situations of Lodovico and Brachiano serve both to define and to highlight the nature of the protagonist. Webster carefully builds each stage image on the preceding one, to establish a complex, cumulative meaning. This kind of dramatic craftsmanship serves Webster particularly well in the first few scenes of a play, in which the world of the play, and the place of the protagonist in that world, must be clearly delineated. In both his major plays, Webster works above all as a professional dramatist, keeping in mind the visual as well as the verbal impact of his art. The first act of *The Duchess of Malfi* also reveals Webster's careful use of repeated stage images to create complex meaning through parallel and contrast.

THE DUCHESS OF MALFI

In his description of the imagery of the first act of *The Duchess of Malfi*, Price contends that "Webster has done far more than introduce certain characters, he has established the idea of treachery, poison, and slow corruption working in individuals and in the state" (192). Similarly, Belsey views the entire first act as an exploration of

Antonio's initial antitheses of "purity and life, or death and diseases" (102). Such observations, however true, fail to account for the particular nature of the stage action in the first act. Above all the act establishes a series of relationships on the stage—first between Antonio and Delio; then between Bosola and the Cardinal; between Ferdinand and his courtiers; between Ferdinand and Bosola; between the Duchess and her brothers; and, finally, between the Duchess and Antonio. The act is in fact composed of a succession of intense private interviews between two or three characters, and this pattern is sustained even in the central court scene, which is transmitted through the comments exchanged between Antonio and Delio. The dramatic impact of this series of juxtaposed dialogues cannot be described adequately in Price's thematic terms. Nor can it be reduced to a simple political lesson, as Bliss suggests: "In playing off Antonio's recipe against a leisurely exploration of princes' courts, Webster has suggested Malfi's urgent need for attention to public matters. . . . Unconcerned with her duchy's political health, the Duchess seeks private happiness at the expense of public stability" (145). Antonio's political model is undercut before it can serve as a standard for the Duchess's behavior. Her private action is measured against other private actions, not against a public we do not see. The successive vignettes establish a momentum, a restless, jerky rhythm of performance that will be countered at the end of the scene, and in addition they emphasize the dynamics of power and submission with which the play will be concerned.

Though most modern editors print the first act of *The Duchess of Malfi* as a single continuous scene, the original quarto of 1623 divides it into two separate scenes at line 82. In his edition, John Russell Brown adopts the customary practice while pointing out that separate scenes may well have been intended.[2] In fact, the first eighty-two lines exhibit typical scene construction, with the exchanges between Antonio and Delio framing the central confrontation between Bosola and the Cardinal. The formal symmetry of the scene is in inverse proportion to its moral complexity. As in *The White Devil*, the opening scene invokes ideals of conventional social order and justice only to illuminate their inadequacy before a complex dramatic situation. In this way Webster introduces the terms in which his protagonists are to be evaluated.

The scene begins with a dialogue between Antonio and Delio.

The importance of the opening mood was emphasized by Martin Holmes in his review of Donald McWhinnie's 1960 Royal Shakespeare Company production. In McWhinnie's production, "a shouting, cachinnating crowd of odds-and-ends rushed across the stage" at the beginning, making "a very awkward and incongruous introduction to the quiet conversation with which Webster has chosen to begin the play." Holmes goes on to say that McWhinnie's apparently deliberate decision to work at variance to the text "is particularly unsafe in handling an author who planned his dramatic effects, visual as well as aural, as clearly as did Webster" (450). Like the beginning of many Shakespearean plays, the opening interchange moves the play in a direction that will soon be contradicted by the ensuing action. Here, the warm, relaxed tone of the men greeting one another, and Antonio's measured, philosophical account of the French court are, like the first part of the first scene of *King Lear*, false indications of the nature of the play to come. Moreover, the stage image of these two men as friends and equals will remain a comment on the rest of the action, where characters bid for power over one another. Antonio's lengthy account of the French court establishes the complementary functions of ideal ruler and ideal subject. Antonio describes both what a ruler should do in purging his court of "dissolute / And infamous persons" (I.i.8–9), and what a subject should do in instructing his prince and informing him of corruption (I.i.20).[3]

Antonio's lengthy speech, which sets forth the ideal relationship between ruler and subject, is immediately complicated and challenged by the episode that follows. In Antonio's scheme, the Cardinal may appear to be the ideal ruler shaking off a sycophant, a "dissolute / And infamous" person. Yet Bosola seems to be equally an instructor, rather than a flatterer—a "court gall" (I.i.23) who "haunts" the Cardinal to remind him of what he is, and who does what Antonio himself is perhaps incapable of doing. The ambiguity is captured by Antonio's introduction as Bosola enters:

> Here comes Bosola,
> The only court-gall:—yet I observe his railing
> Is not for simple love of piety;
> Indeed he rails at those things which he wants,
> Would be as lecherous, covetous, or proud,

> Bloody, or envious, as any man,
> If he had means to be so.
>
> (I.i.22–28)

After declaring that instructing princes is a "noble duty," Antonio introduces Bosola as "the only court-gall." That the first words he uses to describe Bosola are intended approvingly becomes clear when the next clause begins its string of qualifications with the negative conjunction, "yet." As the episode continues, the ambiguity increases; for all his desire to become a sycophant, Bosola's cynical pragmatism is at the same time directed toward instructing the Cardinal. Whigham points out that in Bosola "the distanced moralist and the envious parasite coincide in uneasy dissonance" (177).

Furthermore, as the relation between master and servant, introduced by Antonio, becomes increasingly difficult to disentangle, the play's emotional range broadens in preparation for the rest of the action. When Bosola comes on the stage, he interrupts the discursive complacency of Antonio's speech with a burst of primitive energy. As Wardle put it in a review of the 1971 Royal Court production: "Lines like Bosola's, 'I do haunt you still' are like fateful entries in a concerto, prophetic magical utterances that should send a thrill round the house and change the configurations on stage" ("Uninhabited Nightmare"). The line gives a hint of the kind of play that is to come. Its tone of injustice and betrayal, channelled into aggressive energy, cuts through the measured idealism of Antonio at once. And this is to be a play at least partly about the tension between peace and intrusion, between ideas and instincts. In the figure of Bosola in the first scene, the play's contradictions and complexities find early expression. The images he uses indicate his simultaneous attraction to, and distaste for, corruption and power:

> could I be one of their flattering panders, I would hang on their ears like a horse-leech till I were full, and then drop off. (I.i.52–54)

The simultaneous repulsion and attraction prepare us for Ferdinand's horrified fascination with the Duchess. The series of general analogies Bosola finds for his own situation by implication engages the other characters and so expands the range of vision in the play.

The first scene generates images that are repeated and varied later on. From Antonio's vision of an ideal world where hopes are fulfilled, the scene moves to Bosola's image of "Tantalus" (I.i.57), eternally hopeful and eternally disappointed. The episode itself is a dramatization of frustrated energy and restless desire. The Cardinal exits quickly and Bosola is left with no outlet. Antonio's diagnosis of Bosola's problem as due to "want of action" (I.i.80) is picked up in the next episode, when Ferdinand cries wearily, "When shall we leave this sportive action, and fall to action indeed?" (I.i.91–92). The restless energy generated by both Bosola and Ferdinand is finally satisfied by the Duchess's striking assertion before she woos Antonio:

> even now,
> Even in this hate, as men in some great battles,
> By apprehending danger, have achiev'd
> Almost impossible actions—I have heard soldiers say so—
> So I, through frights, and threat'nings, will assay
> This dangerous venture.
>
> (I.i.343–48)

Our satisfaction with the Duchess's decision to act is based on the frustrated, idle energy built up through the scene.[4] The image used by the Duchess highlights her strength and resolution, rather than suggesting "the Arragonian family penchant for self-aggrandizement" (Bliss 144). It both exploits and releases the associations of images used earlier with relation to Ferdinand and Bosola.

Successive dialogues and poetic imagery throughout the act build an atmosphere of energy and violence that will be exploited only to be defused in the wooing scene. Further, repeated stage images continually explore the relation between master and servant that is set forth by Antonio at the beginning of the play. In the interview between Bosola and the Cardinal, the tension in this relation is immediately apparent. The problem clearly arises of how to interpret these two characters in terms of Antonio's scheme. Is Bosola a "dissolute" (I.i.8) who should be purged, or a good instructor who should not be neglected? The stage image does not clarify this, nor do the contradictory assessments of Antonio and Delio. For Antonio, Bosola is "very valiant" (I.i.76); for Delio, he is guilty of "a notorious murder" (I.i.71). Moral ambiguity clouds the master-servant relation in the early stages of the play and persists until the very end.

If, in the first scene, Bosola appears to be an aggressively ambitious servant, in the second Ferdinand is a tyrannical master. Both represent possible abuses of Antonio's ideal. Again, the staging clarifies this repeated concern with the dynamics of power. Ferdinand, surrounded by his courtiers, is awarding a prize. The conversation centers on the functions of a prince. "It is fitting a soldier arise to be a prince, but not necessary a prince descend to be a captain" (I.i.96–97), says Castruchio, thus compounding the moral problem with a new variation on the theme first introduced by Antonio. Castruchio's ideal, like Antonio's, allows both absolute power for the ruler and upward mobility for the servant. The results can lead to despotism or rebellion—to Ferdinand, or to Bosola. In a brief episode that serves no other apparent purpose apart from displaying another aspect of the master-servant relation, Ferdinand suddenly bursts out in anger at his courtiers.

> Why do you laugh? Methinks you that are courtiers should be my touch-wood, take fire, when I give fire; that is, laugh when I laugh. (I.i.122–24)

Ferdinand asserts his power as a ruler in a ridiculous context and blocks the natural pleasure of his audience's laughter. The courtier who causes the incident, identified as Silvio, has a significant function throughout the scene, more obvious on the stage than in the study. His bawdy jest about Ferdinand's jennet—"True, my lord, he reels from the tilt often" (I.i.120)—is seen by Ferdinand as a threat to his dignity and hence his control. The sinister implication should be clear when at the end of the episode Ferdinand says,

> I would then have a mathematical instrument made for her face, that she might not laugh out of compass:—I shall shortly visit you at Milan, Lord Silvio. (I.i.136–38)

Silvio, moreover, stands at the visual center of the court scene that follows. Ferdinand introduces him to the Duchess and Cardinal with, "Here's the Lord Silvio, is come to take his leave" (I.i.151).

And, while Antonio and Delio observe and comment on the scene, it is reduced to a dumb show of ceremonial farewell, as the three rulers bid goodbye to Silvio. Promptbooks for stage performances of the play suggest his visual importance. In the 1892 Poel production, he conversed with the Duchess throughout the dumb show; in the 1960 Royal Shakespeare Company production, he "kisses Duchess's hand"; in the 1980 Royal Exchange production, he knelt before the Duchess. In all these productions, it is Silvio who takes the jewel from Ferdinand and hands it to Antonio (I.i.91); in all productions, Silvio exits with the Duchess. At the end of the episode, Ferdinand reiterates the visual importance of what has passed:

> We are now upon parting: good Lord Silvio,
> Do us commend to all our noble friends
> At the leaguer.
>
> (I.i.219–21)

Silvio's temporary function as a central character ends with the Duchess's offer to bring him "down to the haven" (I.i.223), and finally the two exit together. The choice of an otherwise minor character to perform an important function in the first scene indicates a deliberate dramatic strategy. Silvio incurs Ferdinand's wrath, stands at the center of a ceremonial farewell in dumb show, and finally exits with the Duchess. The function of Silvio, barely perceptible in a reading of the play, becomes in performance an anticipation of Antonio's future lot.[5] As a slight hint, a shadow of a theatrical suggestion, it sketches the outlines of a major movement of the play in little. Ferdinand's irrational tyranny, the ceremonial banishment, the Duchess's warmth and kindness to a servant—all are suggested in an understated form of analogical probability.[6] Thus, while the verbal text expounds on corruption in high places, the visual image again directs our attention to the master-servant relation.

During the central court scene dominated by the commentary of Antonio and Delio, Cariola reminds Antonio that he is still a servant when she interrupts:

> You must attend my lady, in the gallery,
> Some half an hour hence.
>
> (I.i.210–11)

The episode that follows reanimates the problem of master-servant relations. In the interview between Ferdinand and Bosola, the issues of control and exploitation are perhaps clearest because the struggle of wills is most intense. While the earlier episodes between the Cardinal and Bosola, and between Ferdinand and his courtiers, presented stage images of either the ambitious servant or the despotic master, in this confrontation both wills are evident and in conflict. The interview begins with dynamic thrust and counter-thrust; two strong characters with concealed motives encounter one another. After verbal fencing, Ferdinand gives Bosola some gold, promising him "a higher place by't" (I.i.263). Bosola at first resists and refuses the gold, but finally accepts it. The encounter dramatizes the despotic will of a prince corrupting and exploiting the vulnerable position of a servant. Bosola's usual mercenary attitude is suppressed here by Webster in order to make this dramatic point. The episode is clearly constructed to anticipate and heighten, both by parallel and by contrast, the wooing of Antonio that follows.

The wooing scene begins with a clear dramatic reassertion of the relation between the Duchess and Antonio as mistress and servant, respectively. She speaks to him first in a firm tone of command:

> I sent for you—sit down:
> Take pen and ink, and write: are you ready?
> (I.i.361–62)

As the scene continues, it builds in tension and energy as the pressure of unspoken desire mounts. The conventional relation between mistress and servant becomes less and less clear, as Antonio enters into the conversation with spirit and the Duchess allows him to become her equal, encouraging him with questions. Yet, at the significant and crucial moment when she gives him her wedding ring, she at the same time reasserts their relative positions:

> One of your eyes is blood-shot—use my ring to't,
> They say 'tis very sovereign—'twas my wedding ring,
> And I did vow never to part with it,
> But to my second husband.
> (I.i.404–7)

The Duchess's pun—conscious or not—on "sovereign," at the very moment she discloses her motives to Antonio, broadens her meaning slightly, allowing overtones of the mistress offering a bribe or reward to her servant to complicate the direct suggestion of marriage. As usual in Webster, the exchange or movement of a stage property (a bag of gold, a ring, a dead man's hand, a poniard), initiates and underlines a moment of dramatic crisis. Here, the Duchess's wedding ring recalls the gold offered to Bosola by Ferdinand in the earlier episode, particularly in the manner in which it is received. Bosola's reference to the gold coins as "devils" (I.i.263) is echoed in Antonio's fearful reference to the "saucy and ambitious devil" (I.i.411) dancing inside the wedding ring.[7] The Duchess's reassurances to Antonio all carry double meanings, activated especially by the recollection of Ferdinand's corruption of Bosola. The Duchess tells Antonio to "raise" (I.i.418) himself, and helps him to his feet in a gestural equivalent to her proposed elevation of his social position. She invites him to rejoice in her offer by using another double entendre, saying,

> So, now the ground's broke,
> You may discover what a wealthy mine
> I make you lord of.
> (I.i.428–30)

The metaphorical connotation of the word "wealth" is uncomfortably close to its literal meaning here. Antonio's speech on the dangers of "ambition" (I.i.420–28), followed by his visible doubt and withdrawal, forces such underlying meanings to the surface. In the promptbook for the 1960 Royal Shakespeare Company production, though the "ambition" speech was cut, Antonio's hesitancy was suggested visually when, at line 425, he removed the ring and held it out to the Duchess, provoking her anger and frustration as she in turn withdrew physically. The gesture recalls Bosola's initial rejection of Ferdinand's gold (I.i.263). The 1892 Poel production visually strengthened connections between the two episodes by staging both around a table, a physical barrier which may have suggested the class difference.[8] In the first episode, the class barrier forces Bosola's submission and impedes his individual freedom to refuse Ferdinand's offer. These overtones carry over into the wooing scene, complicating and challenging it. Yet the class barrier in the wooing scene, like the balcony in *Romeo and Juliet*, prevents not freedom but union, and so the terms of the encounter have changed. The dramatic result of such clear parallels to the preceding series of successive tableaux in which masters and servants bargained for power and control is not to undercut the wooing scene but rather to heighten it. The potentially disturbing overtones of this socially and politically sensitive encounter are not ignored, but are deliberately forced to the surface. Webster's dramaturgical need to insulate the wooing scene from moral ambivalence dictates his choice of preceding episodes.[9] The wooing scene activates all the moral and political abuses in the relation between master and servant only to dismiss them. This it does partly through context and partly through gesture.

That Webster himself understood the dramatic impact of juxtaposition is evident from the Duchess's whimsical remark to Antonio later in the play:

> Did you ever in your life know an ill painter
> Desire to have his dwelling next door to the shop
> Of an excellent picture-maker? 'twould disgrace
> His face-making, and undo him.
>
> (III.ii.49–52)

As in the opening scenes of *The White Devil*, Webster's dramatic construction in the first act of *The Duchess of Malfi* places a number of stage pictures side by side in order to emphasize their common meaning through repetition. Then the wooing scene is set against them, so that its dramatic meaning is established by comparison. Its moral status thus becomes relative, not absolute. Or, to put it more precisely, Webster sets up a context, a particular moral range within which the Duchess is to be judged. He is not content to depend on the prejudices his audience brings to the theatre, nor to trust the Duchess to the mercies of conventional attitudes.

The suggestion of a power struggle between mistress and servant in the wooing scene is evoked only to be mitigated by the mutuality and equality shown in the rest of the scene. If Antonio kneels quickly in a servile gesture (I.i.415) at the Duchess's suggestion of marriage, thereby fearfully reasserting his position as a social inferior, later in the scene the Duchess and Antonio kneel together (475) in a united act of worship. If the Duchess first kisses and embraces Antonio (469), telling him,

> All discord, without this circumference,
> Is only to be pitied, and not fear'd
>
> (I.i.469–70)

later in the scene she welcomes his embrace, saying,

> O, let me shroud my blushes in your bosom,
> Since 'tis the treasury of all my secrets.
>
> (I.i.502–3)

And if the Duchess helps Antonio up with her hand in the early part of the scene, she later asks him to do the same for her:

> I would have you lead your fortune by the hand
> Unto your marriage bed.
>
> (I.i.495–96)

The Duchess initiates the motions of love with delicate tact and consideration for Antonio's vulnerable position. She protects him from any contaminating hint of vulgar ambition by making all the moves herself and by playfully continuing to allude to his mixed fortune in obtaining her. The verbal equality and mutuality that develop during the scene are reinforced by gesture, thus neutralizing the earlier overtones of social inequality and moral exploitation.

The first act of *The Duchess of Malfi* is a lengthy one, composed of a series of tenuously connected incidents, an example of what one critic calls Webster's concern "with perfection of detail rather than general design" (Bradbrook, *Themes* 186). Yet closer examination reveals that the scene is carefully constructed. It deliberately draws attention to meaningful juxtapositions by clearly dividing one unit of action from another by means of abrupt shifts of focus. The scene opens with Antonio's set speech on the complementary functions of the ideal ruler and the ideal subject. The episode that immediately follows makes the audience sensitive to the difficulty of making moral judgments in such matters. Immediately Antonio's oversimplified view shifts into the moral complexities of the play which are beyond good and evil, for Bosola is both a would-be sycophant and a satiric instructor of his prince. Later, in the wooing scene, Webster creates a delicate balance of feeling that exploits the energy of power and ambition to dramatize the beginning of love. The ideal relation between prince and subject envisaged by Antonio is again put into a context which challenges and complicates it. The series of dramatic tableaux that precede the wooing scene present, again and again, the relation between master and servant, tyranny and ambition. The moral complexity of Bosola introduces a range of feeling that prepares the ground for the wooing scene. And the dramatic vignettes which explore the tyranny of power activate, only to defuse entirely, the political and moral contexts of the wooing scene.

The careful craftsmanship of the first act of *The Duchess of Malfi* owes a good deal to Webster's experimentation with similar principles of construction in the opening scenes of *The White Devil*. As in the earlier play, the repetition and juxtaposition of dramatic situations allow Webster to build cumulative contrasts and parallels within the carefully defined context of his tragedy.

CHAPTER THREE

〜〜〜〜〜〜〜〜〜〜〜〜〜〜〜〜〜〜〜〜〜

WOMEN OF PLEASURE AND MEN OF CONSCIENCE:
Subplots and Final Acts

〜〜〜〜〜〜〜〜〜〜〜〜〜〜〜〜〜〜〜〜〜

MODERN critics have drawn attention to the Elizabethan dramatists' frequent use of subsidiary action to mirror the main action of their plays. Beckerman observes that "a central, repeating element within the rhythmic pattern of extension-contraction is the arrangement of scenes or incidents in a combination of contrasting and comparable circumstances. Whether the scenes used are central or peripheral to the story, they repeatedly gain illumination through mirroring similar situations" (59). The subplot of *King Lear*, for example, illuminates the main plot through parallel and contrast. Similarly, Rowley's comic madhouse subplot scenes in *The Changeling* counterpoint the tragic madness of the main plot written by Middleton. Critics have virtually ignored Webster's use of subsidiary action in his plays. In his study of the multiple plot in Renaissance drama, Levin goes so far as to claim that Webster "avoided" subplots in his tragedies (*Multiple Plot* 221). Yet for the final act of each play, Webster invented a prominent subsidiary action which has long been dismissed or ignored by critics. In this chapter, Webster's use of subsidiary action will be considered as another example of his persistent use of repetition. We will see that the subsidiary action repeats the main action, not for contrast or intensification, but for final recapitulation. In both *The White Devil* and *The Duchess of Malfi*, the subsidiary action not only recapitulates and thus clarifies the play's tragic action, but also allows Webster to create a final, collective tragic vision.

THE WHITE DEVIL

During the first four acts of *The White Devil*, dramatic interest centers on the protagonists, Brachiano and Vittoria, and culminates in their intense confrontation at the house of convertites in IV.ii. Flamineo remains a secondary, though significant, character. In the final act, however, Brachiano and Vittoria are distanced from the audience while Flamineo and other hitherto minor characters assume a more prominent role in the action. In fact, these minor characters become involved in a fully articulated subsidiary action, which is coexistent with the main action and increasingly demands the attention of the audience.

In the first scene of the final act, Francisco appears in Brachiano's court disguised as Mulinassar and plots with his conspirators to murder Brachiano. Before they can effect their plan in V.iii, however, an independent action emerges in which Cornelia and Marcello attack Flamineo for conducting an affair with Zanche. In response to their attack, Flamineo unexpectedly murders his brother Marcello, an action which causes his mother Cornelia to plunge into grief and madness. Brachiano's death scene follows, framed and distanced by commentary exchanged between Francisco and Flamineo. After Brachiano's death, the consequences of Flamineo's act of murder increase. Giovanni ejects Flamineo from the court; Cornelia grows more distracted and delivers a poignant meditation on death while winding Marcello's corpse; and Brachiano's ghost threatens Flamineo with emblems of mortality. Driven by despair, Flamineo stages a mock death before Vittoria and Zanche; this is followed by the real death of all three characters at the hands of Francisco's henchmen.

Although editorial division of the final act into scenes may obscure its basic design,[1] it is clear that the main action alternates with the subsidiary action in a pattern that is repeated for clarity and emphasis. Thus, in the main action, the villainous, disguised avengers are twice pitted against a noble Brachiano, first in their initial meeting with him (V.i.44–85), and second in their horrible murder of him (V.iii.80–175). In the subsidiary action, Zanche woos Mulinassar twice (V.i.212–32; V.iii.215–70), and Flamineo twice faces the consequences of his murder of Marcello in his mother's grief and madness (V.ii.17–83; V.iv.50–123). As elsewhere, Webster uses repetition in this act for the purpose of intensification; the simple juxtaposition of heroes with villains in V.i shifts into the death agonies of V.iii, while Flamineo's *anagnorisis* deepens when he is confronted with his mother's heightened despair. The two plots, though they remain independent of one another, are woven together by the presence of Flamineo and Francisco in both, and by lengthy interlinking passages of commentary between them. Characters from the main plot—Brachiano and the court conspirators, Carlo and Pedro[2]—appear as judges and witnesses of the subsidiary action (V.ii.17 s.d.), while Flamineo is an observer of the main action. Because of the rhythmic alternation of the plots, the reaction of characters and audience to one plot is affected by the other; Brachiano's death (V.iii), a major climax of the main action, is theatrically upstaged by the preceding quarrel and murder of the minor action (V.ii), while Flamineo's despair is increased by both Brachiano's death and his ghostly augury. Finally, although the minor action's point of entry into the play is very small, beginning as it does with a ten-line exchange between Marcello and Flamineo regarding Zanche (V.i.86–96), it dominates the final act increasingly until, after Brachiano's death, it carries the tide of events and brings the play to its resolution.

The significance of the subsidiary action in the final act of *The White Devil* appears even more striking in light of its originality. No suggestion is contained in any of Webster's many sources for the wooing of Zanche, the murder of Marcello, the madness of Cornelia, or the despair of Flamineo (John Russell Brown xliv; Boklund, *White Devil* 99–104). The same is true of the last act of *The Duchess of Malfi*, for which Webster invented the madness of Ferdinand, the love and death of Julia, and the moral reformation of Bosola (Boklund, *Duchess* 123). In both plays, Webster elaborates on his source material most significantly in the final act.

The reluctance of critics to treat the Flamineo-Marcello-Zanche episodes as authentic "subplot" material often disguises their distrust of Webster's multiplicity. Dallby completely dismisses the idea that the episodes have any significant relation to the action of the play: "*The White Devil* . . . cannot be said to have any real subplot. . . . The Flamineo-Marcello conflict (III.i, V.i and V.ii) and Cornelia's reaction to Marcello's death (V.ii, V.iv) have a rather indirect bearing on the main plot but, to my mind, they constitute an episodic (and thematic) digression rather than a completely self-sufficient subplot" (39). Most subplots in Elizabethan and Jacobean drama are not completely self-sufficient, however. Levin argues that main plots and subplots may be linked in a variety of ways. The "efficient" relation allows causal interaction between plots; in Levin's view, this is "a more meaningful way to combine plots, because their mutual interaction knits them more closely together and makes them, quite literally, part of the same dramatic universe" (*Multiple Plot* 8). The dependence of a minor action on a major one does not disqualify it as a subplot. Furthermore, the subsidiary action of *The White Devil* is clearly far too important to the play to be dismissed as a mere digression. With some bewilderment, Boklund remarks on its extensive treatment:

> Although the logic of the events ending with Cornelia's madness can hardly be assailed, the attention lavished on the catastrophe seems out of proportion with the importance of the episode itself. Marcello is not only murdered, he is murdered in the presence of his mother; Cornelia is not only overcome with grief, she goes most spectacularly mad with grief. This concentration and elaboration of horrors is not demanded by the structure of the play. Whatever the ultimate reasons behind these scenes, they were also written with the purpose of providing additional intrigue, terror and pathos. (*White Devil* 153)

Boklund acknowledges the dramatic importance of the episodes, yet he views them as a structural redundancy in Webster's supposed accumulation of horrors. He does not attempt to elucidate the "ultimate reasons" for the scenes, though he implies that such reasons may exist. Most critics simply deplore what they see as an unintegrated addition to, and distraction from, the main action. Champion complains, "Marcello's murder and Cornelia's madness are never effectively integrated into the major action" (457), though, like Boklund, he justifies their inclusion in Webster's play on the grounds that "the atrocity itself . . . underscores again the vicious and animalistic nature of his stage world" (454). Jenkins deplores Webster's "fatal tendency to complication" in *The White Devil* and contrasts it with *The Duchess of Malfi*, in which "there is now no ghost, no mad wailing mother, no good brother to be killed by a bad" (53). The subsidiary action of *The White Devil*, regardless of its dramatic prominence in the final act, has been dismissed by critics as an irrelevance.

Elizabethan and Jacobean drama, as a drama of "multiple unity," is built on complication. Beckerman points out that, in such a drama, "the events frequently are extensions of the implications of the story exactly as the shattering of glass may be the effect of an explosion" (57). In Webster this is literally so; in the final act, the shattering of the glass is most evident as the implications of the story are explored. Those critics who dismiss the subsidiary action of the last act of *The White Devil* resemble the critics identified by Levin, who "approached the subplot as alien matter illegitimately attached to the main action, which was tacitly assumed to be the *real* play, and which could only be appreciated after it had been abstracted by the charitable reader from these distracting and disfiguring excrescences" (*Multiple Plot* 2). Thus when Dallby claims that "the multiplicity of the play and the overloading with detail . . . may on occasion obscure the basic structure of the events" (44), he ignores the simple fact that the play's multiplicity *is* its structure.

The argument in favor of the multiplicity of Elizabethan drama does not justify the subsidiary action of *The White Devil*. Yet that action cannot be dismissed on the grounds that it is merely a complication or an unintegrated digression. Only close examination of the double plot structure of the final act can determine the significance, and the effectiveness, of the invented episodes in the play as a whole. Insofar as they comprise an independent, subsidiary line of action coexistent with, yet independent from, the main action, these episodes can conveniently be treated as a "subplot." For though most subplots in Elizabethan and Jacobean drama counterpoint the main action throughout the length of the play, "the age was multiple in its artistic means" (Beckerman 48). The subplots of Webster's final acts appear to be characteristic of his dramatic construction, and hence of his artistic vision. In *The Duchess of Malfi*, the subplot reappears in a more conventional, extended form, but is still reserved primarily for the final act. Significantly, Webster's final acts have attracted as much critical censure as the subplots of other dramatists.

The final act subplot of *The White Devil* is itself complex and contains two distinct but interrelated actions. The first centers on Zanche, who becomes both the object of Marcello's and Cornelia's scornful anger, and the apparent reason for Flamineo's fratricide. Rejected by Flamineo, Zanche then pursues and amorously woos Francisco in his disguise as Mulinassar. The second action centers on Flamineo. Provoked by Marcello's moral condemnation of himself and Zanche, Flamineo unexpectedly murders Marcello in his mother's presence. He then becomes a witness to his mother's overwhelming grief at the destruction of her sons. The two actions are interlinked; Zanche is the cause of the quarrel between Flamineo and Marcello, and she appears later with Cornelia, "winding Marcello's corse" (V.iv.65 s.d.). Moreover, both actions involve characters who have appeared throughout the play: their significance consequently depends in some measure on how these characters are presented in the rest of the play.

Critics are divided in their views of Zanche's dramatic function. Elizabeth Brennan sees her as Vittoria's foil, "dark-skinned and treacherous, a black devil who offsets her mistress' whiteness" (xvi). Boklund, on the other hand, views her as a parallel to the protagonists: "Her conduct parallels that of the leading characters closely; she is ready to commit the same crimes as lightheartedly as they and fits perfectly into Webster's picture of an amoral world. She also becomes the victim of an uncontrollable passion" (*White Devil* 173). Such different views of Zanche's function imply different readings of the protagonists. Brennan, in the Lamb tradition, views Vittoria as a romantic heroine, while Boklund reads the play as a cautionary tale about the consequences of crime and passion. Yet both critics agree in their basic view of Zanche as a stock whore whose blackness is symbolic as well as real.[3] Such a view is more easily maintained in the study than on the stage, however. When Forster saw the 1920 Cambridge production of *The White Devil*, Zanche's wicked exuberance won his interest and sympathy. He wrote, "The Moorish confidante was far more vital [than Vittoria] and, seductive yet humorous, gave a vivid impression of low class sin" (Forster review). Lucas complained that the stock treatment of Zanche in the 1925 Scala production distorted Webster's intention: "Why . . . make up Zanche so like a comic negress that it was inconceivable how Flamineo could ever have become entangled with her? True, she is a Moor and gibed at as such; but so was Othello" (Lucas review). Both Forster's impressions of a successful Zanche and Lucas's criticisms of an unsuccessful one point to something more complex than a stock character who invites quick moral condemnation.

Recent productions of *The White Devil* have tended to represent Zanche as more menacing than she is in Webster's play. In an amateur production by the York Graduate Theatre Company in Toronto in 1983, Zanche was doubled with the conjuror in the dumb show scene. As a result she appeared to be, if not a murderer, at least a sinister conspirator with demonic supernatural powers. In the 1984 Greenwich Theatre production, director Philip Prowse invented a scene in which Zanche is hired by Brachiano to murder Isabella, and substituted it for the dumb show in which Isabella is murdered by Dr. Julio. According to Irving Wardle, the invented scene was simply confusing and sacrificed "theatrical logic . . . for an arresting flow of stage pictures" (Review, "Greenwich"). More important, such theatrical exaggerations of Zanche's villainy contradict Webster's own decision to downplay any suggestions of her villainy contained in his sources. In the major source, a Bolognese chambermaid to Vittoria named Caterina actively participated in the plot to murder Vittoria's husband and later died at Vittoria's side (Boklund, *White Devil* 94–95). In the final act of Webster's play, although Zanche casually admits she "had a hand / In the black deed" (V.iii.249–50), this hint of her guilt is undeveloped.

Throughout most of *The White Devil*, Zanche remains a minor character who is neither demonic nor particularly comic. She is primarily an accomplice and appreciative observer of the affair between Brachiano and Vittoria; during their wooing scene, she fetches cushions for them (I.ii.204 s.d.) and murmurs her encouragement at their union (I.ii.214). She retains this association with the lovers' passion throughout the play. Her mute presence throughout Vittoria's arraignment, as she stands silently beside her mistress for the duration of the trial[4] reminds the audience of Vittoria's real "crime," her sexual passion, even as she defends herself vigorously against the exaggerated charges of her accusers. Zanche's silent presence reinforces Vittoria's indignant reply to Monticelso:

Sum up my faults I pray, and you shall find
That beauty and gay clothes, a merry heart,
And a good stomach to a feast, are all,
All the poor crimes that you can charge me with.
(III.ii.207–10)

In the first four acts, Zanche remains in the background, a shadowy figure who, like Vittoria, is frankly sexual but not openly villainous. In the final act, Zanche suddenly emerges into the foreground, and Webster suggests a new complexity in her character. As a major character at the center of a subsidiary action, Zanche is drawn by Webster with vivid particularity. She is introduced, briefly at first, in the first scene of the final act. In the main action, the conspirators led by Mulinassar are courteously received in Brachiano's court. Then they remove their disguises to exult horribly at length over their murderous plans (V.i.63–85). Immediately afterward, Marcello turns on Zanche and calls her a "devil" (V.i.86). The juxtaposition is ironic, for the real devils remain undetected while Marcello's claim against Zanche has no apparent foundation. His allegation that Zanche is Flamineo's "shame" (V.i.91) seems as unwarranted as the relationship itself is unexpected.[5] The altercation between Marcello and Flamineo subsides with Zanche's disappearance, and the main action continues as the court prepares for the "barriers" announced by Brachiano (V.i.56). The subplot develops more fully upon Zanche's reappearance. Though Zanche has been rejected by Marcello, she is described by the more objective Hortensio as Flamineo's "sweet mistress" (V.i.151) who "claims marriage" (V.i.157) of him. Though Flamineo describes Zanche as a "wolf" and himself as a "frighted dog" (V.i.155,159), Zanche's words soon contradict Flamineo's degraded comic assessment of her. Her expectation of serious commitment from Flamineo is emphasized by contrast with Flamineo's jocular evasiveness. An outcast among the "perfum'd gallants" (V.i.165) of the court, Zanche cannot compete with the "painting and gay clothes" (V.i.169) of the other court ladies.[6] Her obviously plain appearance and direct speech reinforce her earnest enjoinder to Flamineo to remember his "oaths" (V.i.175) to her. The picture of Zanche that is briefly suggested is far from that of a promiscuous, unprincipled whore. Flamineo's expansive, comic generalizations throw Zanche's terse, personal remarks into relief. The brief episode not only hints at greater underlying complexity in the hitherto simple character of Zanche, but also suggests a more complex dimension in the play as a whole, which belies simple moral judgments.

The subplot gains momentum when Cornelia enters suddenly and strikes Zanche (V.i.185). Marcello quickly follows suit, berating Zanche as a "strumpet" (V.i.189) and kicking her. Flamineo reacts to the insults directed against Zanche with mild irritation at first; irritation grows to anger as Marcello threatens him violently. The episode clearly echoes the wooing of the first act, in which the voice of outraged morality had similarly intervened. Cornelia's brief appearance may be intended to reinforce the analogy between the two episodes, in both of which an observer (in the first episode, Cornelia; in the second, Marcello[7]) suddenly interrupts a lovers' meeting with a tirade of threats and insults, provoking in turn a violent response and setting off a fatal chain of events. In the first act, Cornelia uses the metaphor of the poisoned "garden" (I.ii.272–78) to describe the affair between Brachiano and Vittoria; here, Marcello refers to Zanche as a scarecrow in "some new-seeded garden" (V.i.195). Repeated poetic and stage images link the two episodes. Flamineo, a minor figure during the first episode, has become the central figure in the second one, and both end in his conflict with a family member. Of course the second episode, unlike the first, immediately issues in murder, as Flamineo unexpectedly stabs Marcello.

At this point in the play the two strands of action in the subplot separate. As Flamineo goes off to fetch the weapon with which he will attack Marcello, Zanche pursues Mulinassar as a lover of her own "complexion" (V.i.213). The meeting of the two "Moors" on the stage draws attention to Webster's color symbolism in the play. Eldred Jones views Webster's treatment of black characters in *The White Devil* as conventional racism: "The devil, hell, and their accompanying colour of black are woven into the language of the play as if Webster were repeatedly reminding his audience that behind the fair exteriors of his characters hell constantly lurked. To make symbol flesh, he intermingled black faces with his white characters on the stage" (78). Forker sees Zanche as "the 'black fury' (V.vi.227) whose face matches 'the black deed' of double murder" (270). However, the "black" villainy of the white Francisco in blackface far exceeds the villainy of Zanche, who is actually black. Webster's color references, Schuman observes, "establish an ethical perspective on characters and actions which Webster actually seeks not to reinforce, but to question" (35). Zanche's approach to Mulinassar highlights her vitality, resilience and humor, in contrast to his simple hypocrisy. The physical resemblance between them emphasizes their differences. As all those about her murder or die violently, Zanche blithely pursues her own heart's desires; this lighthearted indifference is emphasized by the structure of the final act. Zanche's first amorous encounter with Mulinassar comes as a relief after the rising tension of Flamineo's altercation with Marcello, and the second one follows immediately upon Brachiano's death agonies. In both encounters, while Zanche is a victim of both the outrage of Cornelia and Marcello and the evil manipulations of Francisco, she is also a comic survivor.

In the second encounter with Mulinassar, Zanche recounts an erotic dream, reveals the "secret" of the murders, and plans her escape. Again the stage image recalls the first-act wooing scene; Zanche and Mulinassar exchange embraces in the presence of observers, as Vittoria and Brachiano had done earlier. Again a wish-fulfillment dream is related by a woman to her prospective lover. Pearson claims that Zanche's dream "recalls the previous seduction scene, and as in the previous scene a dream is to lead to murder. The chain of cause and effect behind the action of the play is stressed by these repetitions, and because of it the complex events of the play never become confusing" (58). Yet in fact Zanche's dream does not lead to murder. It has no other end than its expressed desire for pleasure and sexual fulfillment; "Methought sir, you came stealing to my bed" (V.iii.227), Zanche says coquettishly. Immediately Francisco takes over and insists on recounting his own dream (V.iii.236). The murders, when Zanche discloses them, are as disconnected from the logic of her dream as they are disconnected in Zanche's revelation from those who incited them:

> Isabella
> The Duke of Florence' sister was empoison'd,
> By a 'fum'd picture: and Camillo's neck
> Was broke by damn'd Flamineo.
> (V.iii.243–46)

The audience finds out no more than it knew in the second act; Vittoria's ambiguity is confirmed rather than removed. Nor does Zanche's revelation have a significant effect on Francisco's revenge. When Lodovico exclaims, "Why now our action's justified," Francisco replies, "Tush for justice" (V.iii.267). Zanche's explicit recollection of the protagonists' crimes in a context that recalls their passion and leads to their retribution may suggest a causal relation between them, but this relation is suggested only to be undermined by the tone and structure of the episode. In the complex world of

The White Devil, sexual desire cannot be linked directly with murder, as murder cannot be linked directly with justice.

In the final act subplot, Webster invents episodes in which Zanche clearly recalls Vittoria at the beginning of the play. Because Zanche is a simpler and baser character, she emphasizes by contrast Vittoria's dignity and intelligence; she would not have been capable of Vittoria's performance at the trial. In this respect, Zanche is Vittoria's foil. From another perspective, Zanche could equally be intended as a parody of Vittoria, reducing her actions by association to a baser level. Thus the lascivious Zanche in the final act could represent Vittoria's real nature, unclouded by ambiguities—a nature without moral compunction, intent on satisfying its own self-interested lust. The alternate possibilities of parody or foil seem equally suspended; the structural significance of Zanche appears to be as ambiguous as much else in the play. Yet by presenting either a foil to Vittoria or a parody of her at this point in the play Webster wins few advantages. The final act already risks providing an oversimplified resolution to the play's complexities by elevating the protagonists in contrast to their villainous enemies. By using Zanche to highlight Vittoria's heroic qualities, Webster would achieve only a superficial solution to the problems he explores throughout the play. On the other hand, reducing the protagonists to common sinners in the last act lends Francisco's revenge the spurious appearance of justice. Webster can hardly mean to sacrifice the complexity of his protagonists in the important final act. A director should try to preserve this complexity.

In the final act, Webster fills out his portrait of Zanche and places her at the center of a significant subplot. Small touches, like Zanche's injured silence with Flamineo and her good-natured humor with Mulinassar, suggest a new complexity in her nature that, on a smaller scale, approaches Vittoria's. Webster's sudden amplification of this minor character indicates deliberate parallelism. Yet the parallel that develops between Zanche and Vittoria is not primarily one of character, but of situation. Like Vittoria, Zanche inhabits a world in which sexual passion is considered a crime, by both the guardians of conventional morality (Cornelia and Marcello) and the hypocritical villains (Francisco and Monticelso). Again like Vittoria (in IV.ii), Zanche finds that lovers also betray. In such a world, hemmed in by an overbearing morality, a despotic villainy, and an inconstant love, choices are severely restricted. Before she seeks out Mulinassar as a lover, Zanche is put off by Flamineo, attacked by Cornelia and kicked by Marcello. The victimization is continued by Mulinassar; as a "Machivillian" (V.iii.193) who "tickles you to death; makes you die laughing" (V.iii.196), he literally turns on Zanche to tickle her (V.iii.237–39) and, finally, to have her murdered. Zanche's world in the last act recalls Vittoria's world throughout the play. Condemned by her own mother, yet frustrated with her impotent husband in the first act, arraigned by hypocritical judges for her "lust" in the third act, suspected by her own lover in the fourth act, and relentlessly pursued by a murderous villain in the last act, Vittoria must be judged in light of this oppressive world. Zanche's situation in the last act is a compressed, caricatured recapitulation of Vittoria's. Webster uses her as an extreme example with which to test and suggest his heroine's legitimacy. Zanche is a baser, more limited character than Vittoria, yet they share the same moral predicament. When, in response to such a predicament, Zanche's vitality and humor appear credible and attractive, Vittoria's moral actions in the play become by the same token retrospectively clearer. Faced with a context that is so limiting, both Vittoria and Zanche choose to re-main true to their own natures. Zanche's experience in the last act at the hands of Cornelia and Marcello recalls Vittoria's experience in the first act; such recapitulation reminds us of the sexual vitality for which Vittoria has been unjustly persecuted throughout the play.[8]

The subsidiary action of *The White Devil* takes shape in V.i, with Cornelia's and Marcello's attack on Flamineo and Zanche. It then follows the adventures of Flamineo and Zanche separately; while Zanche pursues Mulinassar, Flamineo reacts to his family's insults, murders his brother, and watches his mother go mad with grief.

Most critics who have ventured to explain the significance of this minor plot have viewed it as the "catastrophe" of the play; as Greg puts it, "the keynote of a losing game" (125) for the protagonists or, in Forker's words, "a domestic analogue to the social, moral, and political breakdown of the tragedy at large" (271). According to this view, Flamineo's murder of Marcello becomes another example of the social fragmentation and destruction brought about by the pro-tagonists. The fratricide violates natural familial bonds as Brachiano and Vittoria have violated them earlier in the play; by implication, retribution for their crimes becomes necessary and inevitable. Bliss maintains that in the last act, "the family unit is indeed consuming itself" (128). Ewbank is critical of what she sees as the overt symbolism of Flamineo's actions in the last act: "Family relationships are very important in *The White Devil*, but they are, it seems to me, mainly used as pointers to the theme of social disintegration rather than being explored *as* relationships—so that, for example, the brother-brother killing moves away from human reality towards symbolism" ("Webster's Realism" 173–74). Yet while Ewbank finds the fratricide too symbolic, Boklund deplores the "detailed realism" of the subsidiary action in the final act (*White Devil* 183). This "realism" emerges particularly clearly in performance. In a review of the 1976 Old Vic production, Irving Wardle found that by playing Webster with the "personal definition of Shakespeare,"—with an attention to naturalistic detail—"the plot emerges with much more clarity than usual. One understands better the background motives of the malcontent Flamineo, the Florentine intrigue, and the *volte face* assassination of Marcello" ("Old Vic"). "Detailed realism" appears to be effective in playing the last act in the theatre, and such realism precludes a purely symbolic interpretation. Webster carefully suggests the "background motives" behind the fratricide, and places it in a detailed context in order to complicate its symbolic impact.

Flamineo's murder of Marcello in V.ii is violent and unexpected, yet not without provocation. Marcello initiates the dispute between them by kicking and insulting Zanche and aggressively threatening Flamineo himself. His unwarranted violence is emphasized by contrast with Flamineo's attempts to defuse the situation with his usual good humor. Undeterred, Marcello issues his challenge to Flamineo and gives it mythic proportions:

> Now by all my hopes,
> Like the two slaught'red sons of Oedipus,
> The very flames of our affection
> Shall turn two ways. Those words I'll make thee answer
> With thy heart blood.
>
> (V.i.204–8)

In Act I, Cornelia's violent, disproportionate response to the hitherto comic wooing between the lovers has the effect of immediately elevating and dignifying the affair. Here, Marcello's extreme assault on Flamineo, based on the same rigorous moral code as Cornelia's, immediately suggests a more complex moral dimension in Flamineo and his relation to Zanche than is apparent in Flamineo's comic banter. What we have seen of the affair suggests more than just "a sexual experiment between a dyspeptic misogynist and a 'gypsy' that degenerates fast into an intensity of loathing" (Forker 271). Marcello's moral challenge to Flamineo elicits a moral response from him that is more than simply "sterile egoism" (Bliss 127). On the contrary, Flamineo's violent reaction to Marcello's provocation shows him to be a staunch defender of individual moral freedom. Flamineo's act of murder, far from being casual, imitates precisely Cornelia's sudden attack on Zanche,[9] theatrically emphasizing that the murder is a direct response to tyrannical moralism. In *The White Devil*, as in *The Duchess of Malfi*, individual moral freedom is impossible in the morally restrictive world of the play. Yet its champions remain the closest alternative to heroism in each play, however qualified that heroism may be in *The White Devil*.

Throughout the play, Flamineo's voice counterpoints the main action with its cynical, reductive interpretation of human events and relationships. Only occasionally does the surface of Flamineo's posture suddenly crack to reveal the contradictions lying beneath. Shortly after Vittoria's arraignment, Flamineo pretends madness and rails at the world's corruption, crying, "O gold, what a god art thou! and O man, what a devil art thou to be tempted by that cursed mineral!" (III.iii.21–23). Such speeches are double-edged; only in theatrical poses can Flamineo both scorn his own contaminated self-interest and rail at the corrupt world of which he is part. The moral contradictions of Flamineo's role that are thus forced to the surface are followed by a sudden violent action that moves him beyond such contradictions. In response to Lodovico's contention that Vittoria is a "damnable whore" (III.iii.111), Flamineo erupts unexpectedly and strikes him. The episode illuminates Flamineo's moral complexity as well as his capacity for moral action. His behavior in the final act follows the same basic pattern.

The main action of the final act is linked to the subsidiary action by means of lengthy passages of commentary exchanged between Francisco and Flamineo. These passages frame and distance the main action, and increasingly absorb the attention of the audience. During these exchanges, Flamineo continually undermines Brachiano, cynically claiming that his apparent generosity is only "miserable courtesy" (V.i.139). Yet while Flamineo insists on Brachiano's hypocrisy, his comments are ironically directed at the real hypocrite, Francisco. More important, Flamineo's satire turns back on himself. While he curses Brachiano as "a kind of statesman, that would sooner have reckon'd how many cannon-bullets he had discharged against a town, to count his expense that way, than how many of his valiant and deserving subjects he had lost before it" (V.iii.61–64), he admits that, "for money, understand me, I had as good a will to cozen him, as e'er an officer of them all" (V.iii.57–58). Flamineo's cynicism is clearly, like Bosola's, "the foolish obverse of idealism" (Bliss 157). His disillusionment with the world arises from his high expectations of it. His contradictions are even more striking in contrast to Francisco's simple hypocrisy. Flamineo's double vision, in railing at the vulgar abuses of power while hoping to profit from them, is a kind of figurative blindness that is literally played out in his failure to penetrate Francisco's disguise. Yet, as in the third act, Flamineo's moral contradictions dissipate when he takes action. The sister that Flamineo degraded he later defends against Lodovico's crude allegations; the "sweet mistress" that Flamineo scorned he later apparently upholds by murdering her accuser. Flamineo's murder of Marcello both violates his detachment and clarifies his moral position.

Just before the attack on Zanche that sets off a chain of events, Webster takes great care to establish Flamineo's moral position relative to that of the other characters. Flamineo himself offers his amoral cynicism as an attractive alternative to "the morality of your sunburnt gentleman" (V.i.183–84). Mulinassar's is an utopian morality of social equality:

> what difference is between the duke and I? no more than between two bricks; all made of one clay. Only't may be one is plac'd on the top of a turret; the other in the bottom of a well by mere chance. (V.i.106–9)

Yet his idealistic speeches are undercut by his murderous plans. On the other hand, Cornelia and Marcello offer a conventional morality of social decorum, which judges Zanche to be Flamineo's "shame." Their morality is equally contaminated by their tyrannical inhumanity and by their hypocrisy in mutely accepting the union between Brachiano and Vittoria which they had earlier condemned. Neither moral attitude can offer a positive alternative to Flamineo's malcontent pose, which at least gives expression to the corruption which underlies such moral systems. In Flamineo's morality, humanity is a collection of degraded sycophants: "women are like to burs; / Where their affection throws them, there they'll stick" (V.i.92–93). By extension, he himself longs for "some great cardinal to lug me by th'ears as his endeared minion" (V.i.122–24). Yet while Flamineo longs to partake in court corruption, his "morality" depends on seeing himself as fundamentally incorruptible. At the same time, Flamineo shares Mulinassar's "deep contempt / Of our slight airy courtiers" (V.i.36–37), and proclaims the "Misery of princes, / That must of force be censur'd by their slaves!" (V.iii.201–2). Flamineo's cynical, reductive attitude to Zanche suddenly vanishes when he realizes that his family's tyrannical moralism results in a condemnation of her much like his own. His murder of Marcello not only opposes the moral hypocrisy of the other characters, but also violates his cynical detachment and precipitates his self-awareness.

The detailed context of the murder in the final act, combined with its position relative to the main action, clearly recalls the protagonists' crimes which set the tragedy in motion. In the first act, the conventional disapproval of Cornelia raised the "fearful and prodigious storm" (I.ii.306) of Brachiano's anger, which led to the murders of Camillo and Isabella. Flamineo's murder of Marcello, though a similar violent reaction to the constraints of conventional morality, is more startling because it is devoid of motives of self-interest or advancement. Champion notes that "the murder is the more bizarre because—unrelated to the action of the play—it is so senseless" (454). Flamineo's is the anarchic self-will of the protagonists stripped of any motives beyond simple self-assertion in the face of a restrictive moral code. The murder's unexpected simplicity, combined with its hint of a new moral response in Flamineo, offers us relief from both the complex detachment of Flamineo and the predictability of the main action. Furthermore, coming as it does just before Brachiano's punishment at the hands of Francisco for his original crimes, the episode serves to reemphasize the nature of heroism in the play. Flamineo's crime recalls Brachiano's earlier crimes;

like Brachiano's, Flamineo's action is a brutal one. Like Brachiano's relation with Vittoria, Flamineo's affair with Zanche hardly provides a romantic justification for his act. Yet at the same time, Flamineo's murder of Marcello is set in a moral context that makes it comprehensible and even heroic. In such a world, peopled with tyrannical moralists and hypocritical assassins, the will—even when murderous—appears to offer the only possibility for heroism. By duplicating in the subsidiary action the complex conditions under which the protagonists functioned throughout the play, Webster is able to reassert and emphasize the morally problematic and complex heroism of Brachiano and Vittoria at a crucial point in the play. Flamineo's murder of Marcello, with its detailed, suggestive context, not only theatrically upstages Brachiano's death scene, but also reanimates Brachiano's anarchic heroism in a contaminated world so that, at his death, he appears neither guiltier nor more innocent than Webster intends he should be.

Flamineo's murder of Marcello in the final act is given a detailed and "realistic" context by Webster, and this appears to emerge clearly in performance. Yet at the same time the action has a symbolic weight, gathered partly from its juxtaposition with events running concurrently in the main action, and partly from its echoes of past events. Its symbolic function is not, as most critics assume, merely to reemphasize the protagonists' deserved destruction. On the contrary, the murder is an outrageous, brutal act which challenges both the moralist's rigor and the pragmatist's dismissal, both Marcello's narrow-minded scorn and Francisco's single-minded revenge. The subsidiary action makes clear in the final act that, as Ornstein points out, "the power of *The White Devil* is its dramatization of the *isolated* criminal will shattering moral restrictions" (136).

Though Webster carefully sketches in the details to provide a background for Flamineo's murder of Marcello, the murder itself is shocking, sudden, and brutal. Furthermore, it is rapidly eclipsed by its enormous consequences, as Cornelia plunges into madness. Two stirring scenes of maternal love and grief, precipitated by Flamineo's act of violence, frame Brachiano's horrible death scene. Theatre critics testify that Cornelia's scenes are particularly moving in performance. For example, most critics found the poignancy of Cornelia's distraction a relief from the otherwise poor and horror-laden 1984 production at Greenwich. Michael Billington, in his review in the *Guardian*, wrote: "When the production comes to rest, it is suddenly effective: Ann Mitchell as Cornelia has a lament for her dead son that is lyrically moving and when she summons Flamineo with fluttering fingers, it stops the heart." Ann Donaldson, reviewing the Greenwich production in the *Glasgow Herald*, judged Cornelia's scenes to be integral to the play: "Ann Mitchell as Cornelia beautifully delivers the lament for her lost children. In the end the play triumphs." In his review of the critically well-received 1955 production directed by Jack Landau at the Phoenix Sideshow, Walter Kerr found in the Cornelia scenes evidence of Webster's theatrical brilliance: "One brother kills another for no good reason: but this paves the way for a passage in which their mother, crazed with grief, fondles the victim and flies at the victor. The sequence is not only a theatrical workout of spectacular dimensions; it is humanly true."

Cornelia's maternal grief is not only theatrically compelling but also carefully timed in the play's dramatic rhythm. Her expression of pain, with its suggestion of the irretrievable finality of death, immediately precedes the death of Brachiano, for which the audience has been well prepared by his gloating murderers. The terrible pathos of the scene following Marcello's death, heightened by obvious echoes from the final scene of *King Lear* (John Russell Brown 139n), reactivates those human, emotional responses to death that were otherwise limited to Francisco's childish, clinical attitude or Flamineo's desperate one. Because of Cornelia's painfully human reaction and its effect on an audience, Brachiano's death suddenly appears more horrible than the predictable and appropriate act of retribution for which the audience has been prepared. Cornelia herself enacts the futility of retribution when "she runs to Flamineo with her knife drawn and coming to him lets it fall" (V.ii.52 s.d.). For both Flamineo and Brachiano, the vision they achieve in their different encounters with death transcends the pattern of crime and punishment.

After Brachiano's death, the theatrical impact of the Cornelia scenes is registered on Flamineo, who, faced with the human consequences of his violent action, begins to feel the promptings of "compassion" and "conscience" (V.iv.115,121). Unlike Brachiano and Vittoria, Flamineo must immediately confront the enormous effects of will on the bonds of family and community. Cornelia's grief and madness expand the undeveloped hints of such effects implied in

Giovanni's poignant grief at his mother's death in III.ii. Yet at the same time that Flamineo recapitulates Brachiano's act of murderous self-will, he mirrors Brachiano's own agonized *anagnorisis* when confronted with death. By carefully framing Brachiano's death with a subsidiary action in which Flamineo achieves a confused and painful self-awareness, Webster is able by analogy to shift the emphasis from Francisco's revenge, the crude physical consequences of Brachiano's previous crimes, to the more important inner struggle for understanding evident in Brachiano's death agonies. At this point in the play, Webster uses Flamineo as a "screen" on which to flash "readings from the psychic life of the protagonist" (Mack 24). The hints of guilt and responsibility that are contained in some of Brachiano's speeches are expanded and fulfilled in Flamineo's *prise de conscience*. In his madness, Brachiano cries,

> Indeed I am too blame.
> For did you ever hear the dusky raven
> Chide blackness? or was't ever known the devil
> Rail'd against cloven creatures?
> (V.iii.87–90)

Like Brachiano, Flamineo suddenly accepts himself as a member of the human community, corrupt and vulnerable. His new sense of his own criminality coincides with his "compassion" for others. After witnessing his mother's grief, he feels her "tortures" (V.iv.122) as his own. Yet, again like Brachiano, Flamineo's self-awareness is fragmentary and transitory; he continues his desperate self-seeking pursuit of gain and defies his "fate" (V.iv.144). Brachiano also sees the devil as both inside and outside himself; his self-awareness is balanced against his railing at others' abuses.

> You have convey'd coin forth our territories;
> Bought and sold offices; oppress'd the poor,
> And I ne'er dreamt on't. Make up your accounts;
> I'll now be mine own steward.
> (V.iii.83–86)

At his death, Brachiano has the sense that the events he precipitated have gone beyond his control; the world that he attempted to shape to his will was larger than he imagined. For the audience, his initial responsibility seems almost inconsequential in the face of his enemies' enormous punishment. For Flamineo, the consequences of action likewise far outweigh the action itself. The murder of Marcello is quickly accomplished, but the effects it produces are irretrievable. In both main and subsidiary actions, the protagonists are clearly guilty, yet ultimately they are eclipsed by the consequences of their actions. For both Flamineo and Brachiano, the advent of self-awareness coincides with a sense of powerlessness; individual responsibility is outweighed by a chain of consequences. In his final mad visions, Brachiano refers to Flamineo's murder of Marcello:

> See, see, Flamineo that kill'd his brother
> Is dancing on the ropes there: and he carries
> A money-bag in each hand, to keep him even,
> For fear of breaking's neck. And there's a lawyer
> In a gown whipt with velvet, stares and gapes
> When the money will fall.
>
> (V.iii.109–14)

In his hallucination, Brachiano sees clearly Flamineo's emotional precariousness, as he continues to evade his own despair by pursuing worldly gain. Yet in Brachiano's vision Flamineo is only one link in a chain of corruption; the guilty criminal is preyed on by other members of a hopelessly corrupt society. Brachiano's language and vision in this scene recall Lear's on the heath—"the usurer hangs the cozener" (*King Lear* IV.vi.161).[10] Webster borrows heavily from Shakespeare in this scene because he is striving for a tragic effect that is similar to Shakespeare's in portraying both the visionary glimpses and the limitations of the human mind under enormous stress. The Cornelia scenes are similarly rich in Shakespearean echoes, from *King Lear* V.iii and from *Hamlet* IV.v. This concentration of tragic allusion is too deliberate to be dismissed as mere parody or bombast, as some critics have done. Bliss remarks, "Bracciano ends the helpless victim of a dramatized delirium, and the conventional mixture of small amounts of sense with large swatches of comic babble drains his last moments of dignity or pathos. His death is carefully framed and distanced, then forgotten" (125).[11] In performance, however, such an interpretation is not well received by theatre critics. Irving Wardle deplored the 1976 Old Vic version of the death scene in which Brachiano "turns finally into a gibbering blotch-faced ruin, alive only in the sense that life is described as a disease of matter" (Review, "Old Vic"). Other theatre critics have described Brachiano's death scene in performance as "powerful" (Bryden review) and "tight with menace" (Dawson review 39). The subsidiary action of the final act extends the power and menace of Brachiano's death so that it will not be forgotten.

Because neither Cornelia nor Marcello is a sympathetic character in the rest of the play, Cornelia's lyrical outpouring of grief for Marcello's death after Brachiano's becomes almost an abstract, impersonal expression of loss. Gill points out that "the Cornelia of the lament scene, an animated tableau of considerable beauty, is not the same character who rudely interrupted the earlier episode" (55). Moreover, Brachiano's death scene (V.iii) is theatrically connected with the scene of Cornelia's distracted grief (V.iv) in a number of ways. Brachiano's "distractions" during his death agony (V.iii.83 s.d.) and Cornelia's "distraction" over Marcello's corpse (V.iv.83 s.d.) may have been signalled by conventional stage gestures (Thomson 31–32) and thus clearly linked in performance. Both scenes may have been "discovered" on an inner stage (Reynolds 140). The reviewer of the 1935 production for the *Times* connected Brachiano's death with Cornelia's madness: "The death of Brachiano is designed as a picture of Hell itself, and, for a terrible instant, the gates do indeed open. . . . The scene at the bier of Flamineo's murdered brother has the same visionary power" (Review, "New Phoenix Society").

The juxtaposition of the two plots in the final act of *The White Devil* leads to a richly suggestive correspondence between them that cannot be simply defined. "This power of suggestion is the strength of the double plot," observes Empson. "Once you take the two parts to correspond, any character may take on *mana* because he seems to cause what he corresponds to or be Logos of what he symbolizes" ("Double Plots" 34). Clearly, Flamineo's part in the subplot recalls in a highly compressed form Brachiano's actions throughout the play. By extension, Cornelia's madness, the consequence of Flamineo's action, bears some relation to Brachiano's violent death, the consequence of his original crimes. In one sense Cornelia emphasizes the real human cost of Brachiano's crimes, ignored by the murderous retribution of Francisco. Yet because the subsidiary action emerges so late in the play, when the consequences of the protagonists' actions far outweigh the significance of their crimes, its homiletic function is redundant. Rather, Cornelia's grief and madness appear to be an extension—almost a result—of Brachiano's visionary agony in his death scene. As the first of Cornelia's scenes introduced a compassionate, human response to death that transformed the theatrical impact of Brachiano's death scene, so the second of Cornelia's scenes is an elegy for his loss. In the main action itself, response to Brachiano's death is downplayed; Vittoria rushes off the stage, crying "O me! This place is hell" (V.iii.179), while Flamineo dismisses her pain as merely the "moonish shades of griefs or fears" (V.iii.185). Only in Cornelia's dirge do the emotions generated by Brachiano's horrible death find elegiac expression:

> Call for the robin-red-breast and the wren,
> Since o'er shady groves they hover,
> And with leaves and flow'rs do cover
> The friendless bodies of unburied men.
>
> (V.iv.95–98)

At the heart of Webster's tragic vision, criminal and victim share the same perspective in the face of death. His criminal protagonists transgress, and ultimately transcend, the tenets of conventional morality, for in Webster's world individual acts of will are tangled in a web of wider social chaos and tyranny until they are finally made meaningless by the enormity of death. All that remains to these characters is to achieve some vision, however fragmentary, of the world as it is. To the extent that his protagonists do achieve this vision, Webster's world is a moral one. Like Brachiano at his death, Cornelia and Flamineo do not attempt to assign responsibility for disaster; rather, they acknowledge their part in flawed humanity. In Brachiano's mad visions, he is a "devil" living among "cloven creatures" like himself (V.iii.89–90); in Cornelia's distraction, she offers Flamineo some "heart's-ease" but keeps some for herself (V.iv.78–79). Death is the universal annihilation: "This poor men get; and great men get no more" (V.iv.110). Faced with Brachiano's ghost, Flamineo puts aside the stirrings of remorse and asks "the most necessary question": "how long I have to live?" (V.iv.131–32). The conventional moral questions, of guilt and innocence, justice and injustice, pale beside the final reality of death. Webster's moral protagonists are those who possess the courage to confront this reality.

The final scene of the play brings Zanche and Flamineo, central characters of the subsidiary action, together with Vittoria, a protagonist in the main action. Flamineo absorbs the experience of his mother's grief, while Zanche reappears after wooing Mulinassar. By recombining the characters of the separate plots for the last scene, Webster clarifies the function of his multiple, analogical structure in the last act.

In the first part of the final scene, the three characters are locked in a crude struggle for life, in which apparent self-sacrifice masks blatant self-interest. Vittoria assumes a heroic pose when she prepares to die, vowing:

> Yet I am now resolv'd,—farewell affliction;
> Behold Bracciano, I that while you liv'd
> Did make a flaming altar of my heart
> To sacrifice unto you; now am ready
> To sacrifice heart and all.
>   (V.vi.82–86)

Only forty lines later, however, she is viciously treading upon Flamineo, crying, "I tread the fire out / That would have been my ruin" (V.vi.124–25). Likewise Zanche vows loyalty to both Vittoria and Flamineo:

> How madam! Do you think that I'll outlive you?
> Especially when my best self Flamineo
> Goes the same voyage.
>   (V.vi.87–89)

Yet later Zanche threatens to "drive a stake" through Flamineo (V.vi.145). Similarly Flamineo, who vows to kill himself out of loyalty to Brachiano (V.vi.32–34), stages his own comic resurrection. Webster deliberately highlights the treachery and self-serving villainy that accompany the attractive vitality of his characters, and ruthlessly exposes their noble attitudes. Yet their vigorous fight for life in the first part heightens their courage when faced with death in the second part, and the previous parody of heroism authenticates their real heroism. Heroism in the world of *The White Devil* emerges from the petty acts of will that characterize life. Characters who achieve a heroic vision unflinchingly see themselves as part of a whole world in which, as Flamineo says, "rest breeds rest, where all seek pain by pain" (V.vi.274). In such a world, as Lear puts it, "None does offend" (IV.vi.166) because all are guilty. Webster's tragic vision of imperfect virtue in an unstable world is, like Shakespeare's, buried with the protagonists; Giovanni's conventional moral lesson at the end of the play is reductive:

> Let guilty men remember their black deeds
> Do lean on crutches, made of slender reeds.
> (V.vi.300–301)

In the final scene, main and secondary characters merge; Vittoria, Zanche and Flamineo die "with a joint motion" (V.vi.232). Unlike Shakespeare, Webster diffuses his focus so that there are several centers of interest on the stage at the same time. As his characters mirror one another in death, their separate actions reflect and echo one another in the last act. Several critics have deplored this kind of "group tragedy." Kirsch complains that, throughout the play, Vittoria and Flamineo "are essentially insulated from one another, however congruent their positions or attitudes may be, and the attention we are required to give one of them frequently conflicts with, or distracts us from, the attention we are required to give the other" (107). Ornstein claims, "In the very act of asserting their individuality Flamineo, Vittoria, Zanche, and Lodovico lose it: they imitate one another. Because Webster's dichotomies of strength and weakness are artistically and morally primitive, tragic heroine and whorish servant . . . exit alike into the mist" (139). Yet the multiplicity of *The White Devil*, at the risk of being distracting or simply repetitive, is designed to achieve a number of distinct aesthetic ends in Webster's dramaturgy.

In the last act of *The White Devil*, Webster faced an aesthetic problem which reappeared in a different form in the last act of *The Duchess of Malfi*. His play is constructed to emphasize the moral complexity and humanity of the protagonists throughout. Yet in the last act, the triumph of the villains threatens to shift the play toward melodrama and to oversimplify the protagonists. In the culmination of the revenge, Brachiano and Vittoria might become either the innocent victims of murderous assassins, exonerated for their original crimes, or the recipients of a just nemesis, deservedly punished for their crimes. So as not to jeopardize the delicate balance between passionate heroism and criminal self-will in his protagonists, Webster develops a subsidiary action with which to recapitulate and clarify by analogy his protagonists' complexity. The minor plots involving Zanche and Flamineo reemphasize the protagonists' culpability, while at the same time recreating a world in which the consequences of action are disproportionately great and death is the only measure of heroism. In this way the subsidiary plot replays the primary thrust of the play and de-emphasizes the revenge pattern, which provides only the occasion for death and not its meaning.

By using the multiple plot structure in the final act of *The White Devil*, Webster gains the richness and extension of a new perspective on his main action. The new perspective is an extreme, almost parodic, version of the main action, yet Webster uses caricature to test the resilience of his protagonists. Zanche is a more degraded character than Vittoria, "a more obvious and less dignified figure of female depravity" (Forker 270), simpering while recounting her lascivious dream. Yet even Zanche is caught in a frightening, restrictive world where moral choices are limited. Flamineo commits murder for less substantial reasons than Brachiano, yet even his act of will appears comprehensible. The actions of Zanche and Flamineo are designed "not at all to parody the heroes, but to stop you from doing so" (Empson, "Double Plots" 30). In one sense, Zanche and Flamineo are Vittoria and Brachiano seen through the eyes of a Francisco or a Lodovico, as a promiscuous whore and a casual murderer. Yet Webster so complicates even these characters that it becomes impossible to accept such an oversimplified view.

Finally, repetition of the main action in a subsidiary one clearly places the emphasis on situation rather than on character. Empson notes, "The device sets your judgment free because you need not identify yourself firmly with any one of the characters; . . . a situation is repeated for quite different characters, and this puts the main interest in the situation not the characters" ("Double Plots" 54). The subsidiary action of *The White Devil* both distances and illuminates the main events of the play. Through such repetition, moreover, the play's events are universalized; the problem of individual moral freedom in a restrictive, contaminated world is one which transcends the life and death of the protagonists. In the final act, the compressed recollection of the main action in the minor one also lends it an inevitability in retrospect; the moral will must always violate conventional morality, for which it must always be suppressed. Yet it remains the only measure of the human capacity for heroic action and vision in a corrupt world. This essentially tragic view, emphasized through repetition in *The White Devil*, is repeated and expanded in *The Duchess of Malfi*.

THE DUCHESS OF MALFI

In *The Duchess of Malfi*, Webster's rather sketchy portrait of Zanche in *The White Devil* is expanded into the fully developed figure of Julia. In the earlier play, the stock character of the pandering chambermaid and the highly individualized portrait of a sexually vital woman are inextricably interwoven in Zanche; in the later play, these two roles are clearly differentiated in Cariola and Julia. In *The White Devil*, although Zanche occupies a position as go-between and servant to the heroine much like that of Cariola, her dramatic function more closely resembles Julia's. Throughout *The Duchess of Malfi*, and particularly in the final act, the subplot involving Julia functions as an interpretive key to the main action. Indeed, the Julia subplot, which has received little serious critical attention, illuminates both Webster's loose, multiple dramatic construction and his moral emphasis in the play.

The adventures of the Cardinal's mistress that form the Julia subplot were pure invention on Webster's part. Boklund tells us that Webster did not borrow the subplot from any source, though he was accustomed to borrowing (*Duchess* 42). Nor is the subplot strictly necessary to the main plot, a fact which has led some critics to dismiss it as "a mere excrescence on the play" (Archer, "Webster, Lamb" 142). Yet the structural significance of the Julia subplot need not be limited to its contribution to the linear narrative. Since Webster evidently labored to invent a rough analogy to the Duchess's situation, he presumably intended it to serve a useful dramaturgical function in the play.

William Poel's 1892 production of *The Duchess of Malfi* restored the Julia subplot for the first time since the seventeenth century. A review in the *Nation* complained that "the intrigue of the Cardinal with Julia apparently had no other use in the tragedy save to add one more corpse to the many strewing the stage in that indescribable fifth act." Poel's interpretation of the subplot may be inferred from his remark that Julia is "designed as a set-off to the Duchess; as an instance of unholy love in contrast to the chaste love of the Duchess" (87). This view has become virtually a tradition in Webster criticism, shared by a large number of modern critics.[12] In describing the Duchess in contrast to Julia, many of these critics use language which tends to misrepresent her. The Duchess's wooing of Antonio is profound and convincing precisely because it is not "chaste," as she herself points out.

> This is flesh, and blood, sir;
> 'Tis not the figure cut in alabaster
> Kneels at my husband's tomb.
>
> (I.i.453–45)

The Duchess is a woman of sexual energy and vulnerability; she appears pregnant on the stage in the following act. Theatrical critics have been quick to emphasize these important qualities. The reviewer of the 1971 Royal Shakespeare Company production for the *Listener* felt that the death scene failed because "Miss Dench retained stoic dignity but, never having shared her passion with us, now kept us at a distance" (Lewsen review). Michael Billington of the *Guardian* pointed to the same essential qualities when he complained, in a review of the 1985 National Theatre production, "Even when Ms. Bron's Duchess divests herself of her wrappings, she never finds the virtuous, mettlesome, sexually-charged woman underneath." By way of contrast, several reviewers praised Helen Mirren's portrayal of the Duchess in the 1980 Royal Exchange production—Hughes-Hallett called her "playful, lascivious and vain"; Pearson alluded to "her capacity for affection and her deep sexual awareness." The Duchess's intense sexuality, so vital in performance, has been downplayed by critics who wish to emphasize the differences between the Duchess and Julia. Leech claims that "the general attitudes [in the play] to Julia and the Duchess are polar opposites" (*Duchess* 32), citing the Cardinal's contempt for Julia and Pescara's reference to her as a strumpet (V.i.46), in contrast to Antonio's first idealized view of the Duchess's "divine . . . continence" (I.i.199). Leech's moral distinctions appear doubtful, however, when one remembers the epithets applied to the Duchess by her brothers, for whom she is a "notorious strumpet" (II.v.4). Moreover, the structural justification for this interpretation of the subplot is dubious. If Julia were intended as a foil to the Duchess, she appears utterly redundant. By the final act of the play, Boklund comments, "Reader and spectator have formed definite opinions about the Duchess's conduct, and neither praise nor blame, be it open or implied, will now affect their judgment" (*Duchess* 158).

Other critics have proposed Julia as a parody of the Duchess, designed to undercut and qualify her values. Boklund suggests that "since the main action of the play is based on the consequences of a deliberate flouting of the laws guarding sexual decorum, the by-plot may serve to provide a commentary in word and action on the heroine's behavior" (*Duchess* 78). [13] Such attempts to find a "tragic flaw" in the Duchess, reflected and confirmed in Julia, are difficult to support with the text. Webster's sources, Painter and Belleforest, condemn the Duchess's actions, and Webster's deliberate deviation from them in this regard brings him closer to the spirit of the Italian original, a novella by Bandello which treats the Duchess with "tolerant understanding" and sexual pragmatism (Boklund, *Duchess* 9). As Boklund himself admits, in Webster "there is no case for the prosecution" (*Duchess* 102). If Julia were intended as a parody or ironic reflection of the Duchess, Webster's careful construction designed to emphasize the Duchess's virtue throughout the play would be pointless. Some critics sound alarmingly like the hysterical Ferdinand when claiming, "Lower in her sexual drive than 'a beast that wants discourse of reason,' the Duchess of Malfi, like Hamlet's mother, steps out of the path of duty and marries for lust" (Jardine 71). As William Empson puts it, "A play intended as a warning against marrying a social inferior would have to be constructed quite differently" ("Mine Eyes Dazzle" 298). If the Julia subplot can be explained as an integral part of the play's construction, its function must transcend that of foil or parody.

Clearly, interpretation of the Julia subplot involves moral judgment of the Duchess. Yet often that moral judgment not only fails to allow for the warm humanity of the Duchess on the stage, but also reduces the status of the play as tragedy. Those critics who emphasize the analogies between the Duchess and Julia come perilously close to reading the play as a cautionary tale. Those who concentrate on the differences tend to exaggerate the saintliness of the Duchess and to read the play as melodrama. Underlying both these perspectives is another implicit moral judgment—that Julia is meant to be condemned as a wanton, promiscuous, morally reprehensible woman.

Directors of the play have also tended to impose this interpretation on the character of Julia, sometimes deliberately using stage effects to undercut the immediate import of the language to the confusion of critics and theatre audiences alike. For example, in the 1960 Royal Shakespeare Company production, the scene in which Julia rejects Delio was reinterpreted by Donald McWhinnie's staging. What began as rejection ended in mute consent, as she stalked off with Delio's proffered bribe (II.iv.76).[14] Visual effects contradicted the scene's language and made Delio's bewilderment at her "wit or honesty" (II.iv.77) incomprehensible. In the final act of the same production, Julia's open lasciviousness with Bosola made her a caricature of lust that so jarred with her tragic death that one reviewer commented in utter confusion, "Sian Phillips did not shirk the part of the cardinal's mistress Julia, but what can any actress today make of the last scenes?" (Hope-Wallace review). In the 1985 National Theatre production, director Philip Prowse's conception of Julia was clear from the beginning when she made a dramatic entrance in the first act on the Duchess's cue, only to turn and kneel finally before a much more modest Duchess. The invented stage moment established her clearly as the Duchess's foil as well as her servant.

Critics and directors may have ceased their moral condemnation of the Duchess and instead tended to beatify her, but their moral prejudices continue to vent themselves on Julia. Her contribution to the dramatic texture and design of the play has been largely ignored in favor of the accepted view of her as a stock Jacobean whore. It is Clifford Leech's sensitivity to the text that allows him, however briefly, to entertain a third possibility in the analogical relation between the two plots. He asserts, "How erroneous it would be to regard the Duchess as outside the normal sphere of sexual passion," and declares that, despite the differences between them, "there is enough resemblance between the two actions of the play to keep strongly in our minds the force of the passion that urges the Duchess to speak" (*Duchess* 33). Leech's tentative suggestion moves toward a realistic, human view of the Duchess essential to performance, but it remains a suggestion, which he does not support with close examination of the text.

In fact, few critics provide a detailed reading of the three scenes of the play in which Julia figures. Only close attention to these scenes in their dramatic context can determine their relation to the rest of the play. And such close attention makes some critical claims about Julia's character seem surprising. For Boklund, she is "guided by the two forces of lust and avarice" (*Duchess* 157); for Clifford Leech she is a "rank whore" (*John Webster* 75); for Richard Levin she is a "flagrant adultress [sic]" (*New Readings* 98). Actresses who attempt to play Julia this way, however, must find themselves working directly against the text at several points.

Before Julia appears for the first time in II.iv, the audience is prepared by Bosola for her appearance. After Bosola has picked up the horoscope and discovered that the Duchess has given birth to a son, he gleefully closes the scene (II.iii) with a couplet which carries over into the following scene.

> Though lust do mask in ne'er so strange disguise,
> She's oft found witty, but is never wise.
> (II.iii.76–77)

At the opening of the next scene, the Cardinal echoes Bosola's couplet when he describes Julia as a "witty false one" (II.iv.5). At first Julia appears to be a fulfillment of Bosola's and the Arragonian brothers' degraded vision of the Duchess, which has dominated the stage since the beginning of the second act.[15] The device is similar to that used by Shakespeare in *Othello*, where, Mack points out, "Bianca . . . may be thought to supply in living form on the stage the prostitute figure that Desdemona has become in Othello's mind" (30). Yet just as, in *Othello*, Iago's vision of Bianca as a "notable strumpet" (V.i.78) is cast into doubt by her loyalty to Cassio, very early in the scene Julia's words and stage actions begin to contradict the Cardinal's version of her. Her first speech, with its anxious, halting rhythm, betrays the deep inner struggle of a woman who has compromised herself for uncertain gain and finds herself the victim of a cynical and abusive man.

You have prevail'd with me
Beyond my strongest thoughts: I would not now
Find you inconstant.

(IV.ii.6–8)

These are hardly words that convey the lust and avarice of a flagrant adulteress. On the contrary, they imply that her decision to commit adultery was a painful one, the result of an ongoing struggle between the demands of sexuality and morality. As the interview progresses, Julia defends her own constancy and integrity as the Cardinal attacks them. In the face of his cruel misogyny, she finally bursts into tears when her objections can no longer be heard. If the scene begins as a confirmation of Bosola's degraded perspective on the Duchess, it moves away from that perspective as it continues. The scene is clearly written to overturn an audience's initial impression of Julia. The "whore" and "adulteress" cannot be quite so easily dismissed.

The Cardinal's assault on the "giddy and wild turnings" (II.iv.12) of women both echoes the satiric perspective of Bosola that dominated the previous three scenes and anticipates the crazed misogyny of Ferdinand in the following scene (II.v).[16] The scene suspends and extends the previous action—its precise form is unexpected, and it carries the audience away from the world of the Duchess. At the same time, however, it exploits the tension and energy that have built up during the previous three scenes regarding the Duchess's escalating danger. The scene is an analogical replay of the situation between Bosola and the Duchess throughout the second act, since Julia is another woman victimized by the cruel cynicism of men. Again, the satiric vision is pitted against the vulnerability of human love and sexuality with their inherent compromises. In both cases, two voices are heard in opposition to each other—the tough against the vulnerable, the deeply cynical against the merely human.[17] As Bosola's meditation on death and decay (II.i.45–60) is set against the stage image of the pregnant Duchess, swollen with life, the Cardinal's diatribe on the inconstancy of women is contrasted with Julia's long-suffering silence. Like Bosola (and like Iago in *Othello*), the Cardinal attempts to degrade women by generalizing them and by reducing them to the level of mere animals. The Duchess and Julia both contradict this version of themselves with their stage presences.

Following the interview between the Cardinal and Julia is an exchange between Julia and Delio that has puzzled most critics. Archer simply admits that "the relevance of the passage in which Delio makes love to the Cardinal's mistress utterly escapes me" ("Webster, Lamb" 142). Lois Potter claims that the exchange "must inevitably be confusing in performance," though she suggests that it recalls Ferdinand's bribery of Bosola in Act I and reiterates the play's "service and reward" motif (180). If the echo is there, it is designed to enforce a contrast; Bosola finally accepts the gold while Julia rejects it. In his edition of the play, John Russell Brown suggests that the incident is designed "to aggravate the audience's sense of a growing web of intrigue and an increasing complexity of character" (62). That the exchange is designed deliberately to confuse appears a weak explanation at best. Neither critic accounts for the particular nature of the incident—another kind of exchange would presumably serve just as well to reinforce a theme or to suggest intricacy of plot. Nor does either critic examine the dramatic rhythm of the exchange. Its dramatic impact is, however, unmistakable.

The first part of the interchange between Julia and Delio centers on Julia's old husband, Castruchio, who has already appeared twice in the play. As Ferdinand's poker-faced advisor in Act I, and as an aspiring courtier and the object of Bosola's mockery in Act II, Castruchio quickly impresses an audience as a foolish old man. His marital relationship to Julia, to which Webster suddenly draws attention in this scene, appears to be the culmination of his function in the play, since he disappears completely after his mention here. A foolish, impotent old man married to an obviously desirable young woman—whom Bosola later describes as "very fair" (V.ii.177)—recalls the marriage of Camillo and Vittoria in *The White Devil*. There, the husband's inadequacy helped to exonerate the wife's adultery. Here, the first explicit identification of Julia's deceived husband with foolish old Castruchio (whose name suggests castration) shifts the scene even further in the direction of Julia's redemption in the eyes of the audience. The terse reply Julia makes to Delio's mockery of her husband—"Your laughter is my pity" (II.iv.56–57)—betrays her suffering with its brevity.

Delio then offers her his gold, drawing attention to its physical properties by mockingly treating it as an aesthetic object. Julia rejects not only the gold itself, but also the crude materialism it represents.[18] In reply, she evokes a world of positive aesthetic values and refined sensual beauty—of beautiful birds, music and fragrance. It is a world in which the Duchess also lives, and which she conjures up most eloquently just before her death in lines like these:

> What would it pleasure me to have my throat cut
> With diamonds? or to be smothered
> With cassia? or to be shot to death with pearls?
> (IV.ii.216–18)

The struggle between two polar views of life, between the crudely sexual and the delicately sensual, is articulated throughout the play's main action in the characters of Ferdinand and the Duchess (Warren 65). Here, its mere suggestion is enough to associate Julia with the Duchess's refined sensuality. Finally, Julia's categorical rejection of Delio's sexual offer, combined with the disclosure of her unhappy marriage to Castruchio, is clearly designed to capture audience sympathy for Julia. Together, they confirm the impression of abused integrity suggested in her relationship with the Cardinal at the beginning of the scene. As Julia remains in the foreground, the background shifts around her so that the vulnerable victim of the Cardinal's misogyny can exhibit self-assured integrity. The question of Delio's motives is less important than the dramatic impact of Julia's reassertion of her integrity. And that integrity is not undercut by Julia's witty reply to Delio:

> Sir, I'll go ask my husband if I shall,
> And straight return your answer.
> (II.iv.75–76)

On the contrary, Julia's need to rely on the outward form of conventional morality by calling on her husband illuminates its inadequacy as a standard of human behavior. The courage she displays appears more significant since the audience knows that it is unsupported by the facts of her marital relationship. Delio may wonder, "Is this her wit or honesty that speaks thus?" (II.iv.77), but an audience is left in little doubt. Because Julia, like the Duchess, is forced to exceed the bounds of respectability, her "virtue" must be judged according to another standard. One might say, in the spirit of Empson, that a scene intended to portray a "flagrant adulteress" in clear contrast to the Duchess would have to be constructed quite differently.

Just before Julia's final dismissal of Delio's offer, a servant enters to report,

> Your husband's come,
> Hath deliver'd a letter to the Duke of Calabria,
> That, to my thinking, hath put him out of his wits.
>
> (II.iv.67–69)

The audience is suddenly reminded of what has been going on in the play's main action. Bosola's report of the birth of the Duchess's "illegitimate" child has been delivered by Castruchio to the Arragonian brothers. The servant's report briefly anticipates the following scene, with Ferdinand's reassertion of his crazed view of the Duchess as a "notorious strumpet" (II.v.4). As we are reminded of Ferdinand's distorted vision of the Duchess, Delio imposes his degraded perspective on Julia, making her a sexual offer. Julia's rejection of that offer thus has the effect of salvaging the Duchess's values by association. At this point, Julia's function in the play transcends mere analogy to anticipate the reassertion of the Duchess's integrity after Bosola's and Ferdinand's assaults upon it throughout the second act.

The second act, with its opening parody of the Duchess and Antonio in the figures of the Old Lady and Castruchio, tends to modify, if not to obliterate, the delicate power of the tender wooing scene that closes the first act. While an audience may have little difficulty rejecting the Arragonian brothers' tyrannical moralism in favor of the Duchess's individualism in the first act, it finds few alternatives to Bosola's relentless cynicism in the second. Bosola takes over from Antonio as the Duchess's observer in the second act, and audience response is to some extent conditioned by his vision of life and sexuality as purely physical and subject to decay. Moreover, both times that Julia appears the Duchess has been absent from the stage for a prolonged period. Bosola's gift of "apricocks" to the Duchess sends her into labor in the first scene of Act II; she quickly leaves the stage and does not reappear until the following act. The only momentary reanimation of her presence is an offstage shriek

Bosola hears at the beginning of II.iii, realistically suggesting her offstage labor, but also conveying the deeper suffering that shapes her character in preparation for the death scene. Her absence from the stage throughout most of the second act may represent this implied process of necessary psychic change, what Mack calls the "second phase" in the development of the tragic hero (35). When Julia comes onto the stage, the audience is prepared to judge her as the Duchess's enemies have judged the Duchess. With this scene, however, Webster overturns the simplified prejudices of conventional morality that are inevitably part of an audience's response, a response we share with the Duchess's enemies. Webster's presentation of Julia is consistent with his portrait of Vittoria in *The White Devil* and, ultimately, with his interest in the figure of the Duchess. It allows him to draw attention to something he evidently considered very important—that "whore," a word applied by social convention to someone unchaste, does not exhaust the psychological reality of the woman. This is true of Vittoria, of Julia, and most of all, of the Duchess.[19] The first of Julia's scenes functions as analogical probability at a point in the play when the Duchess is most vulnerable to the attacks of her enemies because she is not present on the stage.

Bosola's cynical, satiric vision presents a challenge to the Duchess's values that intensifies them by contrast when they are reasserted. But Bosola's vision also serves another purpose in the play's dramatic construction by further humanizing and illuminating the Duchess. The Duchess is above all, as she herself makes clear, an intensely sexual woman. The "apricocks" scene (II.i) becomes, in performance, not an indictment of the Duchess, but a further confirmation of the directness and sensual delight she exhibited in the wooing scene. It is precisely this sensual Duchess that Webster wanted to capture in Julia.

When Julia appears again in the first scene of Act V to request Antonio's property from Pescara, she immediately represents those who crudely profit from the ruin of the couple. Yet the focus of the scene shifts quickly from Julia's appropriation of Antonio's land to Pescara's hypocrisy. The scene centers, not on Julia's immoral action, but on the moral turpitude of those who condemn her as a "strumpet" in order to excuse their own actions. Pescara's guilt is thinly disguised by his abuse of Julia; his own fault is greater than hers. He grants Antonio's land to the Cardinal's mistress as "salary for his [the Cardinal's] lust" (V.i.52), defending his sycophantic action with perverse self-righteousness.[20] The moral status of Julia is again made relative, since her moralizing accusers are unreliable. Her appearance here is intended to offset possible moral condemnation from the audience in the following scene.

Julia's appearance in the following scene (V.ii), as in the second act, re-stages for emphasis an aspect of the Duchess's experience that threatens to disappear with her. Whereas Julia's first appearance reflects the Duchess's position as a victim of the cruel cynicism of men and anticipates the Duchess's restoration, her final appearance recalls the Duchess's fate in miniature and anticipates the futile revenge of Bosola.

Julia's wooing of Bosola in the second scene of Act V seems deliberately designed to recall the Duchess's wooing of Antonio in Act I. Webster goes to considerable lengths to establish visual and verbal parallels between the two incidents. In both cases, the woman is the wooer (I.i.442; V.ii.183) and uses roughly similar phrases to express with striking directness her admiration for her man (I.i.435–37; V.ii.167–68). In both cases, the woman puts herself at great risk for her lover. While Webster clearly did not intend the crude seduction of Bosola to be a direct echo of the tender wooing of Antonio, the parallels between the two scenes appear to be as significant as the differences, which have frequently been emphasized by critics. During performances of the play, the later scene is clearly linked to the earlier one, not by its reiterated images, but by its similar effect on an audience. The two wooing scenes are virtually the only extended actions in the play to evoke laughter and delight in an audience predisposed to expect danger. As in Act I, in the last act the play's relentless machinery of crime and revenge is suspended while we watch the digressive banter of lovers.

Noting the differences between the two wooing scenes, critics have proposed interpretations of the later scene as a foil to, or parody of, the earlier one. Yet, as has been argued earlier, the dramaturgical advantages of either at this late stage in the action are limited. A foil appears superfluous, since the stature of the Duchess is by this point fixed. She is clearly exalted beyond all the characters of the fifth act. A parody seems groundless, since it would undercut the tragic intensity of her loss. There is, however, a third possibility, consistent with Webster's treatment of Julia in the second act.

Here, as there, she may be intended as a mirror for the main action, reflecting its broad outlines in simplified analogical fashion from a different moral perspective. Shakespeare uses a similar dramatic strategy in the final act of *Othello*; Bianca, falsely accused by Iago of Cassio's murder, recalls Desdemona's plight as she has also been presented as a "whore" responsible for her man's destruction.

When Julia enters, pointing a pistol at Bosola and accusing him of treachery (V.ii.151), she continues the language of violence, intrigue and deception used by the Cardinal and Bosola in their preceding interview. Similarly, when the Duchess offers her wedding ring to Antonio, visual and verbal echoes recall Ferdinand's bribery of Bosola in the same scene, and the interview is fraught with over-tones of danger. In both scenes, however, the context of love and sexuality defuses the play's threatening language. The oppressive intrigue of the court is mockingly parodied and transformed by Julia. Her wit takes Bosola and the audience by surprise, as she abruptly turns apparent aggression into playful lovemaking. Webster sustains a tone throughout the scene that carefully avoids both romantic and sexual cliché. When Bosola attempts to seduce Julia with a conventional line, saying

> Your bright eyes
> Carry a quiver of darts in them, sharper
> Than sunbeams.
>> (V.ii.179–81)

Julia abruptly cuts him off and asserts her own status as the wooer. When he takes the opposite tack and decides to "grow most amo-rously familiar" (V.ii.185) with her, Julia responds with pragmatic intelligence, again drawing the focus away from Bosola and onto her own power.

> For if I see and steal a diamond,
> The fault is not i'th' stone, but in me the thief
> That purloins it:—I am sudden with you;
> We that are great women of pleasure use to cut off
> These uncertain wishes, and unquiet longings,
> And in an instant join the sweet delight
> And the pretty excuse together.
>> (V.ii.190–96)

While the scene verges on caricature, it develops a sustained contrast between Bosola's limited, conventional attitude and Julia's strong unconventional one. The echoes of the wooing scene of Act I, however distorted or exaggerated, are nonetheless startling in performance. The entire scene is structured to highlight the energy, wit, and exuberance of Julia, glimpsed only briefly in her earlier interchange with Delio. In both wooing scenes, Webster challenges the popular antifeminist stereotype that "a *Harlot* is full of words" (Woodbridge 77), and links the Duchess and Julia in their common deviation from the conventional "good" woman. In the earlier scene (II.iv), the assertion of Julia's sexual integrity was necessary to suggest by analogy the Duchess's dramatic recovery at a point when it seemed threatened. In the later scene, the "splendidly sensual" and "voluptuous" Julia reevokes by association quite a different quality in the Duchess.[21] Again, the recollection is a timely one in the play's dramatic rhythm, since Bosola's perspective on the Duchess as "sacred innocence" (IV.ii.355) threatens to distort her by exalting her. With Julia in the final act as an analogical reassertion of the Duchess's strong sexuality, a balance is restored.

In the final act, Julia reanimates by association, not the Duchess of the recent death scene, but the Duchess of the wooing scene—playful, confident, sensual, and direct. If, as I have argued, Webster attempts to recall such qualities in the Duchess by exaggerating them in Julia, he does so at considerable risk. The success of his strategy rests finally on performance—on an actress who can play Julia in this scene as a strong, vital woman rather than as a vulgar strumpet. Such risks, however, are unavoidable for the dramatist. In this instance, Webster takes the risk of falling into crude burlesque, for the greater advantage of clarifying his tragic construction. The recollection at this point of the young, carefree, and childless Duchess of the beginning of the play leads an audience to appreciate precisely what has been lost and gained in the course of the play's tragic action. The changes that are forced upon the Duchess enrich and develop her as a character who can finally face her death with courage. Yet at the same time those changes rob her of her innocent confidence that "time will easily / Scatter the tempest" (I.i.471–72). With the appearance of Julia in the final act, the audience can measure the distance it has travelled since the wooing scene. Loss of the Duchess's youthful insouciance is balanced against the recollection of the richness of her spirit in adversity. The evocation of this simple tragic paradox is the main dramaturgical function of Julia at this stage in the play.

If the wooing of Bosola is intended as an echo of the Duchess's lighthearted wooing of Antonio, then the subsequent interview with the Cardinal plunges the audience directly into the death scene. The opposed perspectives of the play's main action—the Duchess's youthful vitality and the irrational menace of her enemies—are recalled in the confrontation between Julia and the Cardinal. Julia is still witty and playful, but the Cardinal is dangerously bitter. Comic and tragic perspectives illuminate each other in their dialogue, remaining at cross purposes until the Cardinal confesses his crime:

> By my appointment, the great Duchess of Malfi,
> And two of her young children, four nights since,
> Were strangled.
>
> (V.ii.268–70)

The Cardinal's syntax imitates the dramatic suspense of the interview, delaying the final shock until the end of the sentence, thus heightening its impact. The witty innocence of Julia's playful persuasions acts as a foil to the Cardinal's bald and horrifying declaration. His admission of guilt is directly followed by a re-staging of the crime, for Julia immediately pays for her indiscretion with her death. The death of the Duchess in the fourth act is painstakingly prepared for from the play's very beginning, so that its dramatic shock is greatly mitigated. For Julia, love is more irresponsible, knowledge of evil more sudden, and death more abrupt than for the Duchess, yet the compressed juxtaposition of these extremes of love and death recalls the Duchess's tragic fate with new force. This simplified—almost caricatured—recollection of the Duchess's life and death clarifies the essential tragic meaning of the play's action. In a review of the 1960 Royal Shakespeare Company production, T. C. Worsley summarized, "As we see her first the Duchess is a woman of high natural spirits and vitality, and it is that buoyancy of heart that it is so terrible to see being desolated." Julia's part in the final act is a microcosm of the main action, her cruel death a striking contrast to her strength and vitality. And, unlike Cariola—the

Duchess's foil in death—Julia accepts her death with dignity, though it is undeserved.

During the final act, Bosola's role as an onlooker and accomplice during the Duchess's death is re-staged. After Julia's death, he argues with the Cardinal about "reward," vows vengeance for the Duchess's murder, and drags the body off the stage, exactly as he had done at the end of Act IV. His complaint as he picks up Julia's body—"I think I shall / Shortly grow the common bier for church-yards" (V.ii.311–12)—reinforces the analogue. In the staging of the scene, Bosola's vengeful soliloquy is invariably delivered as he kneels over Julia's body, precisely as he had knelt over the Duchess's body earlier. While it keeps the memory of the Duchess alive, the repetition of the sequence of crime and revenge also suggests the futility of Bosola's attempt at vengeance, futility that is later confirmed in his botched murder of Antonio.

It would of course be dangerous to overstate the case for the parallels between the two plots. Certainly the two women belong to sharply contrasting worlds throughout the play, and such contrasts give the play its richly varied texture. Julia is involved in the petty, broken world of the Duchess's enemies as the Duchess herself never is, and the parallels between the two women heighten their differences. Conversely, however, Webster exploits the obvious differences between them in order to reveal surprising similarities, which serve his dramatic ends. The differences between the Duchess and Julia may emphasize the Duchess's calm self-sufficiency, but the similarities between them suggest the vulnerability of women in a hostile masculine world. These similarities may have been reinforced visually: when Julia visits the Cardinal in II.iv, she likely comes dressed as a pilgrim "for devotion" (5); the Duchess is clearly disguised as a pilgrim during the banishment scene (III.iv), when she, too, suffers abuse at the hands of the Cardinal. Forker notes that "Julia's trifling with religion almost parodies the Duchess's in advance, necessarily complicating our response to . . . the unquestioning decision of [the Duchess] to depart instantly for Loretto" (361). Yet the Duchess's disguise may recall Julia's, not in its trifling with religion, but in its visual reminder of the hypocrisy required in this constricted world of male tyranny. Kathleen McLuskie observes, "Both Julia and the Duchess assert their independence in the only way open to them, by sexual choice, and Webster's drama places these choices against the commonplace and limiting values of the men in the play" (88). The play's final emphasis falls on Julia and, by analogy, on the Duchess—not as a single, heroic individual destroyed by crazed villains, but as an ordinary, vital young woman stifled by misogyny. On the one hand, Julia's startlingly casual murder casts new light retrospectively on the psychotic forces behind the murder of the Duchess, showing them to be merely exaggerations of forces that regularly destroy women in the real world. On the other hand, instead of undercutting or further exalting the Duchess's stature in the final act, Julia restores the Duchess by analogy to the world of common humanity, to which she firmly belonged throughout the play. In a review of the 1971 Royal Shakespeare Company production of the play, the critic for the *Sunday Mercury* described Julia as "the most genteel whore, cooing like a dove in a cage of hawks" (P. W. review), a description which could apply equally well to the Duchess. Like the Duchess, Julia is caged and finally killed by the predatory Arragonian brothers. And like the Duchess, Julia remains sexually alive to the last moment.

The Julia subplot reaches its conclusion as part of a final act which has been considered notoriously problematic by both critics and directors. *The White Devil's* prominent subsidiary action has become the major action in *The Duchess of Malfi*. In *The White Devil*, the major characters are distanced and increasingly overshadowed by the minor characters in the last act; in *The Duchess of Malfi*, the chief protagonist is dead and the remaining characters play out an entirely different scenario stage-managed by Bosola. Indeed, as John Russell Brown points out in his introduction to his edition of *The Duchess of Malfi*, "Perhaps the most pervasive debt to *The White Devil* is the structure of the last Act: both plays depart from their narrative source to widen and complicate the conclusion" (xxxi). The entire final act of *The Duchess of Malfi* has aroused the same kind of criticism as the subsidiary action of *The White Devil*. Both actions are cited by critics to prove that Webster could not make the parts of his play cohere into a total vision.

It is a common critical allegation that *The Duchess of Malfi* is marred by its lengthy final act, which closes the play after the Duchess has been murdered. Archer baldly states that "with the death of the Duchess, the interest of the play is over" (*Nineteenth Century* 96). Lucas asserts that the play "lives too long, when it outlives the heroine" (2:24). These views are repeated by the *Times*'s theatre critic in 1960, who called for "resolution" in the director as "the quality most needed in this sombre Jacobean tragedy . . . to conceal a slackening of tension after the somewhat too early death of the heroine" (Review, "Webster's Play Well Handled"). It is obvious that any serious consideration of Webster's ability to construct must examine the position of the final act in the play's structure.

Modern critics have attempted to justify the final act by claiming that it deliberately steers the play away from tragedy in the direction of tragicomedy. Pearson claims that "in Act Five the play moves away from tragedy: the Duchess' hard-won tragic moment is precarious and collapses as soon as she dies, and the return from tragedy is illustrated in several small inversions or parodies of tragedy" (87). Berlin calls the play a "comitragedy," and relates it to modern "absurdist" drama, claiming that Webster sought to achieve "effects which are not altogether tragic" (362, 353). Potter asserts that in the last act "Ferdinand's madness . . . is funny in a way that the madmen in Act IV are not" (178). Yet this statement comes after her admission that she did not see either the 1960 production in Stratford, England, or the 1971 production in Stratford, Ontario (172)— both major productions that, according to the critics, played the final act (including Ferdinand's mad scene) seriously with success. Irving Wardle's review of the 1971 Stratford, Ontario, production praised "the moral centre . . . implicit in Powys Thomas's Bosola, a maimed eagle who manifestly sustains the play's life through the precarious last act after the Duchess's death" ("Beardsley Garden"), and Herbert Whittaker, reviewer for the *Globe and Mail*, called Ferdinand "a most convincing madman, whose darker motivations haunt us all evening." Of the 1960 production, the reviewer for the *Times* wrote, "Mr. Donald McWhinnie [the director] keeps his confident grip on the play through the perilous fifth act. The mad scene of the lycanthropic Duke Ferdinand is tellingly acted. . . . So from first to last the life of the play is kept going surprisingly well" (Review, "Webster's Play Well Handled"). Although the final act is considered perilous for a director, it appears to be carried off successfully when it is treated seriously on the stage. Irony, absurdity, and low comedy are all possibilities in the study but will not hold the attention or the sympathy of an audience in the theatre.

A comparison of two postwar productions of the play turn up

useful clues to the meaning and function of the fifth act. The first major American production of *The Duchess of Malfi*, at the Barrymore in 1946, was based on a script revised by W. H. Auden and Bertolt Brecht. Reviews of the production were unanimously unfavorable. Brooks Atkinson, the drama critic for the *New York Times*, wrote that "W. H. Auden has revised the script to keep the Duchess as the central figure straight on to the conclusion. But it still leaves the Duchess as a weak figure among brutish men." Mary McCarthy commented, "The cutting done by Auden, while it enhances the Duchess's plight as the play's victim, misunderstands her character by making her its dead center" (93). The New York production was directed by George Rylands, who had directed a production at the Haymarket in London only eighteen months previously, in April 1945. The production in London, which retained Webster's original design, was much more successful. And its success appears to have been related in large measure to its retention and serious treatment of the fifth act. The *Times*'s theatre critic praised the act that some academic critics have dismissed as comic or absurd, and claimed that "the audience . . . followed all that happened on the stage with a respectful curiosity which rose at times to emotional sympathy and never once descended to misplaced tittering." With special reference to the final act, the reviewer goes on to say, "That we do not smile at the heap of corpses on which the final curtain falls implies that the actors have fixed attention with Ferdinand's soul-stricken ravings, with the Cardinal's unequal struggle against implacable fate, and with Bosola's strangely intense remorse—thus flouting Johnson's opinion that the genius of the play comes in and goes out with the Duchess" (Review, "Haymarket Theatre"). Comparison of the New York and London productions is striking and instructive, since they shared the same director and a similar audience. The Brecht/Auden revision, which ends with the death of the Duchess, veers into melodrama, leaving its audience with an innocent victim destroyed by villains, an involuntary, solitary martyr who in life was dedicated to the group, the family. Rylands's London production on the other hand played the final act fully and seriously, and was praised as highly tragic. That theatre critics, reviewing these different productions, directed their attention to the absence or presence of the final act as essential to the play's tragic construction appears very significant.

The final act begins with the reappearance of Antonio and Delio alone together on the stage; this repeated stage image again indicates a new phase in the action. As in *The White Devil*, the first and the third scenes of the final act pursue the main action, with their focus on Antonio's "poor ling'ring life" (V.i.63), while the second and last scenes introduce a different series of actions which finally bring the play to a close. In this alternating rhythm, the main action is increasingly distanced—the Duchess herself dwindles to an echo—while the subsidiary action becomes progressively more predominant.

Dominating and controlling the subsidiary action of the last act is Bosola. Like Flamineo in *The White Devil*, Bosola undergoes a significant moral regeneration while at the same time remaining limited by his own fearful self-interest. Yet while in *The White Devil* Flamineo replicates the complexity of the protagonists as they achieve tragic vision in the last act, in *The Duchess of Malfi* Bosola mirrors the humanity of the antagonists and so completes the tragedy. Furthermore, Bosola also appropriates Francisco's role in the final act of *The White Devil* and illuminates the futility of retribution for the play's villains. The figure of Bosola is necessary to the play's unity—as he has straddled two worlds throughout the play, working for Ferdinand to destroy the Duchess with a steady commitment that seems paradoxically virtuous, so he reanimates the Duchess's virtue and imposes it villainously on her enemies in the final act.

The second scene of Act V introduces the subsidiary action in what may appear to be a rambling, disconnected series of episodes. Closer examination, however, reveals the scene's careful design. At its center are Julia's wooing and death, together an analogical replay of the Duchess's experience. This centerpiece is framed by discussions of equal length between Bosola and the Cardinal regarding the planned murder of Antonio (V.ii.105–50,285–330). Finally, the scene's outer frame shows the effects of the Duchess's murder on her murderers, Ferdinand and Bosola. The first part of the scene shows the madness of Ferdinand, the result of his guilty conscience; the last part of the scene shows Bosola's plan for revenge, the result of his "Penitence" (V.ii.348). Both Ferdinand and Bosola are "haunted" by the Duchess and by their crimes against her. Ferdinand attempts to "throttle" (V.ii.38) his own shadow for haunting him in a mad gesture that suggestively evokes both the original murder and his subsequent self-disgust; Bosola flinches nervously at an imagined spectre (like Francisco in *The White Devil* IV.i):

> still methinks the duchess
> Haunts me: there, there!—
> 'Tis nothing but my melancholy.
> O Penitence, let me truly taste thy cup,
> That throws men down, only to raise them up.
>   (V.ii.345–49)

After the Duchess's death, Bosola's vision of "a perspective / That shows us hell" (IV.ii.358–59) anticipates and mirrors the harrowing agony of Ferdinand's mad scene in the final act. Although many academic critics argue that the scene is comic, theatrical reviews of widely different productions attest to its dramatic power. In his admiring review of the 1980 production at the Royal Exchange, Wardle commented, "Ferdinand does not have the voice for the early homicidal hysterics, and a good thing too as this enables him to secure his real climax after his reason cracks" ("Clearing the Hurdle"). On the other hand, in his review of the 1971 Royal Shakespeare Company production, Ronald Bryden of the *Observer* attributed the failure of the mad scene to the exaggeration of Ferdinand's incestuous motives earlier in the play: "Michael Williams tries to suggest an inner history of incestuous passion for his sister in Ferdinand's jealousy, but the result is to diminish the horror of his collapse into madness." Ferdinand's madness is related not to his individual pathology but to his humanity. The Ferdinand in this production, who, according to Wardle, was "turned completely to ridicule, lurking in the corridors carrying a dead rabbit" (Review, "Stratford"), illuminated the failure of the scene on the stage when it is played as low comedy, or is not convincingly tragic.

A conversation between the doctor and Pescara prepares us for the entrance of Ferdinand in the mad scene (V.ii). The doctor appears to be setting the audience up for a conventionally comic mad scene by describing Ferdinand's disease, "lycanthropia," in vivid comic detail. Yet Ferdinand's first words upon entering— "Leave me" (V.ii.28)—give him immediate control and dignity. He speaks not of wolves but of eagles, contradicting the doctor's version of him.

> Eagles commonly fly alone: they are crows, daws, and starlings that flock together:—look, what's that follows me? (V.ii.30–32)

Ferdinand wants to separate himself from the community and to deny his involvement in humanity, but finds he cannot do so. Even the existence of his own shadow means that he cannot be single and indivisible. Bosola, his accomplice in the murder, hovers nearby. The audience's privileged knowledge of the reason for Ferdinand's agony lends his "mad" actions the dignity of anguished self-recrimination rather than the degradation of comic futility. Ferdinand's deep sense of guilt, as one of the "worst persons" destined for "hell" (V.ii.41–43) is matched by his terrible implied regret. In his madness he vows,

> To drive six snails before me, from this town to Moscow; neither use goad nor whip to them, but let them take their own time:—the patien-test man i'th' world match me for an experiment. (V.ii.47–50)

Yet Ferdinand's earlier attempt to hasten the passage of time, by forcing the Duchess to die "young," cannot be eradicated by his new vow of patience. His guilt is more terrible in its futility. The doctor, who tries to impose his comic version of the scene on Ferdinand, cannot succeed in reducing him to "a comic madman afraid of his own shadow" (Pearson 90). Ferdinand finally overturns the scene's comic potential by beating the doctor and hurling insults at the others as he exits. After Ferdinand's exit, the doctor's under-stated admission that he was "somewhat too forward" (V.ii.84) al-lows the audience to succumb to its thwarted urge to laugh. The laugh, however, is directed not at Ferdinand but at the doctor, and does not erase the harrowing agony of Ferdinand's appearance.

Later in the same scene, Webster again uses comic elements to heighten, rather than to undercut, the tragic. The interview be-tween Julia and Bosola (V.ii.152–223) comes as a relief to the au-dience. It treats the play's serious themes and images of love, weapons, secrets, and dangers in a light-hearted and comic fashion. Yet soon afterward, Julia collapses and dies on the stage, the Cardinal's victim. Her defeat, like that of the doctor, is the defeat of comedy. Comic elements again reinforce the tragic vision. As in the preceding "mad" scene, Webster carefully plants a line that allows the audience to laugh and drains off the scene's comic potential. Bosola, taking up Julia's dead body, complains that he "shall / Shortly grow the common bier for churchyards" (V.ii.311–12). The laugh is, like the earlier one, an uneasy laugh. The audience, in its continual experience of comedy shifting into tragedy, is being trained not to accept comedy's simpler vision.

It is the final scene of the play that unites the characters of both main and subsidiary actions and perhaps best illuminates and justifies Webster's tragic design in the play as a whole. In fact, the last two scenes should be considered as a single, unbroken unit on the stage—as they are in the promptbook for the 1960 Royal Shakespeare Company production. When the Cardinal enters to deliver his brief speech downstage, Bosola and the servant, with Antonio's body, likely move upstage, as there is insufficient time for them to exit and reenter during this time. When the two scenes are considered as a single unbroken scene in performance, the concentric design becomes clear. The final movement of the play, which has often been dismissed as comic confusion, is in reality carefully structured.

The scene begins as it ends, with a group of courtiers surrounding a central figure. The opening fifteen lines are balanced by the closing thirty, and the presence of the courtiers brings the wheel full circle, providing a frame for the action. The Cardinal's instruction to the courtiers at the beginning, that they should ignore his "mad tricks" and cries for help, is ironically recalled in his dying words to them:

> and now, I pray, let me
> Be laid by, and never thought of.
> (V.v.89–90)

At the center of this scenic unit, as a kind of emblematic centerpiece, is the Cardinal's vision of hell:

> I am puzzled in a question about hell:
> He says, in hell there's one material fire,
> And yet it shall not burn all men alike.

> Lay him by:—how tedious is a guilty conscience!
> When I look into the fish-ponds, in my garden,
> Methinks I see a thing, arm'd with a rake
> That seems to strike at me.
>
> (V.v.1–7)

As he speaks, the Cardinal clutches a book. John Russell Brown notes that a book is "an old stage-device for indicating melancholy or introspection" (166n). It is also a visual reminder of the crime for which the Cardinal suffers, his murder of Julia with a poisoned book. The book represents both his crime and his knowledge of its consequences. The dramatic impact of the moment is heightened by the Cardinal's unusual isolation, suffering, and remorse, and by the audience's knowledge that Bosola will return to strike at him. When Bosola appears on the stage, he seems to incarnate the "thing" the Cardinal fears. His last entrance recalls his first, moreover, with its thrilling "I do haunt you still." The end returns to the beginning with a crucial difference; the rest of the scene undercuts Bosola's "revenge," while it confirms the Cardinal's solitary anguish.

Surrounding this "centerpiece" are two actions that exhibit significant parallels. In the first, Bosola attempts to carry out his plan of retribution, but instead accidentally kills Antonio. The irony of Bosola's mistake is underlined by his cry, "Fall right my sword!" (V.iv.45) before he stabs Antonio. As Antonio dies, Bosola likely assumes a kneeling position beside Antonio's prone body that visually recalls his position at the deaths of the Duchess and Julia—indeed, promptbooks for the 1971 productions at the Royal Court and the Royal Shakespeare Theatre both indicate that Bosola knelt here. As Bosola had told the Duchess of her family's survival, he tells Antonio of his family's death. Visual and verbal echoes link the two scenes, as Bosola again finds himself in the position of an involuntary murderer. In the second action, following the Cardinal's vision of hell, Bosola stabs the Cardinal. By this time, his use of the same sword to kill Antonio and Antonio's servant undercuts his triumph. Moreover, the Cardinal's death at Bosola's hands echoes that of the Duchess. He cries "Mercy" to Bosola, as the Duchess had done earlier, and he appears to drop to his knees at the moment of death, again like the Duchess. Bosola's words imply that the Cardinal kneels, then falls:

Now it seems thy greatness was only outward;
For thou fall'st faster of thyself, than calamity
Can drive thee.

(V.v.42–44)

The promptbooks for the 1960 Royal Shakespeare Company production and the 1971 Royal Court production both indicate that the
Cardinal knelt at this point. Rather than exacting retribution for the
Duchess's murder, Bosola repeats it.[22] The courtiers, who are cut
from virtually every production, mistakenly understand the scene
as comedy, and further emphasize the futility of Bosola's attempt
to depersonalize himself as "Justice." Their appearance "above"
(V.v.19 Brown's s.d.) the action suggests a world of arbitrary indifference to which "justice" seems ridiculous. Bosola invokes the same
sense of a cruelly detached universe after he kills Antonio:

We are merely the stars' tennis-balls, struck and banded
Which way please them.

(V.iv.54–55)

Of course, the indifferent fate suggested here and in the courtiers'
detachment is simply the externalization of the tragic process, of
men who cannot but mechanically repeat their crimes, even as they
attempt to redress them. Any notion of just retribution is rendered
ridiculous in the final scene; the tangle of corpses cannot be justified
by Bosola's explanations. Like Francisco's "revenge" in *The White
Devil*, Bosola's attempt to impose the logic of melodrama on the
play's villains illuminates its inadequacy. The two final sequences
are nearly comic in their futility, yet they frame a central image that
is neither comic nor futile. The Cardinal's uneasy vision of hell as
his own guilty conscience occupies a prominent central position in
the final long scene, and is not absorbed into the chaotic futility of
the finale. The hollowness of justice only emphasizes by contrast
the quiet and sinister "thing" that attacks only from within.

While the play's villains suffer for their murder of the Duchess,
they retreat from their own suffering and helplessly repeat the
crime. The Cardinal plans more murders, and poisons Julia; Bosola
finds himself an agent in four more murders; Ferdinand, in his mad
hallucinations, reenacts the crime, crying,

> Strangling is a very quiet death
>
> . . . .
>
> So it must be done i'th'dark: the cardinal
> Would not for a thousand pounds the doctor should see it.
>
> (V.iv.34–38)

Yet Ferdinand's sinister mutterings and the Cardinal's visions transcend the conventional rhetoric of penitence. Like Flamineo and Brachiano in *The White Devil*, Bosola, Ferdinand and the Cardinal all attain a stricken self-awareness that is neither a purgative vision nor a "fatal judgement" (V.ii.85), as Bosola would have it. The villains are eclipsed by an indifferent and unfathomable world that is greater than the sum of their evils. Bosola himself realizes this in his dying words:

> O, this gloomy world!
> In what a shadow, or deep pit of darkness,
> Doth womanish and fearful mankind live!
> Let worthy minds ne'er stagger in distrust
> To suffer death, or shame for what is just—
> Mine is another voyage.
>
> (V.v.100–105)

Like Vittoria in *The White Devil*, Bosola, the Cardinal, and Ferdinand all die with moral lessons on their lips. Such simple formulas illuminate by contrast the complexity of the play they attempt to summarize. Yet Bosola, Ferdinand, and the Cardinal finally subside into a silence which cannot be simply defined. Beyond penitence and beyond justice, it is "another voyage."

When the Duchess dies at the end of Act IV, her death is not a tragic one. If she is seen as merely the innocent victim of fiendish murderers, and dies only a martyr, the play veers into melodrama. Aristotle's formula for tragedy provides that "good men must not be seen suffering a change from prosperity to misfortune; this is not fearful or pitiful but shocking" (24). The final act of the play moves in two different directions to break down this melodrama. First, in the Julia subplot, the Duchess is reanimated as an unconventional, willful and sexually vital woman. Second, the last act casts a new light retrospectively on the forces that led the Duchess to death, and reveals them to be human, frail, and error-prone. In the final act of

The Duchess of Malfi, the Duchess and her enemies become members of the same human community; the Duchess is no longer simply "a weak figure among brutish men," and her commitment to others is confirmed. Such a readjustment in the play's perspective steers it toward the painful vision of tragedy rather than the complacent vision of melodrama.

In literature, as opposed to life, the fact of death can be considered tragic only by virtue of its context—that which produces it, its causes, and that which it produces, its consequences. Though there are many "causes" of Renaissance tragedy, Webster's play satisfies the traditional Aristotelian formula with its final act. It is not until Act V of *The Duchess of Malfi* that the death of the Duchess can be considered tragic. By shifting the focus from the victim to her destroyers, Webster draws our attention away from the fact of death to the context of death. With the humanization of Bosola, the Cardinal, and Ferdinand, the world of the play's evil is suddenly simply frail humanity, and the double vision of tragedy becomes possible. To expose the enemies of the Duchess as pathetic bumblers rather than depersonalized machines of destruction is retrospectively to grant the fourth act tragic status. There can be no real sense of tragic waste or loss without a concomitant sense of what might otherwise have been, combined with a sense that, in this world, this is how things inevitably are. The deluded, misguided creatures of the play's finale suddenly make it apparent that, on the one hand, they are morally capable of change and introspection, and that, on the other, they are destined to repeat their crimes and failures. In the fourth act, the Duchess dies, a victim of either a relentless fate or an overpowering human evil. In the fifth act, these monsters are dispelled, and the Duchess's murder becomes the product of a human world, no longer simply terrible but also wrong. When the Duchess's death can be seen as the result of errors that might have been corrected, yet were not, then the play approaches tragedy.

This kind of construction delineates a complete and irreversible tragic action to which individual characters are subsidiary. Unlike Shakespeare's tragedies, there is no single tragic protagonist on which to focus entirely the tragic experience. Instead, Webster's tragic construction is multiple and diffuse, using a number of characters to convey the tragic vision of a world in which virtue is wasted as a result of human blindness as well as human malice.

Consequently, the Duchess's suffering is still undeserved, but traceable to the terrible inevitable weakness of humanity, *hamartia*—that necessary and sufficient cause for tragedy that is normally embodied in the protagonist in Aristotle's tragic formula. The same moment that reveals the fallibility of the villains also shows their thwarted potential for goodness. The Duchess herself is that potential fulfilled and realized—and, even though destroyed, she remains the index of human greatness.

In the last act, Antonio sees two faces, both sorrowful and both illuminated. The first is that of his wife's ghost, in the echo scene, when, as Antonio tells it, "on the sudden, a clear light / Presented me a face folded in sorrow" (V.iii.44–45). The second is that of Bosola in the next scene, lit up by a dark lantern after he has killed Antonio by mistake (V.iv.51). Stage effects link these two moments in performance. If the first apparition, recalling the Duchess's murder, inspires pity, then the second should inspire terror. The second reveals that the first was produced, not by a cold and mechanical act of deliberate evil, but by human pain, futility, and error.

If *The Duchess of Malfi* is a play in the course of which the innocents die a terrible death and the wicked are punished for it, the audience is left with a feeling of outrage on the one hand and smug satisfaction on the other. These are feelings aroused by melodrama, not by tragedy. Great tragedy, according to Aristotle, arouses pity and terror in its audience—pity, because the consequences of action are terrible; terror, because those consequences are explicable in terms of normal human behavior. The Duchess's death in the fourth act takes place in a bizarre universe of evil that seems quite distant from our own—one that evokes pity, not terror. When we come to the last act, however, both tragic emotions are reanimated. We cannot accept the smug satisfaction expressed by Delio in his final speech:

> These wretched eminent things
> Leave no more fame behind 'em than should one
> Fall in a frost, and leave his print in snow;
> As soon as the sun shines, it ever melts,
> Both form, and matter.
>
> (V.v.113–17)

The villains of the play are finally punished for their crimes, but they don't melt away into insignificance. The horror they confront bears no relation to their punishment. The agent of their punishment, Bosola, is finally as weak and guilty as they, and sinks into death crying that he was "neglected" (V.v.87). Even their penitence is futile, as it only exposes them to the horrible knowledge of the consequences of their own frail humanity. Yet the same universe that renders Bosola's revenge impossible authenticates the Duchess's heroism, and the villains' new humanity reflects the Duchess's ordinary, social values. Both pity and terror are aroused in the final act, since the propelling forces of the play's action are revealed to be both firmly rooted in the human and at the same time deeply mysterious and unfathomable.

Directors of the play have chosen to effect closure in a variety of different ways to convey their own sense of the play's final vision. In Poel's sentimental finale, Bosola lived to deliver Delio's moral lesson, and the Duchess was "seen between the cypress trees . . . looking sadly towards her son"; the 1971 Royal Court production featured a "live sculpture" of bodies at the end, including that of the Duchess; the 1985 National Theatre production closed with the triumphant, sweeping exit of the Duchess and her companion, Death, past the tangled heap of bodies. Yet perhaps the most fitting final image was provided by the 1960 Royal Shakespeare Company production, which ended with Antonio's son on his knees among the bodies, mutely contradicting Delio's moral lesson.[23] At the end of *The Duchess of Malfi*, the audience does not leave the theatre with a feeling of either outrage or smug satisfaction. As Herbert Whittaker put it in his review of the 1971 Stratford, Ontario production: "There is no hope of any great relief through the death of evil, and the small son of Malfi, produced to restore some semblance of right, offers fragile consolation. But we are glad we had the courage to stick it out to the bloody end."

A comparison of the final acts of both plays allows us to trace the development of Webster's tragic vision and formal construction. Clearly, Julia in *The Duchess of Malfi* is a much more fully realized character than Zanche in *The White Devil*, though both women mirror the plays' heroines and their actions from a slightly distorted perspective. Less obviously, the main action of *The White Devil*, emphasized and reflected in the subplot involving Flamineo, is later extended and reworked in the final act of *The Duchess of Malfi*, with some significant differences. The protagonists of the earlier play, who struggle in their fallible way to attain some understanding of a world greater than the sum of their evils, have in the later play become the antagonists. Although academic critics usually treat both Brachiano's death scene and Ferdinand's mad scene as comic material, both scenes have a tragic impact in the theatre, as the reactions of theatre critics have shown. Brachiano's death scene is echoed in Ferdinand's harrowing visions and the Cardinal's chilling self-awareness;[24] like Brachiano and Flamineo, Ferdinand and the Cardinal achieve a fitful glimpse of their own involvement in a corrupt world, and such a glimpse illuminates their humanity. While in the earlier play Flamineo simply mirrors Brachiano's guilty heroism, the villains of the later play reflect and confirm the Duchess's human values.

CHAPTER FOUR

~~~~~~~~~~~~~~~~~~~~~~~~~~~~~~~~~~~~~~

CONCENTRIC DESIGN

~~~~~~~~~~~~~~~~~~~~~~~~~~~~~~~~~~~~~~

THE aim of this chapter is to set the device of repetition in the context of the play as a whole, to relate our experience of the play as it unfolds to our sense of its general contours after it is over. The change in emphasis will require a change in perspective. Keith Brown points out that "any work of art tends to have a twofold structure: a static 'architectural' form (the legs of Brighton pier) and a dynamic form (the wave moving through the legs)" (918d). After riding the wave, we can now get a view of the pier. Previous chapters have shown that our experience of watching a Webster play is neither linear in the classical sense nor abrupt and discontinuous in the modern absurdist sense. The linear sequence of scenes has been shown to be less important than those strategies which allow Webster to intensify or emphasize an important idea, to draw significant parallels or contrasts, or to recapitulate the essence of his play. Though Webster's scenes are designed as independent units, they are meaningfully interrelated to form more than "a succession of merely theatrical tableaux" which "do not function collectively" (Kirsch 104). If we adopt a more "static" view of Webster's plays, in an attempt to discern "the archetypal patterns that are, in a broad sense, 'structure'" (Rose 2), we find that repetition remains a means of heightening differences and suggesting parallels between opposed groups. Yet in this broad context Webster's repetitive dramaturgy chiefly buttresses the powerful dramatic focus at the center of each play. This kind of concentric organization shows Webster striving for a complex unity in his multiplicity and a "strong and single" impact in the theatre (Davies 89).

THE WHITE DEVIL

The second scene of *The White Devil* illustrates in microcosm Webster's spatial organization, and shows the strategy of repetition as it complements concentric form. The scene is a lengthy one, tracing the fortunes of the lovers from Brachiano's initial admission to Flamineo that he is "quite lost" (I.ii.3) in Vittoria's charms, to Flamineo's gulling of the comic Camillo, to the first meeting of the lovers, and finally to Cornelia's moral outrage. The linear sequence of events is spatially arranged, however, to illuminate significant parallels and contrasts between the different parts of the scene. Thus, although the scene's movement from desire to disaster, from comedy to tragedy, reproduces in little the movement of the entire play, its internal organization provides for significant non-linear juxtapositions and emphases which are essential to its meaning.

The scene begins and ends with a dialogue, dominated in both cases by Flamineo. The final exchange between Cornelia and Flamineo recalls the opening exchange between Brachiano and Flamineo, for Flamineo reveals to Cornelia the causes of his bitter struggle for "preferment" (I.ii.329), which sets the scene in motion. That Flamineo's witty, attractive banter at the opening has been revealed to be rooted in profound anger and cynicism not only undermines his reliability as an observer, but also suggests the dark underside of the scene's initial comedy. The shift in the scene's direction, as well as its increased complexity, is reflected in the radical change in Flamineo. Although each episode in the scene is causally linked to the one that precedes it—Flamineo's outburst is provoked by Cornelia's, as hers is a response to the lovers' encounter—the scene gives the impression of coming full circle.

The central emphasis of the scene, both structurally and visually, is the meeting of the lovers on which all eyes are fixed. Leading up to this meeting is Flamineo's gulling of Camillo; leading away from it is Cornelia's furious outburst. Flamineo brings the lovers together by fooling Camillo; they meet, and Cornelia drives them apart. The episodes that frame the lovers' meeting are visual analogues, however different in tone: in both cases, the lovers are physically separated by an intruder, whom Flamineo attempts to drive away. Camillo, the impotent cuckold, and Cornelia, the denying parent, both provide obstacles to the lovers' union. The visual analogy between the two episodes underlines another parallel between them. Though Cornelia and Flamineo differ in their attitudes toward the lovers, their view of the nature of the affair is the same. For Flamineo, the affair is one of mere "lust" (I.ii.19), and he encourages it; for Cornelia, the affair is "violent lust" (I.ii.220), and she discourages it. The organization of the scene illuminates the basic similarity of the opposed perspectives, both intent on degrading the love affair.

Both perspectives converge during the lovers' meeting. Yet there, the colliding points of view are held equally in suspension, so that neither one nor the other is in control. At the center of the scene there is a marked shift in tone. The lovers' affair transcends the crude domestic comedy from which it emerges, and evolves into something grand enough to evoke Cornelia's violent condemnation. The lovers' meeting both confirms and transcends the perspectives of its observers.

At the center of the lovers' meeting is Vittoria's mysterious dream. By recounting her dream, Vittoria physically disengages herself from the surrounding action, and from Brachiano's lewd physical overtures. The dream itself, a dramatic set-piece for the boy actor, focuses and holds the audience's attention, providing relief from the proliferation of commentary and the distraction of intrusive observers. The dream also introduces a new kind of language into the play. In contrast to the brief, staccato utterances of the other characters, Vittoria uses long, rhythmic sentences, drawing them out slowly and deliberately.

> Methought I walk'd about the mid of night,
> Into a church-yard, where a goodly yew-tree
> Spread her large root in ground,—under that yew,
> As I sat sadly leaning on a grave,
> Chequered with cross-sticks, there came stealing in
> Your duchess and my husband.
>
> (I.ii.232–37)

With the startling change in language comes an abrupt shift from the immediate situation to a displaced, imagined one, and a corresponding sense of release. The moment is shaped by verbal, rather than visual, elements, drawing its strength from the simple power of narrative detailing a particular experience.[1] While the staging of the episode, with Cornelia, Flamineo and Zanche as observers, tends to universalize the situation as a morality play or as an allegory, the language of the dream draws our attention to vividly recounted individual details.[2] The impact of the dream is derived from these tensions between its language and the stage situation. While Vittoria confidently controls the stage with her extended account, she represents herself in the dream as a frightened victim. While she is plainly involved in an erotic encounter, her narrative gives her some distance and detachment from that encounter. Because the dream is filled with vivid detail which bears only an indirect relation to the immediate situation, it is ultimately ambiguous.

Because of its richness and ambiguity, the dream resists simple interpretation. As John Russell Brown points out, Vittoria herself "gives, in fact, two opposing interpretations of the dream" (25n); the "yew" on which she puns is alternately Camillo or Brachiano. After the dream, Flamineo and Brachiano compound its ambiguity by giving two more opposed interpretations. While Flamineo reads Vittoria's dream literally, as an incitement to murder, Brachiano prefers to interpret it metaphorically, as a general expression of fear and a plea for safety. Whether it is prophecy, deliberate suggestion, or unconscious desire, the dream's vivid expression of terror and longing suggests much more than a casual liaison with Brachiano. At the center of the scene, the lovers suddenly transcend the terms in which they have been judged by both Flamineo and Cornelia. Brachiano's response confirms Vittoria's elevation of their relationship, while his renewed embraces at the same time reemphasize its frankly sexual nature. While the scene as a whole traces a clear linear movement from the desire to the consummation, and finally to the enforced separation of the lovers, its concentric organization illuminates the similarity of both perspectives that view the affair as one of mere lust, and provides a central focus which challenges, while it confirms, those perspectives.

By no means all of the scenes of *The White Devil* are designed according to this concentric plan. Frequently, however, scenes and groups of scenes establish a clear central emphasis framed by parallel episodes. In the fourth act, for example, the dramatic scene between the lovers in the house of convertites is placed between two scenes in which the opposing faction consolidates its triumph; in the final act, Brachiano's death is framed by the crime of Flamineo and the crime of Francisco. Although the second scene of the play is a rather highly schematic model of concentric organization, it does reveal that Webster's construction is spatial as well as temporal, conceptual as well as linear. This is also true of the play as a whole; its individual parts are interrelated by contrast, analogy and repetition as much as by sequential logic. Furthermore, Webster's plays, like those of Shakespeare, are characterized by "the intensification of action and the change of direction in the middle of a play." This "split structure" (Beckerman 43) allows Webster to do in the play what he does in the scene—establish a central emphasis which transcends the logic of the story, and suggest significant analogies between the two parts of the play that result.

The structure of *The White Devil* has long been a subject of fervent critical debate (Dallby 33–35). Although no act or scene divisions appear in the original quarto, editors have divided the play into the conventional five acts, while critics have postulated anywhere from four to six "movements." Dallby supports the customary five-act division, maintaining that "each act may be seen as devoted to the description of a major event or phase in the story of Vittoria Corombona" (36). Waage, on the other hand, divides the play into five different units of action, combining the first act with the first scene of the second act to form a single movement and splitting the final act into two separate movements (5–8). Glier hypothesizes four movements by consolidating the first two acts into a single unit (Dallby 34). A six-part movement has also been suggested, with the final three scenes forming an addition to a five-act tragedy whose protagonist is Brachiano (Dallby 35). The major drawback of all these approaches to the play's structure is their concern only with the linear narrative, at the expense of other kinds of dramatic organization. The division of a play into "movements," however convenient for editors, tends to obscure its more important nonlinear structure.

However differently critics divide up most of the play, they all agree that a division must be made at the end of the third act, after the arraignment. At this point, the tone and characterization seem subtly to shift and a new revenge motive is introduced. The first part of the play ends with the arraignment, the consequence of the murder of Camillo, while the second part begins with the delayed effects of the murder of Isabella. The double murder, present in Webster's sources, buttresses this two-part structure. Before the arraignment, the sequence of events may be variously divided, but Brachiano's desire and murderous plot are the primary focus; after the arraignment, the major focus shifts to Francisco's murderous plans, even as our commitment to the protagonists is confirmed. Simplified, the basic design of *The White Devil*, like that of the second scene, consists in two roughly symmetrical parts framing a central set-piece, the arraignment. The broad outlines of this structure are emphasized by the recurring figure of Lodovico. A banished Lodovico shouts defiance at the beginning and at the end of the play. At the center, Lodovico is struck by Flamineo (III.iii.123 s.d.); this action is recalled in the final scene when Lodovico strikes back (V.vi.190). Repeated stage actions hint at the play's concentric form.

Webster draws attention to the symmetry of the two parts of his play. As Brachiano dominates the first half, stage-managing the action with the aid of Flamineo, so Francisco manipulates the second half, with Flamineo as his constant companion. Flamineo's similar role in relation to each man connects the two; in the first part, Flamineo is Brachiano's satiric advisor, while in the second part, he offers Francisco "politic instruction" (V.i.133), and "court wisdom" (V.iii.66). Webster's concern for symmetry may also explain some inconsistencies of characterization. As, in the first part, Cornelia provides Brachiano with moral resistance to his murderous plans, so, in the second part, Monticelso unexpectedly attempts to dissuade Lodovico from participating in the murder. Both the Cardinal's and Cornelia's moral injunctions are unconvincing and ineffectual, and ironically serve only to goad the "villains" on to greater evil. Repeated stage actions further emphasize the role reversal of Brachiano and Francisco. In the first part, Brachiano's murders are executed by the comic Dr. Julio, an "abhominable loathsome gargarism" (II.i.310), and distanced by dumb show; in the second part, Francisco's accomplices discuss their planned murder of Brachiano with ghoulish glee (V.i.65–85), and the murder itself is distanced by commentary. Moreover, the murders of the first part are reflected in the murder of the second part. In the dumb show of Isabella's murder, poison is ceremonially prepared by burning perfumes before the unveiled portrait of Brachiano. The image is mirrored later when the disguised "Franciscans" present Brachiano with a "hallowed candle" (V.iii.129 s.d.). The actions of Dr. Julio and his assistant as they "wash the lips of the picture" (II.ii.23 s.d.) anticipate the poisoning of Brachiano's beaver, which contaminates the kiss Brachiano would give to Vittoria.

The mirroring of the first murders in the final one might suggest a simple pattern of retributive justice, were it not that the villainous revengers claim it as such. Nor does the repetition of acts of murder in both parts suggest merely "the underlying unity of all the play's evils" (Murray 114). Since all the acts of murder are distanced from the audience by dramatic convention, Webster's interest would appear to lie, not in villainy itself, but in different responses to villainy. While Francisco's repetition of Brachiano's original act of murder forces the audience to recall Brachiano's act of villainy even as it engenders sympathy for him, it chiefly serves to define the precise nature of Brachiano's brand of heroism by contrast. Brachiano's real heroism lies not simply in the determined imposition of his will—Francisco does this too—but in his understanding of a principle beyond retribution, of "a divinity that shapes our ends." In the final act, this vision is associated with the protagonists, and is variously expressed in Cornelia's madness, Brachiano's death agony, Flamineo's terror and Vittoria's defiance. Though Brachiano immediately grasps the fact that "This unction is sent from the great Duke of Florence" (V.iii.27), he nonetheless ascribes his own fall to a far greater power, that of the "corrupted politic hangman" (V.iii.20), death itself. Brachiano thus connects his ruin with his greatness, and sees himself as the hero of a *de casibus* tragedy in which "horror waits on princes" (V.iii.34).[3] Francisco and his accomplices are, on the other hand, creatures of the revenge tragedy of intrigue. In Lodovico's final speech, he sees himself as the stage-manager and chief agent of destruction:

> I do glory yet,
> That I can call this act mine own:—for my part,
> The rack, the gallows, and the torturing wheel
> Shall be but sound sleeps to me,—here's my rest—
> I limb'd this night-piece and it was my best.
>
> (V.vi.293–97)

Lodovico's words reveal arrogance and physical insensibility, both of which suggest his limited nature. His qualities contrast with those of Brachiano and his faction. For Brachiano and Vittoria, when death comes it is an inevitable consequence of their greatness; that Lodovico and his assistants deliver the death blow is mere coincidence.

That the opposing factions of the play inhabit different kinds of tragedy may account for the divergence of critical opinion concerning the play's genre. Dallby asserts that the play adheres to "the form of the revenge tragedy, with the motives of ambition and lust on one side, and revenge on the other, contending for the upper hand in a pattern of dramatic reversals" (44). Motives of lust and ambition may indeed belong to the Italianate tragedy of intrigue, as Doran maintains (131), but the play's real structure belongs to the *de casibus* type of tragedy, which includes, in Doran's view, Shakespeare's *Richard II*, *Hamlet*, and *King Lear* (124). Francisco's faction may perceive the story as—so Dallby would have it—"an interlacing zig-zag pattern of two opposed lines" (42), but Brachiano's faction seems to grasp that the action traces an inevitable fall from vitality to decay. John Russell Brown points out, "Webster combined a chronicle-play technique with interests and devices derived from medieval narrative tragedy, and so presented the rise and fall of Fortune's wheel" (xl). Of course, the protagonists' recognition of this universal fall from desire to death—of the fact that, according to Flamineo's description, "Fate's a spaniel, / We cannot beat it from us" (V.vi.177–78)—distinguishes them from their enemies.[4] "The revengers adopt the conventional limitations of their role;" Bliss notes, "while striking a theatrical pose, equally conventional in its own way, their victims have momentarily dropped all roles and looked at each other and at themselves to find the complex and lonely humanity they had denied" (135). In *The Duchess of Malfi*, as we shall see, Webster exploits the parallelism of his two-part structure to suggest that, while they are very different, all the play's characters share this glimpse of their "complex and lonely humanity." In *The White Devil*, the symmetrical structure in which the two "great men" are mirrored in one another also suggests that both are involved in this inevitable fall from greatness, though Brachiano alone remains conscious of it.

The mirroring of Brachiano in Francisco thus suggests not only essential differences, but also subtle affinities between the two men as victims as well as villains. Early in the last act, Francisco remarks to Flamineo, "what difference is between the duke and I? no more

than between two bricks; all made of one clay" (V.i.106–8). Brachiano himself draws attention to the analogy between them; after
threatening to "turn dog-killer," he cries, "Rare! I'll be friends with
him: for mark you, sir, one dog / Still sets another a-barking"
(V.iii.94–96). During the death scene, Francisco and Flamineo exchange comments on Brachiano's final end. Flamineo observes:

> To see what solitariness is about dying princes. As heretofore they
> have unpeopled towns; divorc'd friends, and made great houses un-
> hospitable: so now, O justice! where are their flatterers now?
> (V.iii.42–45)

Ironically, Flamineo's catalogue of the misdeeds of great men applies
more accurately to Francisco, his interlocutor, than to the dying
Brachiano. As a disguised intruder in his enemy's court, Francisco is
more solitary than Brachiano, and, further, is actively engaged in
the crimes of violence mentioned by Flamineo. Francisco's reply to
Flamineo—"There's great moan made for him" (V.iii.48)—is as curiously defensive as it is hypocritical. Indeed, one reason that Francisco completely disappears from the last part of the fifth act may be
that he is to be seen as reflected in Brachiano's fate.

At the mid-point of *The White Devil*, protagonist and antagonist
change places. In the fourth act, Francisco parodies Brachiano's role
as a lover by writing a love letter to Vittoria; Brachiano imitates
Francisco's parody of him by announcing,

> the same project which the Duke of Florence,
> (Whether in love or gullery I know not)
> Laid down for her escape, will I pursue.
> (IV.ii.206–8)

In this way, Webster playfully draws attention to the role reversal of
these two "great men" early in the second part. If Brachiano initiates
and controls the events of the first part, Francisco takes over his role
in the second part. Boklund observes, "From the death of Isabella to
the death of Vittoria he is the supreme director." In order to create
this symmetrical structure, Webster was forced to expand the figure
of Francisco from mere hints in his sources (Boklund, *White Devil*
167, 89). The "hour-glass" shape that Webster creates,[5] with the mir-

roring of one character in another, sustains the play's complexity. Brachiano's crimes cannot be forgotten, since they are continually recalled in Francisco's. Francisco's role as a revenger is undercut by the image of his final destruction that is reflected in Brachiano's death. The basic symmetry of the play, instead of suggesting the triumph of one group over another, emphasizes the complexity of the play's world, in which some villains achieve a heroic vision, revengers are unreliable, and all the characters progress toward all-consuming death.

At the structural center of the play, dividing the first part from the second, is the climactic set-piece of the arraignment. The arraignment is both a sustained dramatic focus and a pivot around which the rest of the play is organized. Rose suggests that Webster may have imitated Shakespeare in his tendency to organize his plays concentrically: "Shakespeare's influence can be traced in later writers such as Webster and Tourneur. *The White Devil*, for example, is designed on much the same pattern as *Hamlet* or *Lear*, Vittoria's trial coming in approximately the middle and forming a great emblematic centerpiece for the play as a whole" (ix). Theatre reviewers and academic critics alike have confirmed the central importance of the arraignment. If, as Rose points out, we remember from Shakespeare "striking moments like Hamlet in the graveyard, Lear in the storm, or Lady Macbeth scrubbing her hands" (1), from *The White Devil* we first recall Vittoria's great trial scene. Like Shakespeare's great scenes, it transcends the linear narrative to become an emblem for the whole. The trial not only clearly divides the play into two parts to be contrasted and compared, but also distills the play's essence.

That Webster himself had a strong sense of the central importance of the trial is indicated by its position in the printed text, set off from the preceding scenes by a title. The formality of its textual presentation is matched by the ceremoniousness of its staging. All the major characters are assembled on the stage for the first time in the play (a stage image which recurs only briefly during Brachiano's death scene), and their confrontation is formalized by the public forum of the trial. After the restless fluidity and constantly shifting points of view of earlier scenes, the sustained visual simplicity and order of the trial scene come as a relief. Its impact is virtually undiminished by the asides and commentary usually so characteristic of Webster.

The trial scene has been hailed by some critics as a dramatic exploration of the idea that "conventional morality seems to pale before the imaginative expression of some greatness of spirit" (Stilling 232). Yet the previous acts have shown that the brothers are not simply guardians of conventional morality. As Hilary Spurling put it in her review of the 1969 National Theatre production, "In the Cardinal's tirade at Vittoria's trial . . . the sense conveyed—in odd, stifled gulps and spasmodic, circling movements—is of something ferocious, fighting to break out, something far more monstrous than puritanical disgust at an adulterous whore." Nor are the lovers possessed only of greatness of spirit. For this reason the scene has also been called "an artistic insincerity—a lie in the poet's heart" (Jack 162), and an example of Webster's "emphasis . . . on vivid sympathetic insights at the expense of ethical coherence" (Doran 355). Certainly, the audience is not prepared for the overwhelming impact of the trial scene in favor of the protagonists. While taking care to mitigate their crimes by undermining the credibility of their victims,[6] Webster nonetheless implicates both Brachiano and Vittoria in the initial murders. The trial scene is, therefore, problematic, because its presentation of the moral triumph of the protagonists does not appear to correspond with the earlier suggestions of their guilt.

A number of stage productions have attempted to resolve the "problem" of the trial scene by suggesting that the heroic defense is mere hypocrisy, Vittoria's assertions simple pretense. Such productions assume that, as Price contends, Vittoria "displays a splendid spirit, she is magnificent in intellect and courage, and she is—a whore and a murderess" (185). These stage interpretations of Vittoria during the trial are not well received by critics, however. In a review of the 1925 Renaissance Theatre production, Lucas complained that "Miss Cowie as the heroine . . . seemed in needless uncertainty how far she was a great lady, how far a designing minx." In the 1969 National Theatre production, according to Bryden's review, Geraldine McEwan as Vittoria discarded her white cloak during the trial scene to reveal a scarlet dress beneath it. In his review, Wardle noted that "Geraldine McEwan's Vittoria shares the production's sardonic view of the play. However you regard her, Vittoria is a heroic figure: but here she is shown through Miss McEwan's oblique and quizzical style . . . as an uninvolved comic spectator" ("No Terror"). By way of contrast, Anna Nygh's interpretation of Vittoria in the 1983 Bristol production met with critical approval.

Anthony Masters, while admitting in his review in the *Times* that "it would be easy (and perhaps right) to play her as a monster whose tears and shows of affection point only to her skill as an actress," finally noted approvingly that "Anna Nygh courageously opts to chart a course through the character's contradictions, instigating her husband's murder by an artlessly told dream and keeping a sympathetic dignity in her courtroom defence." Stage productions confirm that the effect Webster intended in the trial scene is one of "sympathetic dignity" rather than ironic duplicity.

Yet, while Webster does not appear to intend to undercut his protagonists, the trial does not depend on a total suspension of disbelief on the part of the audience. Indeed, throughout the scene, various details reactivate the audience's memory of the passionate affair between Brachiano and Vittoria, and of Brachiano's subsequent involvement in the murders of Camillo and Isabella. Brachiano's presence throughout the trial reminds the audience of his crimes. As Pearson points out, his initial gesture of spreading his gown on the floor recalls "the first meeting of Brachiano and Vittoria, where Zanche spread out a carpet with cushions for the lovers (I.ii.204 s.d.). By this apparently casual repetition we are reminded, at the beginning of Vittoria's trial, of the crime of which she is accused" (59). Later Brachiano openly lies to the court in claiming that his relation to Vittoria was prompted by his "charity" (III.ii.161). At the end of the trial, Flamineo reminds the audience in an aside (III.ii.265) of his role as the lovers' pander, again drawing attention to their illicit union. Yet such pointed reminders of the lovers' guilt, far from suggesting that "self-proclaimed innocence and righteousness prove on both sides to be merely acted" (Bliss 112), are integral to the trial's powerful impact. Rather than undermining or contradicting the total impression of the trial, our knowledge of the lovers' violent lust actually buttresses our acceptance of their heroic defiance. During the trial, Webster asks us to reconcile the lovers' culpability with their greatness. The result is complexity rather than confusion or contradiction.

The narrative which precedes the trial does not prepare us for its impact. Yet the trial itself has only a tenuous connection to the murders that precede it; Vittoria's involvement in them is unclear and treated as an irrelevance by her judges. Vittoria's condemnation and subsequent imprisonment are a foregone conclusion rather than a direct result of the trial. As in *The Duchess of Malfi*, it is female sexuality that is on trial at the center of the play. Because sexuality, rather than any specific crime, is the main issue of the trial, it draws our attention to more complex issues than innocence or guilt, good or evil.

At the center of the play, Webster gives dramatic and structural weight to an idea which, though it is essential to the play, transcends the logic of the story. This central idea is the moral complexity of human action, the possibility of the coexistence of guilt and innocence in a world in which moral judgment is corrupted by tyrants. Webster requires his audience to juggle this paradox by treating the theatrical experience as a metaphor for the complex nature of reality. Monticelso continually presents the theatre as a mirage, denying its visual reality along with Vittoria's, claiming, "I will but touch her and you straight shall see / She'll fall to soot and ashes" (III.ii.66–67). Vittoria, on the other hand, reinforces the immediacy of the theatrical experience by implicitly including the offstage as well as the onstage audience in "this auditory / Which come to hear my cause" (III.ii.15–16), and often drawing attention to the physical situation on the stage. As a result, the theatre audience is asked to accept the theatrical experience, which represents reality by its artifice, as an image of the complex experience of life, in which appearance and reality are often inextricable, and moral judgments fallible.

The trial does not stand alone, but is the central and sustained portion of a larger dramatic unit that surrounds it. The entire third act, usually divided by editors into three separate scenes, may be considered as a single unbroken dramatic unit on the stage, unified by a continuous time frame and consistent setting. In fact, according to the promptbook, the 1969 National Theatre production played the third act as a single long scene. The scene that is usually marked III.i opens with a brief appearance by Monticelso and Francisco, continues with a discussion among Marcello, Flamineo, and the lawyer, and ends with the procession of ambassadors across the stage. The following scene, III.ii, begins in the quarto with a mass entry for the ambassadors, Francisco, Monticelso, Brachiano, and Vittoria. Like the formal title which introduces the arraignment, the entry may simply have been intended to mark the opening of a formal set-piece, the point at which all the characters assume fixed positions. Since no reentry is indicated for Flamineo and Marcello, we may assume that the stage has not been cleared. This hypothesis is strengthened by the immediate reappearance of the ambassadors; rather than exiting only to reenter, their procession more likely simply comes to rest at the opening of III.ii. In addition, Francisco and Monticelso may remain on the stage for the duration of III.i, clarifying visually the opposition of the two factions.[7] After the arraignment, Webster again creates two simultaneous stage images: the ambassadors "withdraw a little" (III.ii.322) to confer with Monticelso,[8] presumably about Vittoria's trial, while Giovanni and Francisco discuss Isabella's death in the silent company of Lodovico. After this, no exit is marked for Flamineo, Marcello, Lodovico, or the ambassadors, all of whom reappear in the following scene, designated III.iii by editors. In short, the stage seems at no point to be completely cleared throughout the third act.

When the third act is considered as a single, continuous dramatic unit, its design becomes clear. The trial, punctuated at the beginning, middle, and end by Brachiano's interruptions, is extended to include the brief scene of mourning for Isabella's death. Before this long sequence, Flamineo quarrels with Marcello; afterwards, he quarrels with Lodovico. The act, like the play as a whole, is organized concentrically; the pivotal focus is on the protagonists, and they are framed by episodes involving Flamineo, the play's chief interpreter.

Although Vittoria is removed from the stage after the judges reach their verdict, there is every indication that the trial setting remains in place throughout Giovanni's lament. A continuous setting thus connects Vittoria's arraignment with Isabella's death. However, because the trial precedes the discovery of the more serious crime, and thus cause and effect are reversed in the dramatic sequence, the relation between the two events is neither simple nor direct. At the risk of undermining Vittoria's triumph by immediately presenting a poignant glimpse of Brachiano's victims, Webster strives for further complexity. By choosing to delay the news of Isabella's death until after the trial, Webster not only mitigates any direct causal relation between the two incidents, but also links his protagonists with their enemies in a larger vision of universal destruction.

Giovanni's belated lament for his dead mother does more than simply recall "a world of real suffering ignored by quaint devisers and ingenious rhetoricians" (Bliss 117), though this is part of its function. It also puts Vittoria's vigorous self-assertion into the final perspective of death, against which all the play's characters will ultimately be measured. Giovanni poignantly expresses the final release of death after the fretful chaos of life:

> Good God let her sleep ever.
> For I have known her wake an hundred nights,
> When all the pillow, where she laid her head,
> Was brine-wet with her tears.
>
> (III.ii.328–31)

This vision of the agitation and suffering of life, put into the final perspective of death, extends to all the play's characters. As director Jack Landau put it, "There are ghosts and visions and nightmares, and suddenly there is the simple question of an orphan child, 'What do the dead do, uncle? do they eat, / Hear music?'" (234). It is a question which is repeated in a different form by both the Duchess (*Duchess of Malfi* IV.ii.18–21) and Flamineo (V.iv.127–31) just before their deaths. Far from reinforcing the melodramatic conception of the protagonists as mere villains, Giovanni's lament functions as a chorus, giving voice to the unfathomable and inevitable mystery of death, as Vittoria's trial illuminates the complexity and mystery of human action. Because of the displacement of Isabella's murder in the play's linear sequence, and because of the ambiguity surrounding Vittoria's involvement in her murder, Giovanni's lament is able to express general, irremediable grief at universal destruction, which transcends individual acts of will. The importance of such moments to Webster's tragic vision is emphasized in Lucas's unfavorable review of the 1925 Renaissance Theatre production. Lucas complains, "Not even Webster's poetry could save him or do its part in creating his atmosphere, his sense of the vastness of death and the brave, brief light of human courage in its gloom. At moments, the play showed signs of life—in the scene of Giovanni's questions about the dead." It is significant that Giovanni was excised from the 1984 Greenwich production[9] which, according to John Barber, presented the story of "a scandalous courtesan who entices her lover to murder her husband, survives a trial for her life and plots further infamies with a brother as evil as herself" (Review, "Difficult Nut"). The "melodramatic raving" of this production had no place for the complex heroism of the protagonists, and emphasized, not the brooding power of death, but the petty struggles of the revenge plot. Giovanni's lament articulates, not the simplified vision of melo-drama, but the complex vision of tragedy.

In the central portion of the third act, Webster attempts both to distinguish his tragic protagonists from their enemies and to suggest their inevitable common destruction. The center of the play assures that, as Hilary Spurling commented in her review of the 1969 National Theatre production, "What sticks in the mind is not the play's fiendishly quaint murders, not the feckless rapacity nor even the misery and fear of its protagonists, but rather that subtle, tragic distillation." The center of the play not only distills the play's essence but also marks a significant shift in its direction. "Giovanni's unexpected interruption is also the play's turning-point," Bliss remarks (117). The frame which surrounds the central episode clari-fies the nature of this shift and registers the impact of the trial on Flamineo, chief observer of the main action.

Before the trial, the lawyer's ribald references to the "lechery" (III.i.25) of Brachiano and Vittoria parodically anticipate the sexual voyeurism of Monticelso during the trial. Flamineo himself mocks the trial, while at the same time he defends his own "quest of gain" (III.i.52) before his brother Marcello. While he justifies his merce-nary pursuit of "reward" (III.i.49), Flamineo points out that Mar-cello's virtue has gone unrewarded:

> what hast got?
> But like the wealth of captains, a poor handful,
> Which in thy palm thou bear'st, as men hold water—
> Seeking to gripe it fast, the frail reward
> Steals through thy fingers.
>
> (III.i.41–45)

Flamineo's self-justification is undercut, however, by his situation: both he and Marcello, regardless of their beliefs, are under arrest. Similarly, his jocular tone is undercut by his own admission that he "put on this feigned garb of mirth / To gull suspicion" (III.i.30–31). Even before the trial, Flamineo's pose as an amoral, cynical satirist begins to break down.

After the trial, Flamineo feigns madness and heaps scorn on worldly corruption. His "mad" scene is followed by his violent and "strange encounter" (III.iii.65) with Lodovico. These scenes, which frame the trial, can hardly be explained by their contribution to the plot, as Dent attempts to do by contending that, in the third act, Flamineo "has an anticipatory quarrel with Marcello, acquires the personal enmity of the tool revenger whose station is most like his own, and estranges the already contemptuous duke on whom his 'preferment' depends" ("White Devil" 183–84). Foreshadowing is an inadequate explanation for such scenes, written out in full with enormous theatrical energy. Indeed, as A. J. Smith remarks with reference to the encounter between Lodovico and Flamineo: "One can't question the dexterity of the writing or the sheer sense of the stage it shows. Yet finally the episode is hardly important to the plot and only marginally relevant" (74). The dramatic significance of the scenes framing the trial transcends mere foreshadowing or comic relief.

Before the trial, Flamineo observes the ambassadors as they file past him in ceremonious procession. His comments deflate their pomp, and he thus controls our response to the mock justice of the impending trial. After the trial, Flamineo is in turn observed by the ambassadors. Their presence connects the two episodes, while the change in their position from observed to observers marks a basic shift in the play as a whole. After the trial, Flamineo is no longer the moderator of audience response to the main action; he becomes the object of commentary and hence is placed at one remove from the audience. The new distance created between Flamineo and the audience allows increasing complexity to be suggested both in Flamineo and in the protagonists, who are no longer simply deflated by his interjections. After the trial, Flamineo is profoundly divided within himself, and our response to the play becomes correspondingly complex.

Flamineo's "mad" scene follows immediately after Giovanni's poignant lament, and its opening lines seem at first to be a grotesque parody of Giovanni's grief:

We endure the strokes like anvils or hard steel,
Till pain itself make us no pain to feel.
                    (III.iii.1–2)

Yet the lines also function like a chorus, recalling the accumulation of painful "strokes" in the last scene. They are not unlike real expressions of grief elsewhere in Webster; the formality of the couplet, with the double blow of its rhyme, is frequently used to contain and emphasize such expressions.[10] As Flamineo continues, however, his breathless inventory of odd occupations takes him further in the direction of absurd pretense. He harangues Brachiano, complaining, "Who shall do me right now? Is this the end of service?" (III.iii.3–4). The gap between Flamineo's pose as an abused servant and his real mercenary attitude is clearly visible. Yet as the scene proceeds and Flamineo responds to the ambassadors' attempts to placate him, his speech gathers momentum, moving from the personal to the general: "O gold, what a god art thou! and O man, what a devil art thou to be tempted by that cursed mineral!" (III.iii.21–23). On the one hand, the speeches appear to be mere hypocrisy; we know that Flamineo himself, by his own confession, is motivated by a desire for gold. On the other hand, it is significant that Flamineo introduces the new and apparently groundless notion of money as the source of all corruption; at once his words seem to apply to himself more than to the cardinal or the lawyer. At the end of his fit of "mad humour" (III.ii.305), he includes himself by implication among the corrupt priests and usurers he deplores:

> For if there were Jews enough, so many Christians would not turn usurers; if priests enough, one should not have six benefices; and if gentlemen enough, so many early mushrooms, whose best growth sprang from a dunghill, should not aspire to gentility. (III.iii.45–49)

That Flamineo himself is an "early mushroom," we know from his revealing speech to Cornelia in the first act (I.ii.315–32). Throughout his diatribes in this scene, Flamineo rails at the contaminated world and bitterly mocks his own involvement in it. While his condemnation of those who "sell justice" (III.iii.28) recalls the corruption of Vittoria's trial, his words at the same time betray his moral dilemma. And if we would doubt this and instead view his invective as mere pretense, we need only turn to Lodovico's murmured observation at the end:

> This was Bracciano's pandar, and 'tis strange
> That in such open and apparent guilt

Of his adulterous sister, he dare utter
So scandalous a passion.
(III.iii.55–58)

This directs us back to Flamineo's own explanation of his tactics in the previous scene:

I will feign a mad humour for the disgrace of my sister, and that will keep off idle questions,—treason's tongue hath a villainous palsy in't, I will talk to any man, hear no man, and for a time appear a politic madman. (III.ii.304–8)

If, however, Flamineo's behavior during his "mad" scene seems neither "mad" nor entirely "feigned," it has also not been "politic," according to Lodovico. Flamineo's treasonous diatribe is "scandalous" because Vittoria is clearly guilty. His "passion" does not appear to have succeeded in its professed aim of diverting attention, but has in fact opened him to suspicion. Flamineo is obviously no longer a reliable interpreter of his own actions. The "mad" scene begins with the striking of an attitude, but moves toward genuine outrage and self-disgust. Flamineo is still the cynical malcontent he always was, but at this point he becomes increasingly the object of his own cynicism. In the final act, Flamineo confirms the earlier dark hints of a divided self:

sometimes, when my face was full of smiles
[I] Have felt the maze of conscience in my breast.
Oft gay and honour'd robes those tortures try,—
We think cag'd birds sing, when indeed they cry.
(V.iv.120–23)

After the "mad" scene, the "strange encounter" (III.iii.65) between Lodovico and Flamineo follows the same basic pattern. The encounter begins with a parody of antagonism—a highly artificial exchange of ingeniously phrased insults replacing conventional forms of greeting. This flyting provides comic relief, as well as focusing and releasing, through parody, the accumulated tension of the last few scenes. The satire of melancholy is a comic lightning-rod for all the professed and felt grief of the preceding scenes. The two men clearly adopt a pose, and this clear inversion of appearance and reality comes as a relief after the complexity and ambiguity of the trial. Both Flamineo and Lodovico have reason to be melancholy—Flamineo for his sister's disgrace, and Lodovico for his mistress's death. Yet the melancholy they profess is pushed absurdly toward hyperbole, so that it becomes merely the occasion for a theatrical set-piece. Despite its comic release, however, the scene is unsettling because it endangers the techniques Webster has used so subtly up to this point, threatening as it does to reduce the play's complexity to a simple inversion of appearance and reality. Ewbank notes that "the curious dialogue between Flamineo and Lodovico after Vittoria's trial is a very blatant demonstration of language as attitudinising" ("Webster's Realism" 175). Flamineo sees the world as pure hypocrisy; in his eyes, the laughing Gasparo and Antonelli in fact "grieve" (III.iii.84), and he enjoins Lodovico to be merry "with a crabbed politician's face" (III.iii.110). His cynical vision denies the possibility of appearance and reality being the same, and the episode appears to confirm his view.

As the two "great men" of the play, Brachiano and Francisco, are reflected in one another, so in this scene Flamineo finds his mirror image in Lodovico.[11] Because they both depend on great men for their advancement, they remain bitter outcasts when the world fails to reward them. Flamineo draws attention to their common situation by proposing that

> all the creatures that hang manacled,
> Worse than strappado'd, on the lowest felly
> Of Fortune's wheel be taught in our two lives
> To scorn that world which life of means deprives.
> (III.iii.94–97)

Again, Flamineo's words are ambiguous in their application to himself. As both an ardent fortune-hunter and a self-conscious hypocrite, his contempt for fortune seems sheer posturing. Yet at the same time, his desire for reward contends with his real scorn for the kind of world in which he must seek reward; for him, Fortune's wheel *is* a wheel of torture. The pact between the two villains is suddenly interrupted when news of Lodovico's pardon arrives, initiating a "clear-cut movement of reversal, which turns on the abrupt shock of that unmotivated announcement" (A. J. Smith 73). In Lodovico's joyous response to his good fortune, Flamineo sees his own miserable dependency reflected. Flamineo recoils from Lodovico's open delight, cynically enjoining him to maintain his previous hypocrisy. Only when Flamineo is confronted with Lodovico's ephemeral melancholy, which disappears with his pardon, does his real contempt emerge to confirm what seemed merely a pose. The derision with which he regards Lodovico is matched by his own implicit self-disgust.

As soon as Lodovico is in a secure position, supported by corrupt figures of authority, he passes moral judgment on Vittoria. Flamineo's contemptuous suggestion of his earlier hypocrisy probably leads to Lodovico's enraged outburst: "Your sister is a damnable whore" (III.iii.111). What follows salvages the integrity of Webster's technique in the third act. Lodovico's accusation gives crude expression to the central issue of the play, while Flamineo's unexpected outraged response retrospectively confirms the melancholy that seemed a posture at the beginning of the episode. If Lodovico's abrupt reversal illuminates his previous hypocrisy, Flamineo's throws any such simplification into doubt. In both the "mad" scene and the "strange encounter," Flamineo's role-playing becomes an instrument of self-knowledge. His violent defense of Vittoria demonstrates that theatrical pose and underlying feeling can support rather than contradict one another. This is of course an important confirmation of the trial itself. Flamineo, in his curious mixture of amoral self-interest and deeper moral vision, takes us into the heart of Webster's complex play.

The lengthy third act of *The White Devil* is the dramatic and structural center of the play, as well as the point which separates the play's two distinct parts, allowing them to be compared and contrasted. Like the second scene, this concentric form allows Webster to highlight a central paradox of the play, the lovers' simultaneous involvement in and transcendence of the petty and corrupt world around them. This paradox is of course at the heart of many of Shakespeare's tragedies, most notably *Antony and Cleopatra*. Because Webster also evokes a powerful image of irrevocable and universal death in both his major tragedies, questions of guilt and innocence, good and evil, are eclipsed by the protagonists' courage and self-knowledge in the face of death. In both plays, the protagonists centralize Webster's concern with the complexity of the human will as it struggles, often in vain, against death and contamination. In both plays, the tool-villains Flamineo and Bosola further elucidate the nature of this struggle by alternately adopting and rejecting a simple view of the play. In *The Duchess of Malfi*, Webster exploits the same concentric form to convey a wider, collective vision of tragedy.

THE DUCHESS OF MALFI

Even more frequently than in *The White Devil*, Webster organizes scenes in *The Duchess of Malfi* concentrically, creating a strong, central dramatic focus framed by significantly opposed sequences of action. One of the most obvious examples of this kind of scenic construction is III.ii. The scene is important to the plot, tracing as it does the rapid fall of the Duchess and Antonio, from the intimacy of their bedroom exchange that opens the scene, to their separation and, finally, to the Duchess's unwitting betrayal of Antonio to Bosola. This is the clear linear movement of the lengthy scene. Yet the scene's internal organization complicates this simple linearity by establishing significant contrasts and emphases. The scene is clearly divided into five dramatic sequences; the first two are juxtaposed, as are the last two, while the central sequence links the two main parts. Finally, the last sequence of the scene recalls the first one; the Duchess's virtue remains constant even as her fortunes fail.

The first part of the scene is composed of two clearly juxtaposed dramatic episodes. The loving, domestic interview between Antonio and the Duchess as they prepare for bed is placed in sharp contrast to the highly charged interview between Ferdinand and the Duchess that follows. Between the two interviews, after Antonio and Cariola have left the stage and before Ferdinand has entered, the Duchess sits alone before her mirror. She talks aloud with warmth and confidence to an Antonio who is no longer there.

> Doth not the colour of my hair 'gin to change?
> When I wax gray, I shall have all the court
> Powder their hair with arras, to be like me:—
> You have cause to love me; I enter'd you into my heart
> Before you would vouchsafe to call for the keys.
>
> (III.ii.58–62)

This is the still center of the episode, and it emphasizes visually both the Duchess's strength and her vulnerability. Her strength is conveyed by her confident pose, even as she is at her most vulnerable physically (almost certainly clad only in a nightdress). While her vulnerability emerges as she looks anxiously for signs of aging, her confidence is clear in her gay response to her own question. The movement of thought in the Duchess's soliloquy is characteristic. From an anxious sense of her own mortality, she moves to a confident reconciliation with it, and finally to a self-assured declaration of her own courage. She will display the same characteristic ways of thinking and speaking at the moment of death. Yet even as she speaks, Ferdinand enters. While she speaks of the keys to her heart, her brother uses the keys to her bedchamber (a property to which attention has been drawn in the preceding scene), to gain entrance (Forker 350). The lines crystallize perfectly the contrast between the two worlds—the lovers' emotional world is set against the crude, literal world of Ferdinand. The stage property of the key draws attention to the ironic contrast. Yet the moment, even as it juxtaposes Ferdinand and Antonio, also implicitly compares them in their relation to the Duchess. As Ferdinand creeps into her bedchamber, the Duchess appears to be directing the lines to him. The bonds of family are as ineluctable as the bonds of love. The central point of the first half of III.ii places equal emphasis on the Duchess's strength and vulnerability. The Duchess is framed by the love of Antonio and by the fury of Ferdinand, both of which render her vulnerable, yet confirm her strength.

The dramatic encounters that frame this powerful central moment exhibit parallels as well as contrasts. In the first one, Antonio answers a question posed by Cariola regarding a choice between wisdom, riches, and beauty. His light-hearted response implies that judgment itself is confounded when faced with love and beauty. By going on to cite the case of Paris, Antonio introduces a range of mythological associations that become significant in the context of the scene. Of course Paris, like Antonio, chose Beauty, and the result was the Trojan war, undertaken by Helen's family for revenge. In the second encounter, Ferdinand makes reference to another triumvirate—this time of Love, Death, and Reputation. His identification of himself with Reputation is especially clear in performance, when he relates the parable in direct speech.

> "Stay," quoth Reputation,
> "Do not forsake me; for it is my nature
> If once I part from any man I meet
> I am never found again." And so, for you:
> You have shook hands with Reputation,
> And made him invisible:—so fare you well.
> I will never see you more.
>
> (III.ii.130–36)

If, in the first segment, love and beauty are clearly chosen by the Duchess and Antonio at the expense of wisdom and riches, here Reputation, in the self-appointed image of Ferdinand, deserts them. The design clearly restates in emblematic form the Duchess's choice in favor of Beauty at the expense of Reputation. Yet the emblematic level is at odds with the dramatic level of meaning. In fact, Ferdinand only imagines himself as his sister's reputation; Antonio is merely playing at being Paris. The formal, emblematic identifications point up the contradictions and ironies of the dramatic texture. Though in one sense the Duchess has indeed sacrificed her reputation for love, in another sense she has been absurdly punished for doing the right thing. The formal symmetry of the design not only allows a startling change of focus, but also invites comparison of the meaning of the clearly opposed episodes.

At the center of the entire scene, following Ferdinand's assault on the Duchess, there is a brief recapitulation and anticipation of its action. Antonio and Cariola reappear; in a replay of Ferdinand's attack on the Duchess, Antonio threatens Cariola with a pistol, and brandishes Ferdinand's poniard at an imaginary Ferdinand. The simultaneous exit of Antonio and entrance of Bosola at line 160 restages the preceding incident with new fear and urgency. The Duchess is again seen wheeling from her lover to her enemy—a stage image of the reversal of her fortunes. The choreography of this moment is replayed later, in III.v, when once again Antonio leaves the stage at the same time that Bosola enters with a guard. Again, a dramatic crisis, the reversal of the Duchess's fortunes, is evoked visually. She turns from bidding farewell to her family to heralding the arrival of a troop of men. Whether or not Bosola and his officers wear vizards, they are given impersonal significance by the Duchess when she says,

When Fortune's wheel is overcharg'd with princes,
The weight makes it move swift.

(III.v.96–97)

While she calls attention to herself as a victim of Fortune, she at the same time retains control of the stage, firing a series of questions at Bosola. Her deliberate allegorizing of her enemies as agents of Fortune also minimizes their hold over her as Ferdinand's henchmen. In both scenes she controls the exits and entrances of the other characters, ordering them on and off the stage and standing firmly at the center.

The second part of III.ii is, like the first, constructed as a pair of contrasting segments with parallel features. In the first segment, the "feigned crime" (III.ii.179) of Antonio is played out by the Duchess and Antonio before an onstage audience composed of Bosola and the officers; in the second segment, the feigned defense of Antonio is played out by Bosola before the Duchess and Cariola. In both cases, of course, the pretense is clear to the audience in the theatre, though it is accepted by the onstage audience. The officers believe the Duchess's account of Antonio and despise him, while the Duchess believes Bosola's account of Antonio and confides in him. In both sequences, pretense becomes entangled with reality. In the Duchess's confrontation with Antonio, she both rejects him and declares her love for him in a series of double entendres. Bosola's speech about Antonio is likewise both a pretense (as he is an intelligencer), and a clear repetition of his usual reflections on the abuse of good men like himself. The onstage audience in both cases selects the version of the "play" that they are disposed to hear and accept, though the offstage audience remains conscious of the ambiguity. The juxtaposition of the two episodes serves to illuminate, at a crisis in the narrative, the opposed perspectives that are at work in the play as a whole. There are those—like the officers—who are always prepared to believe the worst of someone else, while there are also those—like the Duchess—who are always prepared to believe the best. The scene is constructed to emphasize the opposition between them.

In the final segment of the scene, the staging is concentric, visually recalling that of the morality play. The Duchess stands at the center, attended on the one hand by Bosola, who coaxes her to reveal her secret marriage with his words of praise for Antonio, and on the other hand by Cariola, who silently tries to prevent her mistress from making any such revelations. Cariola's role during this scene is not immediately apparent from the text, but emerges chiefly in performance; she cannot remain simply a bystander while the Duchess betrays the secret she was so earnestly enjoined to keep. The Duchess finally listens to Bosola and ignores Cariola. The scene gathers its impact from its morality-play staging; its meaning, however, is rather more complex. The Duchess gives in to Bosola, her demonic tempter, and precipitates her downfall as a result, but the trustful openness of her confession is a sign of her virtue rather than her weakness. The final segment brings the scene full circle, dramatically reasserting the Duchess's virtue even as her enemies gain the upper hand in the plot.

The second scene of the third act is long and filled with action. Its formal design must have greatly simplified the construction of lengthy scenes like this one. Webster constructs the scene to emphasize important oppositions while advancing the narrative. At the center of the scene, the hurried exits and entrances of Antonio and Bosola clarify both the Duchess's firm centrality and the decisive turn in her fortunes. The parallelism between the segments that form each half of the scene, framing its center, is too deliberate to be coincidental. In the first half of the scene, Antonio's playful banter is juxtaposed with Ferdinand's psychotic rage; in the second half, the Duchess's account of Antonio's "crimes" is followed by Bosola's account of his virtues, the officers' meanness by the Duchess's trustfulness. In both the first and second parts of the scene, Webster sets the episodes side by side for maximum dramatic shock. Both the sudden fury of Ferdinand and the sudden warmth of Bosola come as dramatic surprises. Both characters prey on the Duchess's vulnerability as they find her virtually alone (in the first case, after the exit of Antonio and Cariola; in the second case, after the mass exit of the officers). The split structure of the scene allows an important concept to be emphasized through repetition and variation. Over and over the Duchess's choice of love is challenged by different forms of hatred. The crazed fury of Ferdinand and the coolly divided nature of Bosola are in fact built on an entire world of banal evil, represented in the officers. The scene begins and ends, however, with the Duchess's clear choice in favor of love and trust. As the centerpiece that links the two parts shows, the Duchess retains control even as her fortunes collapse.

Not all of Webster's scenes in *The Duchess of Malfi* are constructed according to this concentric plan. This scene does reveal, however, that Webster was a careful dramatic craftsman, and a master of what he himself calls "the ingenious structure of the scene" (Shirley 4). Different parts of the scene explore different aspects of Webster's main theme, contributing not only to the linear progression of the plot, but also to the elaboration of the dramatist's vision. The analogical relation between different segments of the scene, like that between different scenes or groups of scenes, binds Webster's "discontinuities" into a coherent whole that is nonetheless richly varied.

The same playwright who devoted laborious attention to the individual scene has been accused of carelessness in the whole play. Webster has frequently been criticized for his alleged failure to combine the parts of his play into a total vision. The chief target of this criticism is *The Duchess of Malfi*'s final act. In this chapter, it will be considered as the second of a two-part structure which, like that of *The White Devil*, allows for a significant reversal in the overall pattern. Like the trial scene of *The White Devil*, the death scene of *The Duchess of Malfi* is a climactic set-piece that brings to a close the play's first part. Antagonists and protagonists change places at the midpoint of both plays. In the earlier play, the central scene only hints at a vision of universal suffering, in Giovanni's lament; in the later play, this vision is fully realized in the Duchess's death scene. The dramatist, who clearly understood the importance of scenic construction, applied the same formal principles to each play as a whole.

There is no doubt that *The Duchess of Malfi* shows evidence of the "split structure" that has been identified in many of the plays of Shakespeare and his contemporaries.[12] Plays like *Richard II*, with its inversion of the characters and fortunes of Richard and Bolingbroke, or *The Winter's Tale*, with Polixenes in the second part assuming Leontes' former role as a jealous tyrant, are designed in two parts which mirror one another. And, as Emrys Jones points out, "Most of Shakespeare's other histories and tragedies gain in clarity if they are considered as plays conceived in two unequal movements" (81).[13] The total form of *The Duchess of Malfi* is probably closest to that of *Hamlet*. It has been suggested that Shakespeare's play, like

Webster's, can be divided into a lengthy first part (ending at IV.iv), and a shorter second part. In the first part, Hamlet is the avenger of his father's murder; in the second part, Laertes assumes this role, while Hamlet becomes the object of his vengeance. Emrys Jones notes that the play's two-part structure clarifies their exchange of roles: "The second part of the play opens with a new situation, an ironical reversal of the first. Laertes is now the injured son, whose father has been murdered; Hamlet is now, from this point of view, the murderer who must be put to death" (80). In the second part of *The Duchess of Malfi*, the villainous revengers become the objects of revenge. As, in *Hamlet*, Shakespeare complicates our view of the hero by casting him as a murderer in the second part, so, in *The Duchess of Malfi*, Webster changes our perspective of the villains by presenting them as victims in the final act.

The two parts of *The Duchess of Malfi* are clearly defined. The play proceeds in one direction, culminating in the death of the Duchess, and then changes direction for the final act. The Duchess is present in the first part, absent in the second part. There are clear differences in tone and characterization between the two parts; the Arragonian brothers are cruel monsters in the first part, pathetic victims in the second.[14] Critics have frequently noted the shift from a strong, unified world of order and value in the first part to a fragmented world of disorder and chaos in the second. As important as the differences between the two parts, however, are the parallels. In the first part, the Arragonian brothers carry out their "revenge" against the Duchess for marrying beneath her station; in the second part, Bosola perpetrates his revenge against the brothers for their murder of the Duchess. In both parts, the revenge accomplishes its desired end, while at the same time it is revealed to be futile; the victims of revenge cling to their "crimes" and evade simple formulations of necessity or justice. The actions of Bosola in particular serve to emphasize the symmetry of the play's two parts. Before and after the Duchess's death, Bosola appears a curiously muddled figure in whom blatant self-interest always masks a strong sense of loyalty and virtue. In the first part, he murders the Duchess in order to appear a "true servant" (IV.ii.333) to Ferdinand, and in pursuit of his "reward" (IV.ii.294); in the second part, he turns against the Arragonian brothers not only for their murder of the Duchess, but also for their neglect of his services to them. In the first part, Bosola incriminates the Duchess and delivers her up to her brothers; in the second part, he repeats the action by putting Julia at the Cardinal's mercy and thus becoming an unwitting accomplice in her murder. In both parts, Bosola's treachery is emphasized by stage action; twice he accepts a key from one of the Arragonian brothers (I.i.280; V.ii.327). In the first part, Ferdinand sets Bosola to spy on the Duchess; in the second part, the Cardinal sets Bosola to spy on Antonio. Bosola kills the Duchess almost unwillingly in the first part, and murders Antonio accidentally in the second part. The dignified deaths of both protagonists are followed by the desperate struggles for life of Cariola in the first part, and the Cardinal in the second, both of whom are finally murdered by Bosola.

The repeated actions that link the first part with the second clearly undercut Bosola's revenge and call into question the ethic of revenge itself. But more important is the readjustment of perspective on the villains that such parallels make clear. In a sense, the victim and the perpetrator of revenge have merely changed places in the final act, if Bosola can in the second part be considered the Duchess's self-appointed representative. When the antagonists are put into the same position as the protagonist, as victims of a driving and relentless revenge action, the audience's view of them must change. Bosola, despite his apparently radical reformation at the end of Act IV, remains consistent in both parts of the play; Ferdinand and the Cardinal change as the world of the play changes. The inhuman monsters of the play's first part become desperate, self-questioning men, struggling to sustain their inhumanity through their defenses of violence or madness, yet ultimately failing to do so. Tomlinson notes that, in his speech at the beginning of V.v, "the Cardinal is alive here, in a sense in which he wasn't earlier. He speaks personally, not merely with depersonalized brilliance, and he really is puzzled in a question about hell . . . so, indeed, is everyone else, including, notably, the mad Ferdinand: 'Strangling is a very quiet death . . .' Included in the beautifully Jacobean horror of this, there is a grimly striking note of genuine feeling" (153). The "genuine feeling" that suddenly emerges in the play's villains in the final act links them with the Duchess earlier in the play. The symmetry of the two-part structure of *The Duchess of Malfi* includes both protagonists and antagonists in a common tragic vision. And in Webster's tragic vision, as in Shakespeare's, human greatness is intimately linked to human weakness.

Webster strengthens the links between the opposed forces of his tragedy, and connects the two parts of the play, with his structural use of the recurring idea of madness. In the first part, Webster shows that the love and the hatred that are the driving forces of his play are rooted in the same mysterious, irrational impulses, while they have different effects. In the second part, Ferdinand's conscience-stricken madness connects him with the Duchess's tender humanity in the first part.

Madness first appears prominently in the tender wooing-scene between the Duchess and Antonio. In response to the Duchess's proposal of marriage, Antonio says fearfully,

> Ambition, madam, is a great man's madness,
> That is not kept in chains, and close-pent rooms,
> But in fair lightsome lodgings, and is girt
> With the wild noise of prattling visitants, ·
> Which makes it lunatic, beyond all cure.
>
> (I.i.420–24)

This is what Maynard Mack has called an "umbrella speech" (26)— one which allows a wider consciousness than that of its speaker to shelter beneath it. It allows all the dramatic possibilities connected with madness to emerge early in the play, while it avoids associating these only with the villains. The speech of course anticipates the prison scenes, but in its immediate context it introduces the idea of madness into a love scene that is otherwise "fair" and "lightsome." Love is its own madness, Webster seems to imply; this is further emphasized by Cariola at the end of the scene when she accuses the Duchess of "a fearful madness" (I.i.506). Though the Duchess acts in accordance with desire in choosing to marry Antonio, her desire is neither logical nor rational, but "mad" in its own way. In Painter's version of the Duchess's story, Webster's chief source, the madness of the lovers is repeatedly invoked. In one of his frequent moralizing digressions, Painter exhorts, "But let us consider the force of Lovers rage, which so soone as it hath seased upon the minds of men, we see how marvellous be the effects thereof, and with what straint and puissaunce that madnesse subdueth the wise and strongest world-lings" (195). Although Webster deviates from Painter in treating the lovers far more sympathetically, he nonetheless retains suggestions of the madness of love. On the stage, Webster chooses to introduce his audience to the irrational not only through Bosola and Ferdinand, but also through the lovers themselves. Throughout the early part of the play, other characters continually draw attention to Antonio's irregular behavior. "You do tremble" (I.i.450), the Duchess remarks to him during the first scene. "Methinks 'tis very cold, and yet you sweat: / You look wildly" (II.iii.19–20), Bosola says to Antonio later. While the lovers remain guiltless, the "madness" of their love, rather than the "madness" of Ferdinand's hatred, appears to propel the action forward, so that they seem less its victims. By the end of the second act, when Ferdinand screams that he has "grown mad" (II.v.2), the lovers have already established the idiom in the play.

Scenic juxtaposition illuminates the different, but equally irrational, perspectives of love and hatred at the beginning of the third act. At the end of III.i, Ferdinand and Bosola exchange views on the nature of love. From their diseased perspective, love is "sorcery" (III.i.63) and "witchcraft" (III.i.78). At the beginning of the next scene, an apparently aimless discussion between Antonio and Cariola centers on the futility of judgment in matters of love. From Antonio's perspective as a lover, love is a magical force which transforms lovers "into the olive, pomegranate, mulberry . . . flow'rs, precious stones, or eminent stars" (III.ii.31–32). Bosola's and Ferdinand's view of love as a demonic force of astrological origin is juxtaposed with Antonio's view of love's mysterious mythological powers of transfiguration. Both perspectives, though firmly opposed to one another, see love as founded on irrationality and mystery. Similarly, the virtuous love of Antonio and the Duchess and the motiveless hatred of their enemies are both ultimately mysterious and unaccountable. Neither of these interchanges has any apparent plot function, but their juxtaposition illuminates the nature of the play's central opposition, and links all the play's characters with some form of madness.

Webster of course makes distinctions between different kinds of madness in his play. Unlike Painter, who places the blame sometimes on the lovers' passion, sometimes on their enemies, Webster clearly presents the lovers' "madness" as a form of sanity. Their decision to marry, however risky and irrational, brings them a new courage and clarity of vision. Throughout the first part of the play, Webster contrasts their sanity with Ferdinand's psychotic rage. In the second part of the play, however, after the death scene, Ferdinand plunges into real madness. While in the first part Ferdinand suffers from delusions fostered by his own diseased "imagination" (II.v.40), in the second part those delusions have become images of his own actions and of his horror at those actions. As the lovers' "madness" is in the first part a sane response to a mad world, so is Ferdinand's madness in the final act a "sane" reaction that the world considers mad. Before her death, the Duchess cries,

> Th'heaven o'er my head seems made of molten brass,
> The earth of flaming sulphur, yet I am not mad.
>
> (IV.ii.25–26)

Her hallucinations are an appropriate response to the chaos engulfing her, and attest to her sanity. After the death scene, Ferdinand's lycanthropia and "cruel sore eyes" (V.ii.64) are an appropriate recognition of his own savagery. The structural repetition of madness in the play allows Webster both to distinguish between his opposed groups, and to suggest their common experience. The play's split structure emphasizes the links between the lovers and their enemies; Ferdinand's madness in the final act connects him with the Duchess and Antonio as much as it recalls his earlier bouts of fury.[15] In the 1985 National Theatre production, in fact, the connection between Ferdinand and the Duchess was reinforced visually. In the first part, the Duchess was the only figure wearing white among a cast clad entirely in black, while in the final act Ferdinand alone changed into white. His tattered garment looked a good deal like a ravaged version of the Duchess's white nightgown, and further emphasized Ferdinand's own admission that they "were twins" (IV.ii.267). "As their physical twinship implies," Forker observes, "the two characters are complementary as well as opposed" (312).

At the structural center of the play, in the death scene, the masque of madmen functions as a rich and complex dramatic focus for the madness throughout the play. Many critics have noted that "the masque and its characters provide a grotesque image of the world of the play, and some of the madmen reflect quite accurately some of the play's central characters" (Pearson 86). Ferdinand's furious jealousy, the Cardinal's misogyny, and Bosola's decayed cynicism are all quite obviously suggested by the madmen's ravings.

The first speech of the second madman, for example, conjures up all three male characters:

> Hell is a mere glass-house, where the devils are continually blowing up women's souls, on hollow irons, and the fire never goes out. (IV.ii.77–79)

The speech recalls by association Bosola's and the Cardinal's images of glass manufacture for female sexuality, as well as Ferdinand's violent fantasy of having the lovers "burnt in a coal-pit" (II.v.67). Yet at the same time the speech describes the Duchess's experience in the play; her enemies are intent on destroying her "soul" by inflicting on her "the greatest torture souls feel in hell— / In hell: that they must live, and cannot die" (IV.i.70–71). The speech conflates the vision of the torturer and the experience of the tortured. The first madman's speech is similarly ambiguous:

> Doomsday not come yet? I'll draw it nearer by a perspective, or make a glass that shall set all the world on fire upon an instant: I cannot sleep; my pillow is stuffed with a litter of porcupines. (IV.ii.73–76)

The mad astrologer's desire to hasten doomsday recalls Ferdinand's impatience to have the Duchess murdered and the Duchess's own urgent wish for death. The apocalyptic imagery echoes both the Duchess's vision of the earth engulfed in "flaming sulphur" and Ferdinand's frequent use of the imagery of fire to describe his revenge (II.v.24,47). The madmen's speeches are sufficiently general to suggest all the play's main characters. The song that opens the masque suggestively conflates Ferdinand's image of the Duchess as a "screech-owl" (III.ii.89) with the Duchess's tenacity in remaining "Duchess of Malfi still" (IV.ii.142) and anticipates her serenity at her death:

> As ravens, screech-owls, bulls, and bears,
> We'll bill and bawl our parts,
> Till irksome noise have cloy'd your ears
> And corrosiv'd your hearts.
> At last when as our choir wants breath,
> Our bodies being blest,
> We'll sing like swans, to welcome death,
> And die in love and rest.
>
> (IV.ii.65–72)

The masque breaks down the distinctions between the Duchess and her enemies; each is deeply affected by the other, and both crave relief from their suffering.

In many productions of the play the Duchess herself becomes physically involved in the masque. In her review of the 1980 Royal Exchange production, Pearson wrote, "Hunched and angular, her hair clipped, she goes among the madmen, immersing herself in the destructive element in order to master it." Though the Duchess herself declares that she is "not mad" (IV.ii.26), the masque replays and releases her deep involvement in the chaos around her. It is a displaced image of both the psychotic frenzy of Ferdinand and the horror and despair of the Duchess herself. As Joan Lord comments, the masque is "a violent exacerbation and release of one side of her nature (the undisciplined squads of emotion) before her sense of ceremony takes over and allows her to create the form of her death" (314). Throughout the fourth act, the play's "climactic plateau" (Beckerman 42), the Duchess is inextricably linked with her murderers. The masque of madmen is a concentrated dramatic image that illuminates the universal chaos in which all are involved, and thus encapsulates the connections explored through repetition and juxtaposition in the two-part structure of the play.

Like the individual scenes examined above, *The Duchess of Malfi* as a whole is concentrically organized. Every other scene either anticipates or recalls the play's "central referent" (Beckerman 61), the long death scene at the end of Act IV, which marks the end of the first part and the beginning of the second. The Duchess's death scene is the focal point of virtually every theatrical review and critical study. Ewbank writes: "It is a part of the play to which no critic of Webster has been indifferent; it stirred Lamb's and Swinburne's most prostrate praise and Archer's most nauseated denunciation, and later critics have only less ardently condemned or lauded it. Its complexity has been sensed, but hardly satisfactorily analysed" ("Impure Art" 204). The complexity of the death scene is reflected in the diversity of stage interpretations of the Duchess. The *Times*'s review of Poel's 1892 production found that Mary Rorke aroused "a certain amount of sympathy for the hapless Duchess" ("Independent Theatre"). Peggy Ashcroft's first performance of the Duchess in 1945 brought praise from the *Times*'s reviewer on her ability "to communicate the horror of the tortures and to reveal the resistant spirit

of the doomed woman" ("Haymarket Theatre"). The conception of
the Duchess as a defiant woman challenges and complicates the pathetic interpretation. Peggy Ashcroft's second version of the Duchess fifteen years later seems to have emphasized a slightly different
quality. According to the *Times*'s critic, she displayed a serene transcendence over her tortures, as "the only one of his characters to see,
or think she sees, beyond the mist" (Review, "Webster's Play Well
Handled"). Similarly, of the 1971 Royal Court production, Wardle
noted that "Judy Parfitt plays the Duchess on a steady note of
quietly masterful resignation. . . . In the death scene she seems
quite untouched by the surrounding events" (Review, "Uninhabited
Nightmare"). From the pathetic to the rebellious; from the merely
stoical to the serenely transcendent—the richness of the scene is
reflected in the diversity of its possible interpretations. That all of
these are possible dramatic choices for an actress playing the Duchess in the death scene implies complexity in the scene itself. And,
though an individual actress must choose to emphasize one interpretation over another, it is the job of the critic to explore the richness
of a text which allows for such choices.

During the death scene, Ferdinand is absent. Bosola, the otherwise morally ambivalent instrument of Ferdinand's revenge, has
taken on the disguise of an old man who reminds the Duchess of her
mortality and delivers her up to death. In his disguise, he seems to
have shed his dramatic function in the play to take on a purely symbolic one, as Death or Time itself.[16] As Ewbank notes, Bosola
"turns the mock wedding-masque into what reminds us of a Dance
of Death" ("Impure Art" 215). The progressive stages of the death
scene unfold as a foreordained ritual rather than as a successive series of shocks. The atmosphere is one of hushed expectation rather
than of ghastly surprise. Bradbrook points out that "the scene is not
laid in a definite place: it is, as it were, in a different dimension;
there is a curious stillness and hush about the scene, a static quality
and a sense of timelessness" (*Themes* 197). In this atmosphere even
the hubbub of the madmen that precedes Bosola's entrance seems
part of the ritual—the feverish futility of life's chaos that must be
followed by the calm, inevitable release of death. Bosola's reminder
to the Duchess that "this flesh" is no more than "a little crudded
milk, fantastical puff-paste" (IV.ii.125–26) gives expression to the
scene's air of heavy fatalism. In his speeches to her, Bosola trans-

forms the death scene from a murderous outrage against an innocent young woman to an inevitable and universal act of fate. Bosola's message, vividly rephrasing the deeply ingrained medieval notions of *contemptus mundi*, becomes even more powerful when it is embraced by the Duchess herself as a means of maintaining her dignity and mastering her fear. While at some points she challenges Bosola, at others she colludes with him, calmly discussing the folly of "fashion in the grave" (IV.ii.155), and taking her final cue from his conceit of the soul imprisoned in the body.

The powerful atmosphere that is created in the death scene, of life as "a slow but irreversible process of decay" (Alexander 95), with death as its inevitable end, is at odds with the dramatic situation itself, however. The audience's knowledge that the Duchess is a vital young woman, "more sinned against than sinning," unjustly brought to a premature death, works strongly to counter the scene's fatalism. The scene derives much of its power from this vital tension. The Duchess's famous assertion, "I am Duchess of Malfi still" (IV.ii.142), is richly ambiguous. On the one hand, the Duchess bravely and rebelliously asserts her individual identity against villainy and death itself. On the other, youth and beauty confront mortality, a familiar emblem of *vanitas*. The Duchess's cry is both a strong, valid self-assertion, and the lost wail of Everyman confronted with his necessary end. Alexander comments, "It is one expression of that continual declaration of human independence which proclaims the unique value of a particular human existence in the face of the inevitable and eternal triumph of death. This self-assertion is both necessary and vain" (95).

The tension between the dramatic and symbolic interpretations of the scene reaches its highest pitch at the moment of execution. The Duchess kneels to meet her death:

> Yet stay; heaven-gates are not so highly arch'd
> As princes' palaces, they that enter there
> Must go upon their knees.
>
> (IV.ii.232–34)

This recalls her kneeling during the wooing scene, a gesture which there suggested her voluntary submission of herself to her lover. Here, her willing gesture of love and humility heightens by contrast the cruelty of her imposed sentence. Her executioners, whether they are the agents of Death or her brothers, are carrying out an atrocity against the Duchess. Her kneeling posture, while it allows her to retain her dignity, silently recalls the love for which she is to be put to death. Just before the Duchess kneels, the executioners may also kneel, as was conventional, to ask her forgiveness. Her words "I forgive them" (IV.ii.207) may well be a response to the executioners' kneeling. In *The White Devil*, Vittoria admonishes Lodovico:

> do thy office in right form;
> Fall down upon thy knees and ask forgiveness.
>   (V.vi.212–13)

Visually, the executioners' kneeling is a ghastly parody of Antonio's earlier prostration to receive the Duchess's wedding ring. By imitating these movements of mutual affection, the death scene becomes a grotesque reenactment of the wooing scene. Rather than suggesting that the Duchess's "need for love [is] the force which dooms her" (Pearson 61), the echoes of the wooing scene simply heighten the death scene's brutality. The Duchess's kneeling is powerfully ambiguous. She is both a humble Christian, quietly kneeling to meet her inevitable fate, and a controlling, assertive individual, still the rebellious victim of a terrible injustice. The kneeling itself is an aggressive, as well as a humble gesture, for it forces the executioners to stoop uncomfortably in order to pull the noose tight around her neck.[17] Visually, the moment is a significant emblem of the play's total action—the Duchess, by "stooping" to marry her inferior in an act of love and humility, has actually exposed the degradation of those around her. The Duchess herself forces the scene's underlying tension to the surface. By appearing humbly to concede the inevitable justice of death, she in fact calls attention to the injustice of Death's ministers. "Regal calm becomes the outward expression both of protest against injustice and of tragic acceptance of the inevitable," Forker observes (326). At the moment of death, she both refutes and colludes with the scene's symbolic dimension. Her final defense is to complete the interpretation that has been forced upon her, crying, "Come, violent death, / Serve for mandragora to make me sleep!" (IV.ii.234–35). In this way she can ignore her illegitimate human executioners and summon up her courage to die. But her final, bitter words to Bosola emphasize again the cruel injustice of the dramatic situation:

Go tell my brothers, when I am laid out,
They then may feed in quiet.
                                        (IV.ii.236–37)

The Duchess is a consummate actress in the death scene. She gains dramatic control over her assassins and maintains her dignity by colluding with Death, who ultimately controls even her brothers. By supporting the scene's symbolic dimension, the Duchess avoids becoming, like Cariola, merely a pathetic victim. Yet her demeanor at the same time exposes the contradictions inherent in the scene, between the assassins' pose as impersonal ministers of death and their brutal, murderous action. The highly formal, ritualistic structure of the death scene allows the Duchess to be both mistress and victim of the occasion, to control a situation over which she has no control. The richness and complexity of the scene are illuminated by the tendency of different actresses to exploit its different aspects; the Duchess is both resistant and pathetic, defiant and humble, as she goes to her death. And this complexity is derived from the "impurity" of Webster's art—from the interplay of allegory and narrative, convention and realism. Ewbank notes that "in this scene he holds the tension between the two and draws strength from both sides—the kind of strength which tempts one to suggest that Webster's art is most 'impure' at the centres of meaning in his plays; that his peculiar skill, not only as a dramatic poet but as a poetic dramatist, lay in the ability to utilize the very impurity of his art" ("Impure Art" 220).

The formal complexity, or "impurity," of the death scene, has a number of important consequences for the play as a whole. First, because the scene's symbolic dimension complicates the audience's response to the Duchess's immediate plight as the innocent victim of her brothers, its pathos and melodrama are attenuated. The scene hints that the play is to transcend mere catastrophe, the destruction of a good character by villains, and will offer some larger vision. In the death scene itself, the play hovers between melodrama and fatalism, injustice and inevitability, but settles on neither. Because the tone and the situation of the death scene are at odds with one another, each tends to neutralize the other's single impact, while at the same time combining to enrich and intensify the scene's meaning. Second, because the death scene also distances the audience from the villains—the brothers are absent, Bosola is in disguise—their crimes are mitigated. Throughout the third act, the brothers are distanced by means of commentary (III.iii) and dumb show (III.iv), while Bosola becomes increasingly depersonalized.[18] As a result, the humanity of the villains in the final act is more credible because it does not sharply contradict their outright villainy. The distance from both the Duchess and her enemies that results from the death scene's ceremony helps to ease the transition from the first part of the play to the second. Finally, at the structural center of the play, Webster deliberately creates a powerful image of the ineluctable universality of death, which, superimposed on the Duchess's individual fate, prepares us for the collective tragedy of the fifth act. Bosola's dirge, for example, reaches beyond the immediate situation to anticipate the universal experience of mortality:

> Of what is't fools make such vain keeping?
> Sin their conception, their birth weeping;
> Their life a general mist of error,
> Their death a hideous storm of terror.
>
> (IV.ii.186–89)

Both the Duchess's courageous virtue and her enemies' struggles of conscience are set against this nihilistic vision of life made meaningless by death. The death scene transcends the personal calamity of the Duchess's destruction at the hands of her brothers to suggest, in its tone and its language, a general struggle for meaning in the face of the inevitable death that embraces all the characters in the play.

The trial scene of *The White Devil* and the death scene of *The Duchess of Malfi* both achieve the "rich florescence that makes the center of a Shakespearean play such an overwhelming dramatic experience" (Beckerman 45). Both scenes gather into themselves various strands of meaning, and powerfully synthesize and transform them into a resonant dramatic experience. The death scene of *The Duchess of Malfi* suggests that the death and the chaos that appear to divide the different groups actually in some sense unite them. The play's two-part structure, with its major role reversal reinforced through repetition, confirms this vision. Thus the death scene marks not only the play's dramatic and symbolic center, but also the shift in direction from the first part to the second. At the end of the fourth act, "we have reached a point of partial fulfilment and rest (a provisional ending), but the situation is rich in unrealized potentialities (a provisional beginning)" (Emrys Jones 73). In *The White Devil*, the same point is reached, as in many of Shakespeare's plays, at the end of the third act. In each of Webster's major tragedies, the major shift in tone and characterization at the end of the first part is marked by a change in the role of the tool-villain. Like Flamineo in *The White Devil*, Bosola abandons his satiric pose and changes his perspective on the main action. As the characters who stand in closest relation to the audience, Flamineo's and Bosola's adjusted view of the play in turn has a significant effect on the audience's response.

Webster makes use of repeated stage action in the death scene in order to clarify the play's change of direction, while at the same time emphasizing the links between different characters. The death scene opens with the Duchess and Cariola alone together on the stage. The Duchess is clearly in despair and suffering deeply. From Cariola's plea, "Pray dry your eyes" (IV.ii. 14), it is obvious that the Duchess weeps. She describes her suffering in terms of an apocalyptic vision:

> Th'heaven o'er my head seems made of molten brass,
> The earth of flaming sulphur, yet I am not mad.
> (IV.ii. 25–26)

Her pain comes from her double vision; she can see simultaneously the perspective of madness, as it is forced upon her, and the perspective of her own sanity. The long scene ends with another pair of characters alone on the stage together. This time Bosola crouches over the corpse of the Duchess, recalling Cariola as he attempts to minister to her needs and call for help. But in his final soliloquy Bosola recalls the Duchess herself. While the Duchess wept at the beginning of the scene, here Bosola weeps.

> These tears, I am very certain, never grew
> In my mother's milk.
> (IV.ii. 362–63)

Like the Duchess, Bosola suffers deeply at the divided perspective he sees, this time one of innocence and guilt.

> O sacred innocence, that sweetly sleeps
> On turtles' feathers, whilst a guilty conscience
> Is a black register, wherein is writ
> All our good deeds and bad, a perspective
> That shows us hell!
>
> (IV.ii.355–59)

The "hell" that Bosola sees and the "flaming sulphur" that the Duchess sees are aspects of the same vision, seen from opposite points of view. The Duchess sees a possible hell of madness even as she remains sane and virtuous in her misery; Bosola's vision of hell emerges from his simultaneous consciousness of the possibility of innocence and goodness. At the center of the same scene, Ferdinand suddenly sees a vision of reality superimposed on his own madness;[19] when he sees his sister's corpse, he suddenly realizes that "she died young," and his eyes "dazzle" (IV.ii.264), starting with tears. The tears shed by the Duchess, Ferdinand and Bosola in the course of the scene unite them. The scene's design allows victim and murderers to share a common human vision, so that the play's meaning deepens into tragedy. Moreover, the shift from the Duchess to Bosola as a moral focus for the action anticipates the play's overall change in direction for the final act.

Bosola's moral regeneration at the end of Act IV depends primarily on his vision of the play as pure melodrama, of the Duchess as "sacred innocence" put to death by a "cruel tyrant" (IV.ii.372). His voice rings with the certainty and purpose of this simplified vision at the end of the death scene:

> Come,
> I'll bear thee hence:
> And execute thy last will; that's deliver
> Thy body to the reverent dispose
> Of some good women: that the cruel tyrant
> Shall not deny me. Then I'll post to Milan
> Where somewhat I will speedily enact
> Worth my dejection.
>
> (IV.ii.368–75)

Yet his confident tone is undercut, both by his awkward action, as he drags the Duchess's body off the stage, and by his own more complex vision of hell, in which good and bad deeds seem to confound each other in a hopelessly futile struggle. This underlying tension at the end of the first part is repeated at the close of the play.[20] At the end of the final act, Bosola gives a reductive summary of the play's action, and his own part in it:

> Revenge, for the Duchess of Malfi, murdered
> By th'Arragonian brethren; for Antonio,
> Slain by this hand; for lustful Julia,
> Poison'd by this man; and lastly, for myself,
> That was an actor in the main of all.
>
> (V.v.81–85)

Bosola's self-righteous tone is undercut, however, by both the debacle surrounding him on the stage and his implied dual role as perpetrator and object of his own revenge.[21] A few lines later, he turns from this apparent moral certainty to cry despairingly,

> We are only like dead walls, or vaulted graves,
> That ruin'd, yields no echo:—Fare you well.
>
> (V.v.97–98)

Bosola's final speeches move back and forth between stoical aphorisms and a deep vision of futility, which casts doubt on the efficacy of his own actions. The underlying tension in Bosola that rises to the surface at the end of both parts lies at the heart of the play itself. On the one hand, like Bosola's neat summary, *The Duchess of Malfi* traces the actions willfully imposed on some characters by others in a clear linear chain of events. On the other hand, it presents all the characters as victims, caught in a tragic universe of "good deeds and bad" (IV.ii.358). This tragic vision is articulated, not primarily through the linear narrative, but through the web of repeated themes and actions that find their most intense expression at the structural center of the play.

Comparison of the overall structures of Webster's major tragedies illuminates his use of similar formal strategies to achieve different ends in the two plays. In *The White Devil*, Brachiano and Francisco are designed as analogues for the purpose of clearly distinguishing one from the other; in *The Duchess of Malfi*, the villains' position as objects of revenge mirrors that of the Duchess, and all find themselves victims grappling with their fear and their humanity. In the earlier play, Webster's tragic vision is focused primarily on the protagonists, while in the later play both protagonists and antagonists share a similar vision of human suffering. Thus repetition, while obviously central to the bipartite structure of both plays, works mainly to achieve contrast in *The White Devil*, and parallelism in *The Duchess of Malfi*. In both plays, moreover, the ends achieved through repetition are fulfilled in the central emblem. In *The White Devil* the contrast between antagonists and protagonists conveyed through the mirroring of the first half in the second is encapsulated in the famous trial scene. In *The Duchess of Malfi*, the affinities between heroes and villains suggested by the play's two-part structure are concentrated in the climactic death scene of the fourth act. And, at the dramatic center of each play, Webster emphasizes the complexity of his play's world: the Duchess is both victor and victim in her death scene; her death itself is both cruel and inevitable. Brachiano and Vittoria, too, are shown in their trial scene as both innocent and guilty, mired in a similar, morally complex world.

CONCLUSION

W EBSTER'S two major tragedies followed one another in rapid succession. *The White Devil* was first performed early in 1612 (Brown, *White Devil* xxii), and *The Duchess of Malfi* saw its first performance in late 1613 or 1614 (Brown, *Duchess* xviii). Webster's first independent effort was evidently still fresh in his mind when he came to write *The Duchess of Malfi*, for the careful construction of the later play owes much to his formal experimentation in *The White Devil*. It appears that with *The Duchess of Malfi* Webster reached the highest point of his artistic achievement. Another tragedy, *The Guise*, has been lost; it is hence impossible to judge its quality, though Webster himself ranked it with his earlier tragedies (Shirley 3). Webster's last independent play, a tragicomedy entitled *The Devil's Law-Case*, was probably written some four or five years after *The Duchess of Malfi*. In her edition of *The Devil's Law-Case*, Shirley suggests that Webster began the play in 1617 or 1618 and continued to work on it until 1619, when it was probably first performed (xiv). In this play Webster, though he continues to exploit dramatic strategies he used successfully in his other plays, fails to achieve anything more than a confused and banal dramatic intrigue. After this last independent effort, Webster returned to the collaborations with which he began his career, working perhaps with Middleton on *Anything for a Quiet Life* (1621), certainly with Ford, Dekker, and Rowley on a play (now lost) entitled *Keep the Widow Waking* (1624), with Rowley and perhaps Heywood on *A Cure for a Cuckold* (1624), and less certainly with Massinger and Ford on *The Fair Maid of the Inn* (1625). It is possible that the classical tragedy *Appius and Virginia* was another independent effort, written either early or late in Webster's career; most scholars, however, have detected Heywood's hand in its composition. Webster's return to collaborative ventures may indicate, as John Russell Brown suggests, "a failure of artistic confidence" (*White Devil* xxv). Certainly, *The Devil's Law-Case* illustrates—if illustration is needed—that the use of repetition alone does not ensure a great play. Its repetitions merely emphasize the predictable nature of its tragicomic ironies, while helping Webster to control and pace an otherwise hopelessly intricate plot. In the major tragedies, on the other hand, the repetitions are never quite exact, and the balance of similarity and difference contributes to the moral complexity of Webster's vision.

Several years ago, Ewbank claimed that Webster's plays, as well as his part in collaborative works, exhibit a characteristic "constructional rhythm." This rhythm, which she examined in the individual scene, moves the action from "a dialogue of brief, pointed, foreboding utterances" to "slowly analyzing speeches," in which characters try out different ways of describing their experience, to finally a scenic climax of "lucid complexity," which "revolves around a paradox central to the action of the play where it occurs." She goes on to suggest that this pattern may also exist in the overall structures of the plays, which show "a gradually increasing intensity of thought and feeling" ("Constructional Rhythm" 169–75). I have shown, concurring with Ewbank's analysis, that the plays open with a series of brief, ominous episodes, interrelated through parallel and contrast. Then, as the play as a whole builds in dramatic power and tension, the larger sequences of dramatic action are drawn out and repeated. In the total work as in the single scene, "an idea or a feeling is taken up, turned over and over and looked upon from different directions" ("Constructional Rhythm" 173). As chapter 1 explains, the repetition of large sequences of dramatic action allows the play's simple linear progression to be de-emphasized and its central experience explored and intensified. Finally, at the climactic center of each of Webster's tragedies, a clear and sustained dramatic experience incarnates the play's central paradox. Chapter 4 discusses this "lucid complexity" at the heart of both plays. Ewbank's examination of the movement of language and action in Webster's individual scenes thus bears an important analogic relation to the structure of the whole, as she herself suggests. Indeed, throughout this study the single scene has often functioned as synecdoche, reproducing in lit-

tle the repetitive and concentric modes of organization which provide the basic structure of Webster's plays.

The work of recent critics has illuminated Shakespeare's tendency to relate parts of his play to each other and to the whole by
means of repetition. Webster's "constructional rhythm," like Shakespeare's, is based on such inherited principles of dramatic form,
though his articulation of those principles is unique. Compared
with Shakespeare, Webster's unity may be more difficult for a modern audience to grasp because of his dazzling and quixotic dramatic
style. John Russell Brown cites Flamineo's description of Camillo in
The White Devil as a typical example of this style:

> a gilder that hath his brains perish'd with quick-silver is not more cold
> in the liver. The great barriers moulted not more feathers than he hath
> shed hairs by the confession of his doctor. An Irish gamester that will
> play himself naked, and then wage all downward, at hazard, is not
> more venturous. So unable to please a woman that like a Dutch dou-
> blet all his back is shrunk into his breeches. (I.ii.27–34)

Brown points out that "there is a connection between all these details, yet the speaker is never at pains to make it fully explicit; his
utterance is staccato and often grammatically incomplete . . . it
must be followed closely to be fully appreciated; being subtle and
complex, it demands detailed attention" (*White Devil* xlviii). Brown
is right to point to the brilliant intricacy of Webster's verbal surface
and its unusually heavy demand on our close attention. But what
makes it possible for us to give it close attention without impossible
strain is the highly repetitive underlying structure of the speech. As
in the play as a whole, a single idea is turned over and over, gaining
in intensity and clarity as it is repeated and expanded. In this sense
Webster's writing exhibits characteristics of the "baroque," anti-
Ciceronian prose style defined by Morris Croll as "a series of imaginative moments occurring in a logical pause or suspension" or "successive flashes of a jewel or prism as it is turned about and takes the
light in different ways" (212). This kind of nonlinear construction,
in both sentences and plays, has been condemned as loose and fragmented. Thus "minds trained solely in the logical and grammatical
aspects of language" dismiss the sentences of Montaigne, Bacon,

and Browne as "quaint failures in the attempt to achieve sentence unity" (Croll 230–31), and advocates of the oratorical style claim that the "baroque" sentence "makes less progress in five or six successive statements than a Ciceronian period will often make in one long and comprehensive construction." Yet, as Croll points out, their "criticism is, of course, sound if the only mode of progression is a logical one, but in fact there is a progress of imaginative apprehension, a revolving and upward motion of the mind as it rises in energy, and views the same point from new levels" (219). As in the individual speech, so in Webster's drama as a whole—in scenes and groups of scenes—the mode of progression is not strictly logical but broadly imaginative, the relation between parts not one of direct causation but one of general analogy.[1]

Comparison of Webster's formal strategies in his two major tragedies reveals his indifference not only to a progressive, causally linked linear structure but also to the conventional division of a play into five acts, with each act marking a definite phase in the action.[2] In each of his two major plays, similar devices appear at different points in the dramatic rhythm. Webster evidently had a fixed repertoire of structural devices, but did not care to articulate them in any particular order. Viewed temporally, the final act of *The Duchess of Malfi* provides a kind of subsidiary action, comparable to the last act of *The White Devil*; viewed spatially, it is the second of two matching parts, like the last two acts of *The White Devil*. Similarly, the fourth act of *The White Devil* is both a replay of previous material for the purpose of clarification (like the third act of *The Duchess of Malfi*) and an inverted image of the play's first part (like the last act of *The Duchess of Malfi*). These differences, though confusing to anyone seeking direct, point-by-point correspondences between the structures of the two plays, illuminate Webster's indifference to any rigid formula of dramatic construction at the same time that they reveal his repeated adoption of similar strategies throughout his drama.

Differences in the structures of the two tragedies also illuminate the development of Webster's formal art and tragic vision. In *The White Devil*, the sustained "climax" falls in the third act, while in *The Duchess of Malfi* it is reserved for the fourth act. In the earlier play, Webster repeats his material for clarity and intensification *after* the climax of the arraignment; in the later play, he de-emphasizes plot

151

progression for a similar purpose *before* the Duchess's climactic death scene. From his first independent effort, Webster may have learned that it is more useful to clarify the play's basic issues before introducing his big central scene. Another difference between the plays reveals the development of a more complex vision in *The Duchess of Malfi*. In *The White Devil*, Webster uses the device of repetition throughout to emphasize important contrasts between his "villains" and his "villain-heroes." In *The Duchess of Malfi*, he uses the same device also to suggest parallels between his opposed groups. In the earlier play, the crude, restricted vision of Francisco's faction serves as a foil to the moral complexity of the protagonists, who combine guilty weakness with heroic energy. In the later play, the villains develop from types of Francisco into images of Brachiano, allowing Webster to expand his sense of human fallibility to include even villainy in a wider, more compassionate vision.

Throughout this study, in my discussion of both Webster's dramatic construction and his tragic vision, I have relied on records of stage performances of Webster's plays. My assumption has been that the testimony of theatre critics, together with directorial decisions recorded in promptbooks, can illuminate something of Webster's original intention when he wrote his plays for stage performance. Although directors, actors, and audiences have undeniably changed since Webster's day, their responses to successful and unsuccessful productions can still serve as a suggestive guide to the intended shape and dramatic effect of his plays. Clearly, any attempt to explicate Webster's basic dramatic structures must concern itself with how they are or could be realized in performance, though performance alone does not necessarily make them obvious. "The Webster scholar will neither expect the theatre to do his work for him nor ignore its findings," Thomson observes (27). Some of the arguments contained in this study are borne out by successful productions of Webster's plays; others remain to be verified by stage performance. Yet despite the fact that "in the theatre . . . a basic deficiency in execution often negates Webster's desired effect" (Moore, "John Webster" 321), the dramatic force of Webster's plays is widely acknowledged. A. J. Smith remarks, "What makes *The White Devil* more than a loose-knit sequence of theatrical effects . . . is a search for the real power of a play which is more in the end than the sum of its diverse parts. One can be confident of the judgement without any prior assurance of one's ability to substantiate it. The proof is the single impact the play makes where it matters, in the theatre" (76). Webster's excellence as a man of the theatre is, as I have argued, inseparable from his careful dramatic craftsmanship.

If there is any controversy surrounding Webster on the stage, it concerns the style in which his plays are to be acted. Many critics have pointed out that Webster includes both scenes of intimate, realistic detail and scenes of overt symbolism; this mixture of styles is symptomatic of a larger problem in interpreting Webster. Modern directors feel they must choose between playing Webster as "an abstract poem to the mysterious forces of darkness and cruelty, in which the characters play an almost ritualistic, emblematic role," or as "an everyday story . . . perfectly explicable in terms of human character" (Leslie review of *Duchess*). The former emphasizes the plays' symbolic dimension, while the latter supports their vivid realism. As Bryden puts it, "Either you believe 'The Duchess' a profound and truthful statement about the human condition, that evil reigns inexorably and inexplicably at the heart of things. Or else you consider that it can be given a human explanation, traceable through the tangle of ordinary men's mixed motives" (Review of *Duchess*). Yet both symbolic and realistic dimensions are present in the play's structure, and at least one recent production has succeeded in integrating them. As Robert Cushman noted in his review, Adrian Noble's 1981 production of *The Duchess of Malfi* for the Royal Exchange Company "cannot merely move easily from one style to another, it can accommodate two simultaneously; which is what Webster's text itself does." In his review of the production, Wardle remarked that "its main achievement lies in the combination of theatrical opposites. In one sense, it is rougher and more down-to-earth than the usual pageant of exquisite cruelties. In another, Mr. Noble has realized the play's ceremonial element" ("Right to the Heart"). On the one hand, the actions of the play, when fully realized in performance, are almost always vividly realistic in their depiction of the tangled intrigues of human life. On the other hand, as we have seen, the use of structural devices like repetition undercuts the immediacy of "story" and emphasizes the underlying symbolic shape of the plays.

By exploiting conventional repetitive and concentric modes of organization for his own aesthetic purposes, Webster was able to control the rich variety of his dramatic materials. One aim of this study has been to account for the theatrical impact of Webster's plays by eliciting the pattern of their events, long dismissed as loose and haphazard. Our examination has led to the discovery of a careful dramatic craftsman as well as a brilliant poet of individual scenes and speeches—a dramatist who, like his contemporary Shakespeare, was able to achieve a "multiple unity" in his drama.

~~~~~~

NOTES

~~~~~~

Introduction: Webster and the Art of Repetition

1. The original study of Shakespeare's image patterns is Spurgeon's. See Kreider for an account of repeated situations in Shakespeare's plays.

2. See especially Beckerman, Hartwig, Hirsch, Emrys Jones, Rose.

3. Jensen comments that in Lamb's anthology "artistic structure, any sense of the whole creation, is sacrificed to the emphasis on a single dominant impression" (216). Lamb's indifference to overall design made him vulnerable to Archer's claim that he "mistook the value of the dramatic setting in which he found his poetic jewels enchased" ("Webster, Lamb" 133).

4. The term is first used by Heinrich Wölfflin in his *Principles of Art History* to describe Renaissance as opposed to baroque art, first adopted to describe Elizabethan drama by Doran (5–6), and reiterated by Beckerman (27).

5. Hazlitt, for example, found that, in the Duchess's death scene, "the horror is accumulated to an overpowering and unsupportable height" (133).

6. For other examples of this tendency to neglect and idealize Shakespeare at Webster's expense, see Charney and Frost. The idealization of Shakespeare recalls nineteenth-century critics like Watson, who praised Shakespeare's "large and lucid vision of life," and condemned Webster's "disordered" world, in which "virtue . . . is merely wasted, honour bears not issue, nobleness dies unto itself" (13, 17). In both Shakespeare and Webster, of course, virtue is usually wasted or destroyed.

7. For a more complete discussion of the critical controversy surrounding Webster's moral vision, see Whitman 1–57.

8. See Kirsch's attack on John Russell Brown (101–2), and McElroy's response to it (295ff.).

9. See Ewbank's articles "Impure Art," in which she discusses the

155

Duchess's death scene as an inversion of the traditional wedding masque, and "Webster's Realism," in which she explores Webster's use of perspective art.

10. Forker elaborates on the parallels between Webster's two great plays (354–57).

11. Dessen makes this point (59), as does Pearson (59).

Chapter One: Winding and Indirect: Nonlinear Development

1. Landau, who produced the play for the Phoenix in New York in 1955, writes that "critical tradition labels the trial scene as one of the great moments of the English stage. It clearly is" (234).

2. Bliss makes a similar point (124).

3. The differences between the two scenes are glossed over by critics who claim that both simply reveal the internal divisions in each faction (Dallby 43).

4. The analogy may have been reinforced by staging. Reynolds claims that both III.ii and IV.ii were designed to be played on the "rear stage" (140).

5. For an exhaustive review of the possible applications of Flamineo's tale, see Blanton 191.

6. Bliss makes a similar point in asserting that "*The White Devil* concentrates on distinguishing among them, and not on opposing murderous egoism with transcendent romantic passion" (125).

7. Dent identifies such "delayed revelations" as flaws in Webster's structure: "Unaware of Francisco's purpose in sending his 'love letter' to Vittoria, we witness the magnificent quarrel scene intent on Brachiano and Vittoria rather than on how they are fitting into their enemy's plan" ("White Devil" 187).

8. Most critics treat the structural repetition in Act IV as mere redundancy: for Bliss, it "illustrates man's capacity to fall, self-deluded, over and over again" (133); for Dallby, it is "the repetition on a microcosmic scale of the main pattern" of conflict and division (44).

9. Neither court scene has any foundation in Webster's sources. In Belleforest's story, translated by Painter in his *Palace of Pleasure*, "the whole secret investigation into the Duchess's private life is directed by her brothers from Rome" (Boklund, *Duchess* 43).

10. In I.i, Ferdinand's words to Bosola, "this will gain / Access to private lodgings" (I.i.280–81) suggest that a property like a key changes

hands, while in III.i, Bosola clearly hands Ferdinand "a false key / Into her bed-chamber" (80–81).

11. Details about each production were provided by the promptbooks.

12. Baker hints at the same kind of structural repetition when she claims that "the drama is . . . structured as succeeding reenactments of the [Duchess's] informing choice. The play's pattern is not developmental but tautological" (344). She goes on to point out that "in scene after scene, the integrity of the Duchess, her commitment to a self-defined identity, is challenged and affirmed," while at the same time, "each of the succeeding scenes in which she appears increases the magnitude of the threatened encroachments on her integrity" (347).

13. In his review of the production, Emrys Jones applauded the changes made by Prowse in "tightening the temporal sequence and further helping to integrate the play into a close-knit unity." In my opinion, such unity was gained at great expense.

14. A similar point is made by Ornstein: "Time moves in the *Duchess*, as in some of Shakespeare's plays, at more than one rate; for Webster must, on the one hand, stress Ferdinand's irrational fury and, on the other hand, emphasize the careless indifference of the Duchess and Antonio to their ignominious position" (130).

15. Details were provided by the promptbook held by the Royal Exchange Theatre, Manchester. The Duchess's children also appeared in another successful production by the Royal Shakespeare Company in 1960.

16. Details of Poel's production were provided by the promptbook.

Chapter Two: An Excellent Picture-Maker: Opening Parallels and Contrasts

1. This relation disappears later in the play, when all three become conspirators in the pay of Francisco. The suggestion of Lodovico's social superiority here corresponds with historical sources (Boklund, *White Devil* 147), and may have been intended to set up a parallel with the following scene.

2. Brown suggests that "Antonio and Delio may well leave the stage after line 82 to enter again in the wake of the state entry to the 'presence'; this is the customary arrangement for Camillo and Archidamus between I.i and I.ii of *Winter's Tale*" (14n).

3. There is scholarly disagreement about whether this speech was added by Webster between the play's first performance in 1613 and its publication in 1623, as a topical allusion to the coup d'état in France in 1617, when the

king's favorite, Concino Concini, was murdered. Both Lucas (2:4–5) and Stoll (22–30) support this view. However, in his edition of the play, John Russell Brown rejects it. He claims that the passage is borrowed from Sir Thomas Elyot's *Image of Governance* of 1541, "or some other early book," and thus owes nothing to contemporary events. Furthermore, in Brown's view the passage is too well-integrated into the body of the play to have been a later addition. He points out that "some reference to France must always have stood at the beginning of the play, for without this account of Antonio's visit abroad two later references (I.i.140–42 and II.i.118–25) would have been markedly obscure" (xxvi). The concerns of this passage are, moreover, commonplaces of Webster's day.

4. This image pattern is related to images of sleep and waking that appear throughout the play. Ferdinand is continually weary and on the point of exhaustion (III.i.38); the Duchess alone remains "awake" until she is put to sleep in the death scene and Bosola in turn awakens from a "sweet and golden dream" (IV.ii.324). Such patterns of verbal imagery, reinforced by dramatic action, provide a texture of subliminal associations that support the Duchess's actions. Forker also notes images of waking in his discussion of the play (358).

5. Boklund notes that Silvio Savelli was the commander of an army that besieged the French garrison in the castle of Milan in 1512–13 (*Duchess* 42), and appears in Bandello as "Antonio's protector" (7).

6. For a discussion of Shakespeare's use of this strategy, see Aldus.

7. General parallels between Antonio and Bosola have been drawn by recent critics, usually at Antonio's expense. Forker remarks, "The roles of passive consort to a duchess and cynical toady to a duke are felt as alternative possibilities in a sycophantic court where probity and fortune stand in close but unstable relation to each other" (329). Whigham openly views Antonio as "one who, like Bosola, is a man in the way of opportunity, a man with a fortune to make" (175). Peterson notes the precise analogies between the two episodes, but uses them to support her extreme view of the play as a cautionary tale (52–54).

8. Details of the Poel production were provided by the promptbook. A table is almost always present in performances of the wooing scene, suggested by Antonio's task to "write somewhat" (I.i.363) at the beginning. In many productions a table is on the stage from the beginning of the act, and may reasonably be used in the Ferdinand/Bosola exchange as well as in the wooing scene.

9. There is of course an established critical controversy surrounding the moral status of the Duchess's marriage to Antonio. For a view of the marriage as a violation of decorum, see Leech, *Duchess*. For the opposite view, see Empson's review of Leech's book, "Mine Eyes Dazzle."

Chapter Three: Women of Pleasure and Men of Conscience: Subplots and Final Acts

1. The authoritative first Quarto of 1612 has no act or scene divisions (John Russell Brown lxix).

2. John Russell Brown argues that these characters, who appear for the first time in the last act, are "some of those in Brachiano's court who are of Francisco's 'faction,'" and not, as others have claimed, the names taken by Gasparo and Lodovico in disguise (*White Devil* 126).

3. See also Eldred Jones 78.

4. The first Quarto gives Monticelso's command at III.ii.8 as "Stand to the table gentlewomen," though most editors have needlessly emended the plural to a singular. John Russell Brown follows their example, though he concedes that "Q might just possibly be right" (*White Devil* 65).

5. Flamineo's instruction to Zanche to flee upon Cornelia's appearance at I.ii.270 is the mere shadow of a suggestion that there is any illicit involvement between them.

6. Zanche's words to Flamineo—"A little painting and gay clothes make you loathe me"—would seem to mean this. The fourth Quarto of 1672 emends "loathe" to "love" and, based on this emendation, Tokson interprets the line as a racial slur: "Her unsightliness, she hopes, can be mitigated by cosmetics and dress" (86). John Russell Brown's interpretation seems closer to Webster's meaning: "Some one finer than I has taken your love, so that now you hate me" (*White Devil* 132). The late emendation may represent a Restoration attempt to stereotype Zanche as a stock painted whore.

7. Marcello speaks at V.i.116, and no exit or entrance is indicated for him before his outburst at V.i.189, so we may assume that he remains on stage as a silent witness throughout the encounter between Zanche and Flamineo.

8. Webster's treatment of both his minor and his major female characters reflects a general trend in the drama of the second decade of the seventeenth century. Dramatists increasingly overturned stereotyped images of women, and, as Woodbridge notes, "even the image of prostitutes underwent a face-lifting in the drama" (261).

9. On this point see Thomson 39 and Pearson 59.

10. The echoes in this scene from *King Lear* IV.vi and III.iv are noted by Pearson 75n.

11. See also Mulryne, "White Devil" 213 and Pearson 75.

12. See Baker 350, Berlin 356, Bliss 160, Bogard 138, Bradbrook, *John*

Webster 155, Forker 361–62, Leech, *Duchess* 32, Levin, *New Readings* 98, Pearson 61, and Whigham 172–73.

13. See also Berry 38–41, Lagarde 2:851, Leech, *John Webster* 75, Mulryne, "Tragicomedy" 153, and Peterson 88–104.

14. Details about this production were provided by the promptbook.

15. Price also makes this point (195).

16. There are some precise verbal echoes of Bosola in the Cardinal's speeches; both use images of glass manufacture for female sexuality (II.ii.6–10; II.iv.13–14), as well as animal imagery (II.i.47–55; II.iv.27–34).

17. For the notion of "two voices," I am of course indebted to Mack 19–20.

18. I find it difficult to accept Peterson's view that Julia's refusal indicates that Delio "simply has not offered enough" (93).

19. Although she does not discuss the Julia subplot, Woodbridge's view of Webster's manipulation of antifeminist stereotypes in his plays is similar to my own when she remarks that, in *The Duchess of Malfi*, "the question of female sexuality is precisely what Webster seems interested in exploring" (259), and, in *The White Devil*, "the moral ambiguity readers experience in the play stems partly from Webster's attempt to achieve sympathy for a fallen woman, to turn a whore into a hero" (261).

20. I cannot agree with the reading of this scene proposed either by Bliss, who claims, "Some courtiers, or a Julia, seek to 'fortify themselves' with others' ruin, but Pescara displays an innate sense of justice" (163), or by Forker, for whom Pescara also "symbolizes a concern for justice" (344).

21. The descriptions of Julia are from the D. H. and Shulman reviews of the 1960 Royal Shakespeare Company's *Duchess of Malfi*.

22. Forker notes the verbal parallel linking the deaths of the Duchess and the Cardinal, but claims that it "only reinforces an ironic contrast, for whereas the Duchess had directed her final appeal to God, the churchman seems to address his to a human being, the threatening Bosola" (318). Yet in both cases, it seems to me, the appeal is more ambiguous, and the parallel stronger than the contrast.

23. Details about the 1892, 1960 and 1971 productions were provided by the promptbooks; the 1985 production was seen by the author.

24. Forker also remarks that "Bracciano's ravings may be considered an early study for the more extended anatomy of madness in Ferdinand" (357).

Chapter Four: Concentric Design

The methodology for this chapter was suggested to me chiefly by Rose's *Shakespearean Design*, although Emrys Jones's *Scenic Form in Shakespeare*, Hirsch's *The Structure of Shakespearean Scenes*, and Beckerman's *Shakespeare at the Globe* were all extremely helpful. For an account of the work done by critics on spatial form in classical and Renaissance poetry, see Rose's first chapter, "Contexts of Design."

1. For a useful distinction between visual and verbal moments in drama, see Ewbank, "More Pregnantly than Words."

2. For a discussion of possible stagings of the scene, see Schuman 74–78. Panofsky discusses the iconography of Bronzino's famous allegory "The Exposure of Luxury," which bears some strong resemblances to this scene in *The White Devil* in its depiction of an embracing couple kneeling on cushions, framed on the one hand by an old woman tearing her hair with rage, and on the other by a young, nubile figure, encouraging the couple by pelting them with roses (86–91). Bradbrook maintains that the dream "is vivid enough to draw off attention from its sinister purport, if the Elizabethan interest in the surface meaning of words is remembered" (*Themes* 188).

3. Forker makes a similar point about the Duchess: "By seeing herself as one of the numerous tragic 'princes' with which 'Fortune's wheel is overcharg'd' (III.v.96), the Duchess connects herself psychologically with a whole pattern of history and literature, at once establishing a traditional context for her fall and serving, for the moment, as her own chorus" (328).

4. Similarly, Forker remarks that "the characters who at least intermittently command our pity or respect must come to terms with the omnipresent menace of a world in which, as Flamineo puts it, 'Man may his fate foresee, but not prevent' (V.vi.180)" (292).

5. Forster uses this term to describe the geometric patterning of Henry James's novels (137).

6. Camillo is a stock comic cuckold. Isabella's role as a devoted wife is considerably undercut by her violent attack on Vittoria in II.i, and after her death, she is mourned by both Giovanni, her virtuous son, and Lodovico, the play's villain, thus further compounding her ambiguity.

7. Webster exploits a similar strategy of simultaneous staging in II.i.279–323.

8. Most editors add an exit at this point for the ambassadors, but this seems both unnecessary, since they reappear in the next scene, and counter to Monticelso's meaning.

9. The promptbook, held by the theatre, provides this information, as does Billington's review in the *Guardian*.

10. See, for example, *The Duchess of Malfi* III.v.10–11, 74–75, 143–44, and IV.i.109–10.

11. Bliss also notes that "Lodovico is Flamineo's apparent double" (119).

12. The term is Beckerman's (43), but see also Emrys Jones 66–88 and Rose 20–21.

13. Emrys Jones also points out (85) that the Elizabethan and Jacobean

dramatists expanded, but did not invent, the bipartite structure which is evident in many morality plays.

14. An interval after the first part may have facilitated this major shift. See Emrys Jones 66–88.

15. Of course many commentators emphasize the differences between the Duchess and her enemies. John Selzer, for example, remarks, "Where the Duchess died with silent dignity, with acts of virtue, Ferdinand acts and howls like a beast; while Ferdinand had hoped to drive the Duchess mad, it is he who actually goes mad" (95).

16. Death and Time were linked in conventional iconography, and both were generally represented by an old man. See Panofsky's chapter on "Father Time" (69–93). See also Ewbank, "Impure Art" 214–15 and Forker 339.

17. I am grateful to Professor A. M. Leggatt for this suggestion.

18. Bosola may already be wearing a disguise when he comes to apprehend the Duchess in III.v. See John Russell Brown, *Duchess* 103n.

19. For a lengthy discussion of this, and other aspects of Webster's "perspective" technique, see Ewbank, "Webster's Realism."

20. Emrys Jones identifies this kind of repetition in Shakespeare's plays as "structural rhyming": "the two parts of the play having like endings" (77).

21. Whigham makes a similar point about Bosola, who "casts himself finally and summarily as an agent, a vicarious actor on behalf of all the victims, not least for himself, murderer and murdered at once. . . . The supposed restorative of revenge has littered the stage, but the body count, though lavish, is sterile" (181).

Conclusion

1. In drawing attention to the analogy between "baroque" prose style—as defined by Croll—and Webster's dramatic construction, I do not wish to suggest that Webster is a "baroque" artist. First, the term "baroque" is a vague and problematic one. As John M. Wallace points out, "'Baroque' as a literary term is so involved in defining itself and so committed to metaphorical descriptions of literary qualities and analogies between the arts that its value is highly questionable" (Croll 203n). Second, Croll's essay is out of date in its insistence on the spontaneous asymmetries of "baroque" style. Later scholars have pointed to "many cases of disguised symmetry" which Croll overlooked (205); indeed, nonlinear "baroque" expansion may not be incompatible with the circular symmetries of the Ciceronian style described by Croll (224, 228). And so it is with Webster's drama: while his

prose is clearly in the tradition of Montaigne, Bacon, and Browne—of whom Croll writes so perceptively—his multiple, nonlinear play construction is traditional rather than "avant-garde" (Berry 6), deeply ingrained rather than newly inspired.

2. Webster's deviation from "classical" form in this respect is illuminated by Greg's futile attempt to fit the events of *The White Devil* into the "Aristotelian" divisions of introduction, evolution, climax, and catastrophe (124–26).

WORKS CITED

Books and Articles

Aldus, Paul J. "Analogical Probability in Shakespeare's Plays." *Shakespeare Quarterly* 6 (1955): 397–414.

Alexander, Nigel. "Intelligence in *The Duchess of Malfi*." Morris 95–112.

Archer, William. *Nineteenth Century* 87.515 (1920). Rpt. in Hunter 94–98.

——. "Webster, Lamb and Swinburne." *New Review* 8 (1893): 96–106. Rpt. in Moore, *Webster: The Critical Heritage* 132–43.

Aristotle. *On Poetry and Style*. Trans. G. M. A. Grube. New York: Bobbs-Merrill, 1958.

Arnold, Matthew. *On the Classical Tradition*. Ann Arbor: U of Michigan P, 1960. Vol. 1 of *The Complete Prose Works of Matthew Arnold*. Ed. R. H. Super. 11 vols. 1960–77.

Baker, Susan C. "The Static Protagonist in *The Duchess of Malfi*." *Texas Studies in Literature and Language* 22.3 (1980): 343–57.

Beckerman, Bernard. *Shakespeare at the Globe, 1599–1609*. New York: Macmillan, 1962.

Belsey, Catherine. "Emblem and Antithesis in *The Duchess of Malfi*." *Renaissance Drama* ns 11 (1981). Rpt. in Bloom 97–113.

Berlin, Normand. "*The Duchess of Malfi*: Act V and Genre." *Genre* 3 (1970): 351–63.

Berry, Ralph. *The Art of John Webster*. Oxford: Clarendon, 1972.

Best, Michael. "A Precarious Balance: Structure in *The Duchess of Malfi*." *Shakespeare and Some Others: Essays on Shakespeare and Some of His Contemporaries*. Ed. Alan Brissenden. Adelaide: U of Adelaide, 1976. 159–77.

Bevington, David. *From "Mankind" to Marlowe: Growth of Structure in the Popular Drama of Tudor England*. Cambridge, MA: Harvard UP, 1962.

Blanton, Cynthia Lanham. "'A Perspective That Shows Us Hell': Form and Vision in Webster's Major Tragedies." Diss. Princeton U, 1977.

Bliss, Lee. *The World's Perspective: John Webster and the Jacobean Drama*. New Brunswick: Rutgers UP, 1983.

Bloom, Harold, ed. *John Webster's* The Duchess of Malfi. New York: Chelsea House, 1987.

Bogard, Travis. *The Tragic Satire of John Webster*. Berkeley: U of California P, 1955.

Boklund, Gunnar. The Duchess of Malfi: *Sources, Themes, Characters*. Cambridge, MA: Harvard UP, 1962.

———. *The Sources of* The White Devil. Cambridge, MA: Harvard UP, 1957.

Bradbrook, Muriel Clara. *John Webster: Citizen and Dramatist*. London: Weidenfeld, 1980.

———. *Themes and Conventions of Elizabethan Tragedy*. Cambridge: Cambridge UP, 1957.

Brennan, Elizabeth, ed. *The White Devil*. London: Methuen, 1966.

Brooke, Rupert. *John Webster and the Elizabethan Drama*. London: Sidgwick and Jackson, 1916.

Brown, John Russell. Introduction. *The Duchess of Malfi*. By John Webster. Ed. John Russell Brown. London: Methuen, 1964.

———. Introduction. *The White Devil*. By John Webster. Ed. John Russell Brown. London: Methuen, 1960.

Brown, Keith. "Bringing Shakespeare to Book." *Times Literary Supplement* 22 August 1986: 916–18.

Burke, Kenneth. *Counter-Statement*. 2nd ed. Chicago: U of Chicago P, 1957.

Champion, Larry S. "Webster's *The White Devil* and the Jacobean Tragic Perspective." *Texas Studies in Literature and Language* 16 (1974): 447–62.

Charney, Maurice. "Webster vs. Middleton; or, The Shakespearean Yardstick in Jacobean Tragedy." *English Renaissance Drama: Essays in Honor of Madeleine Doran and Mark Eccles*. Ed. Standish Henning, Robert Kimbrough, and Richard Knowles. Carbondale: Southern Illinois UP, 1976. 118–27.

Coleridge, Samuel Taylor. *Complete Works*. Ed. W. G. T. Shedd. 7 vols. New York: Harper and Brothers, 1884.

Croll, Morris W. *"Attic" and Baroque Prose Style*. Ed. J. Max Patrick, Robert O. Evans, and John M. Wallace. Princeton: Princeton UP, 1966.

Dallby, Anders. *The Anatomy of Evil: A Study of John Webster's* The White Devil. Lund Studies in English 48. Lund: Gleerup, 1974.

Davies, Cecil W. "The Structure of *The Duchess of Malfi*: An Approach." *English* 12 (1958): 89–93.

Dent, Robert W. *John Webster's Borrowing*. Berkeley: U of California P, 1960.

————. "The White Devil, or Vittoria Corombona." *Renaissance Drama* 9 (1966): 179–203.

Dessen, Alan C. *Elizabethan Drama and the Viewer's Eye.* Chapel Hill: U of North Carolina P, 1977.

Doran, Madeleine. *Endeavors of Art: A Study of Form in Elizabethan Drama.* Madison: U of Wisconsin P, 1954.

Eliot, T. S. "*The Duchess of Malfy.*" *The Listener* 26 (1941): 825–26.

————. "John Marston." *Selected Essays, 1917–1932.* London: Faber, 1932.

Ellis-Fermor, Una. *The Jacobean Drama.* 4th ed. London: Methuen, 1958.

Empson, William. "Double Plots: Heroic and Pastoral in the Main Plot and Sub-Plot." *Some Versions of Pastoral.* 1935. London: Chatto and Windus, 1979.

————. "Mine Eyes Dazzle." *Essays in Criticism* 14 (1964): 80–86. Rpt. in Hunter 295–301.

Ewbank, Inga-Stina [Ekeblad]. "The 'Impure Art' of John Webster." *Review of English Studies* 9 (1958): 235–67. Rpt. in Hunter 202–21.

————. "More Pregnantly than Words: Some Uses and Limitations of Visual Symbolism." *Shakespeare Survey* 24 (1971): 13–18.

————. "Webster's Constructional Rhythm." *English Literary History* 24 (1957): 165–76.

————. "Webster's Realism; or, 'A Cunning Piece Wrought Perspective.'" Morris 159–78.

Forker, Charles R. *Skull Beneath the Skin: The Achievement of John Webster.* Carbondale: Southern Illinois UP, 1986.

Forster, E. M. *Aspects of the Novel.* Ed. Oliver Stallybrass. 1927. Harmondsworth: Penguin, 1977.

Frost, David Leonard. *The School of Shakespeare: The Influence of Shakespeare on English Drama, 1600–42.* Cambridge: Cambridge UP, 1968.

Gill, Roma. "'Quaintly Done': A Reading of *The White Devil.*" *Essays and Studies* ns 19 (1966): 41–59.

Goldman, Michael. *Acting and Action in Shakespearean Tragedy.* Princeton: Princeton UP, 1985.

Greg, W. W. "Webster's *White Devil*: An Essay in Formal Criticism." *Modern Language Quarterly* 3 (1900): 112–25.

Hartwig, Joan. *Shakespeare's Analogical Scene: Parody as Structural Syntax.* Lincoln: U of Nebraska P, 1983.

Hazlitt, William. *Lectures on the Dramatic Literature of the Age of Elizabeth.* 2nd ed. London: John Warren, 1821.

Hirsch, James E. *The Structure of Shakespearean Scenes.* New Haven: Yale UP, 1981.

Holdsworth, R. V., ed. *Webster:* The White Devil *and* The Duchess of Malfi: *A Casebook.* London: Macmillan, 1975.

Hunter, G. K. and S. K. *John Webster: A Critical Anthology.* Harmonds-worth: Penguin, 1969.

Jack, Ian. "The Case of John Webster." *Scrutiny* 16 (1949): 38–43. Rpt. in Hunter 157–64.

Jardine, Lisa. *Still Harping on Daughters: Women and Drama in the Age of Shakespeare.* Sussex: Harvester, 1983.

Jenkins, Harold. "The Tragedy of Revenge in Shakespeare and Webster." *Shakespeare Survey* 14 (1961): 45–55.

Jensen, Ejner. "Lamb, Poel, and Our Postwar Theatre: Elizabethan Re-vivals." *Renaissance Drama* ns 9 (1978): 211–34.

Johnson, Samuel. "Preface to Shakespeare." *Johnson on Shakespeare.* Ed. Arthur Sherbo. *The Yale Edition of the Works of Samuel Johnson.* Vol. 7. New Haven: Yale UP, 1968.

Jones, Eldred. *Othello's Countrymen: The African in English Renaissance Drama.* Oxford: Oxford UP, 1965.

Jones, Emrys. *Scenic Form in Shakespeare.* Oxford: Clarendon, 1971.

Kirsch, Arthur C. *Jacobean Dramatic Perspectives.* Charlottesville: U of Virginia P, 1972.

Kreider, Paul Vernon. *Repetition in Shakespeare's Plays.* New York: Octagon, 1975.

Lagarde, Fernand. *John Webster.* 2 vols. Toulouse: Association des Publica-tions des Lettres et Sciences Humaines de Toulouse, 1968.

Lamb, Charles. *Specimens of English Dramatic Poets who lived about the Time of Shakespeare.* London: Longman, Hurst, Rees and Orme, 1808.

Landau, Jack. "Elizabethan Art in a Mickey Spillane Setting." *Theatre Arts* 39 (1955). Rpt. in Holdsworth, 233–35.

Langer, Suzanne K. *Feeling and Form.* New York: Scribner, 1953.

Layman, B. J. "The Equilibrium of Opposites in *The White Devil.*" *PMLA* 74 (1959): 336–47.

Leech, Clifford. *John Webster: A Critical Study.* London: The Hogarth Press, 1951.

———. *Webster:* The Duchess of Malfi. London: Edward Arnold, 1963.

Levin, Richard. *The Multiple Plot in English Renaissance Drama.* Chicago: U of Chicago P, 1971.

———. *New Readings vs Old Plays: Recent Trends in the Reinterpretation of En-glish Renaissance Drama.* Chicago: U of Chicago P, 1979.

Lord, Joan M. "*The Duchess of Malfi*: The Spirit 'of Greatness' and 'of Woman.'" *Studies in English Literature, 1500–1900* 16 (1976): 305–17.

Lucas, F. L. Introduction. *The Complete Works of John Webster.* Ed. F. L. Lucas. 1927. 4 vols. New York: Gordian, 1966.

Mack, Maynard. "The Jacobean Shakespeare: some observations on the construction of the Tragedies." *Jacobean Theatre.* Ed. John Russell Brown and Bernard Harris. Stratford-upon-Avon Studies 1. London: Edward Arnold, 1965. 11–41.

McCarthy, Mary. *Sights and Spectacles, 1937–1956*. New York: Farrar, Straus and Cudahy, 1956.

McElroy, John F. "*The White Devil, Women Beware Women*, and the Limitations of Rationalist Criticism." *Studies in English Literature, 1500–1900* 19 (1979): 295–312.

McLuskie, Kathleen. "Drama and Sexual Politics: the Case of Webster's *Duchess.*" *Drama, Sex and Politics*. Ed. James Redmond. Themes in Drama 7. Cambridge: Cambridge UP, 1985. 77–91.

Moore, Don D. "John Webster in the Modern Theatre." *Educational Theatre Journal* 17(1965): 314–21.

———, ed. *Webster: The Critical Heritage*. London: Routledge and Kegan Paul, 1981.

Morris, Brian, ed. *John Webster*. London: Ernest Benn, 1970.

Mulryne, J. R. "Webster and the Uses of Tragicomedy." Morris 133–55.

———. "*The White Devil* and *The Duchess of Malfi.*" *Jacobean Theatre*. Ed. John Russell Brown and Bernard Harris. Stratford-upon-Avon Studies 1. London: Edward Arnold, 1965. 201–25.

Murray, Peter. *A Study of John Webster*. The Hague: Mouton, 1969.

Ornstein, Robert. *The Moral Vision of Jacobean Tragedy*. Madison: U of Wisconsin P, 1960.

Painter, William. *The Palace of Pleasure*. Rpt. in John Russell Brown, ed., *The Duchess of Malfi* 175–209.

Panofsky, Erwin. *Studies in Iconology: Humanistic Themes in the Art of the Renaissance*. New York: Harper and Row, 1972.

Pearson, Jacqueline. *Tragedy and Tragicomedy in the Plays of John Webster*. Manchester: Manchester UP, 1980.

Peterson, Joyce E. *Curs'd Example:* The Duchess of Malfi *and Commonweal Tragedy*. Columbia: U of Missouri P, 1978.

Poel, William. "A New Criticism of Webster's *Duchess of Malfi.*" *Library Review* 2 (1893). Rpt. in Hunter 85–88.

Potter, Lois. "Realism vs Nightmare: Problems of Staging *The Duchess of Malfi.*" *The Triple Bond: Plays, Mainly Shakespearean, in Performance*. Ed. Joseph G. Price. University Park: Pennsylvania State UP, 1975.

Price, Hereward T. "The Function of Imagery in Webster." *PMLA* 70 (1955): 717–39. Rpt. in Hunter 176–202.

Puttenham, George. *The Arte of English Poesie*. Ed. Gladys Doidge Willcock and Alice Walker. Cambridge: Cambridge UP, 1936.

Reynolds, George Fullmer. *The Staging of Elizabethan Plays at the Red Bull Theatre, 1605–25*. New York: Modern Language Association; London: Oxford UP, 1940.

Works Cited

Richards, I. A. *Principles of Literary Criticism.* 2nd ed. London: Kegan Paul, 1938.

Rose, Mark. *Shakespearean Design.* Cambridge, MA: Harvard UP, 1972.

Rylands, George. "On the Production of *The Duchess of Malfi.*" Preface. *The Duchess of Malfi.* By John Webster. London: Sylvan Press, 1945.

Schuman, Samuel. *"The Theatre of Fine Devices": The Visual Drama of John Webster.* Jacobean Drama Studies 88. Salzburg: Universität Salzburg, 1982.

Seiden, Melvin. *The Revenge Motive in Websterian Tragedy.* Jacobean Drama Studies 15. Salzburg: Universität Salzburg, 1972.

Selzer, John L. "Merit and Degree in Webster's *Duchess of Malfi.*" *English Literary Renaissance* 11.1 (1981). Rpt. in Bloom 87–96.

Shakespeare, William. *Hamlet.* Ed. Harold Jenkins. London: Methuen, 1982.

———. *King Lear.* Ed. Kenneth Muir. London: Methuen, 1972.

———. *Othello.* Ed. M. R. Ridley. London: Methuen, 1958.

Shirley, Frances, ed. *The Devil's Law-Case.* By John Webster. Lincoln: U of Nebraska P, 1972.

Smith, A. J. "The Power of *The White Devil.*" Morris 71–91.

Smith, James. "The Tragedy of Blood." *Scrutiny* 8 (1939): 265–80. Rpt. in Hunter 116–32.

Spurgeon, Caroline. *Shakespeare's Imagery and What It Tells Us.* New York: Macmillan, 1935.

Stilling, Roger. *Love and Death in Renaissance Tragedy.* Baton Rouge: Louisiana State UP, 1976.

Stoll, Elmer Edgar. *John Webster.* 1905. New York: Gordian, 1967.

Thomson, Peter. "Webster and the Actor." Morris 23–44.

Tokson, Elliott. *The Popular Image of the Black Man in English Drama, 1550–1688.* Boston: Hall, 1982.

Tomlinson, Thomas Brian. *A Study of Elizabethan and Jacobean Tragedy.* Cambridge: Cambridge UP, 1964.

Waage, Frederick O. The White Devil *Discover'd: Backgrounds and Foregrounds to Webster's Tragedy.* New York: Peter Lang, 1984.

Ward, Adolphus William. *A History of English Dramatic Literature to the Death of Queen Anne.* 2nd ed. 3 vols. London: Macmillan, 1899.

Warren, Roger. "*The Duchess of Malfi* on the Stage." Morris 47–68.

Watson, William. *Excursions in Criticism, Being Some Prose Recreations of a Rhymer.* London: Elkin Matthews and John Lane; New York: Macmillan, 1893.

Webster, John. *The Complete Works of John Webster.* Ed. F. L. Lucas. 4 vols. 1927. New York: Gordian, 1966.

———. *The Devil's Law-Case.* Ed. Frances Shirley. Lincoln: U of Nebraska P, 1972.

————. *The Duchess of Malfi.* Ed. John Russell Brown. London: Methuen, 1964.

————. *The White Devil.* Ed. Elizabeth Brennan. London: Methuen, 1966.

————. *The White Devil.* Ed. John Russell Brown. London: Methuen, 1960.

Whigham, Frank. "Sexual and Social Mobility in *The Duchess of Malfi.*" *PMLA* 100 (1985): 167–82.

Whitman, Robert Freeman. *Beyond Melancholy: John Webster and the Tragedy of Darkness.* Salzburg: Universität Salzburg, 1973.

Wilson, Thomas. *The Arte of Rhetorique.* Ed. G. H. Mair. Oxford: Clarendon, 1909.

Woodbridge, Linda. *Women and the English Renaissance: Literature and the Nature of Womankind, 1540–1620.* Urbana: U of Illinois P, 1984.

Wright, Abraham. "Excerpta Quaedam per A.W. Adolescentem." Rpt. in Moore, *Webster: The Critical Heritage* 35.

Theatrical Reviews

The White Devil

Agate, James. *Brief Chronicles: A Survey of the Plays of Shakespeare and the Elizabethans in Actual Performance.* Rev. Renaissance Theatre, Scala, 11 Oct. 1925. Dir. Edith Craig. New York: Benjamin Blom, 1943.

Barber, John. "Difficult Nut." Rev. Greenwich Theatre, 1 Feb. 1984. Dir. Philip Prowse. *Daily Telegraph* 3 Feb. 1984.

————. "Triumph for Designer in Jacobean Tragedy." Rev. National Theatre, Old Vic, 13 Nov. 1969. Dir. Frank Dunlop. *Daily Telegraph* 14 Nov. 1969.

Billington, Michael. "*The White Devil.*" Rev. Greenwich Theatre, 1 Feb. 1984. Dir. Philip Prowse. *Guardian* 3 Feb. 1984.

Bryden, Ronald. "Swamped by Opulence." Rev. National Theatre, Old Vic, 13 Nov. 1969. Dir. Frank Dunlop. *Observer* 16 Nov. 1969.

Coveney, Michael. "*The White Devil*/Greenwich." Rev. Greenwich Theatre, 1 Feb. 1984. Dir. Philip Prowse. *Financial Times* 3 Feb. 1984.

Dawson, Helen. "*The White Devil.*" Rev. National Theatre, Old Vic, 13 Nov. 1969. Dir. Frank Dunlop. *Plays and Players* 17.4 (1970): 38–39.

Donaldson, Anne. "*The White Devil.*" Rev. Greenwich Theatre, 1 Feb. 1984. Dir. Philip Prowse. *Glasgow Herald* [March 1984].

Forster, E. M. "*The White Devil* at Cambridge." Rev. Marlowe Society, Cambridge, 1920. *New Statesman* 20 March 1920. Rpt. in Holdsworth 226–29.

Hope-Wallace, Philip. "A Classic and a Musical." Rev. National Theatre, Old Vic, 13 Nov. 1969. Dir. Frank Dunlop. *Guardian* 14 Nov. 1969.

Kerr, Walter F. "A Lively Sideshow in Phoenix's 'Devil.'" Rev. Phoenix Theatre, New York, 14 March 1955. Dir. Jack Landau. *New York Herald Tribune* 27 March 1955.

Lucas, F. L. "Playing the Devil." Rev. Renaissance Theatre, Scala, 11 Oct. 1925. Dir. Edith Craig. *New Statesman* 17 Oct. 1925.

Masters, Anthony. "An Infernal Glow." Rev. Bristol Old Vic, Theatre Royal, 9 Feb. 1983. Dir. Celia Bannerman. *Times* 14 Feb. 1983.

"New Phoenix Society: *The White Devil*." Rev. New Phoenix Society, St. Martin's Theatre, 17 March 1935. Dir. Allan Wade. *Times* 18 March 1935.

Ratcliffe, Michael. "Slipping on Blood." Rev. Greenwich Theatre, 1 Feb. 1984. Dir. Philip Prowse. *Observer* 5 Feb. 1984.

Shulman, Milton. "Passion and the Poisoner." Rev. Greenwich Theatre, 1 Feb. 1984. Dir. Philip Prowse. *Evening Standard* 3 Feb. 1984.

———. "Well, When in Medieval Rome . . ." Rev. National Theatre, Old Vic, 13 Nov. 1969. Dir. Frank Dunlop. *Evening Standard* 14 Nov. 1969.

Spurling, Hilary. "Devil Incarnate." Rev. National Theatre, Old Vic, 13 Nov. 1969. Dir. Frank Dunlop. *Spectator* 22 Nov. 1969.

Wardle, Irving. "No Terror, No Pity, and No Mortality." Rev. National Theatre, Old Vic, 13 Nov. 1969. Dir. Frank Dunlop. *Times* 14 Nov. 1969.

———. "*The White Devil*: Greenwich." Rev. Greenwich Theatre, 1 Feb. 1984. Dir. Philip Prowse. *Times* 6 Feb. 1984.

———. "*The White Devil*: Old Vic." Rev. Old Vic, London, 12 July 1976. Dir. Michael Lindsay-Hogg. *Times* 13 July 1976.

The Duchess of Malfi

Ansorge, Peter. "Stratford: *The Duchess of Malfi*." Rev. Shakespeare Memorial Theatre, Stratford-upon-Avon, 15 July 1971. Dir. Clifford Williams. *Plays and Players* 18.12 (1971): 26.

Atkinson, Brooks. Rev. Barrymore, New York, 15 Oct. 1946. Dir. George Rylands. *New York Times* 16 Oct. 1946.

Barber, John. "This Sane 'Duchess of Malfi' Won't Do." Rev. Shakespeare Memorial Theatre, Stratford-upon-Avon, 15 July 1971. Dir. Clifford Williams. *Daily Telegraph* 16 July 1971.

Billington, Michael. "Well-Dressed Decadence Without Relief." Rev. National Theatre, London, 4 July 1985. Dir. Philip Prowse. *Guardian* 6 July 1985.

Bryden, Ronald. "Blood-Soaked Circus." Rev. Shakespeare Memorial Theatre, Stratford-upon-Avon, 15 July 1971. Dir. Clifford Williams. *Observer* 18 July 1971. Rpt. in Holdsworth 241–43.

Cropper, Martin. "Horror Story of Perverted Logic." Rev. National Theatre, London, 4 July 1985. Dir. Philip Prowse. *Times* 6 July 1985.

Cushman, Robert. "Malfi and Merchant." Rev. Royal Exchange Theatre Company, Roundhouse, London, 1 April 1981. Dir. Adrian Noble. *Observer* 5 April 1981.

Dawson, Helen. "*The Duchess of Malfi.*" Rev. Royal Court, London, 18 Jan. 1971. Dir. Peter Gill. *Plays and Players* 18.6 (1971): 38–39.

D. H. "Magnificent Make-Believe." Rev. Shakespeare Memorial Theatre Company, Aldwych, London, 15 Dec. 1960. Dir. Donald McWhinnie. *Bristol Evening Post* 16 Dec. 1960.

"Haymarket Theatre." Rev. Haymarket Theatre, London, 18 April 1945. Dir. George Rylands. *Times* 19 April 1945.

Hewison, Robert. "Blood, Lust and Bad Jokes." Rev. National Theatre, London, 4 July 1985. Dir. Philip Prowse. *Sunday Times* 7 July 1985.

Hobson, Harold. "The Duchess is Dead." Rev. Shakespeare Memorial Theatre Company, Aldwych, London, 15 Dec. 1960. *Sunday Times* 18 Dec. 1960.

———. "Gill's Muted 'Malfi.'" Rev. Royal Court, London, 18 Jan. 1971. Dir. Peter Gill. *Christian Science Monitor* 19 Feb. 1971.

Holmes, Martin. Rev. Shakespeare Memorial Theatre Company, Aldwych, London, 15 Dec. 1960. Dir. Donald McWhinnie. *Quarterly Review* 299: 450–52.

Hope-Wallace, Philip. "The Stratford Company Goes to Town." Rev. Shakespeare Memorial Theatre Company, Aldwych, London, 15 Dec. 1960. *Guardian* 17 Dec. 1960.

Hughes-Hallett, Lucy. "*The Duchess of Malfi.*" Rev. Royal Exchange, Manchester, 16 Sept. 1980. Dir. Adrian Noble. *Now* 26 Sept. 1980.

"Independent Theatre." Rev. Independent Theatre Society, Opera Comique, London, 21 Oct. 1892. Dir. William Poel. *Times* 22 Oct. 1892.

"Is Murder Really Necessary?" Rev. Royal Exchange, Manchester, 16 Sept. 1980. Dir. Adrian Noble. *Sunday Times* 21 Sept. 1980.

Jones, Emrys. "Worldly and Other-Worldly." Rev. National Theatre, London, 4 July 1985. Dir. Philip Prowse. *Times Literary Supplement* 19 July 1985: 799.

Kareda, Urjo. "*Duchess of Malfi* a Breathtaking Night of Tension." Rev. Festival Theatre, Stratford, Ontario, 8 June 1971. Dir. Jean Gascon. *Toronto Daily Star* 9 June 1971.

Leslie, Ann. "Theatre." Rev. Shakespeare Memorial Theatre, Stratford-upon-Avon, 15 July 1971. Dir. Clifford Williams. *Punch* 28 July 1971: 129–30.

Lewsen, Charles. "Sick Stallion." Rev. Shakespeare Memorial Theatre, Stratford-upon-Avon, 15 July 1971. Dir. Clifford Williams. *Listener* 22 July 1971: 125.

McCarthy, Mary. *Sights and Spectacles, 1937–1956*. Rev. Barrymore, New York, 15 Oct. 1946. Dir. George Rylands. New York: Farrar, Straus and Cudahy, 1956.

"Manchester: *The Duchess of Malfi*." Rev. Royal Exchange, Manchester, 16 Sept. 1980. Dir. Adrian Noble. *Stage* 25 Sept. 1980.

Nation 10 Nov. 1892. Rev. Independent Theatre Society, Opera Comique, London, 21 Oct. 1892. Dir. William Poel. Rpt. in Moore 128.

P. W. "A Tidy Murder." Rev. Shakespeare Memorial Theatre, Stratford-upon-Avon, 15 July 1971. Dir. Clifford Williams. *Sunday Mercury* 18 July 1971.

Pearson, Jacqueline. "Man Bites Man." Rev. Royal Exchange, Manchester, 16 Sept. 1980. Dir. Adrian Noble. *Times Literary Supplement* 26 Sept. 1980: 1064.

Ratcliffe, Michael. "Glasgow Style Comes South." Rev. National Theatre, London, 4 July 1985. Dir. Philip Prowse. *Observer* 7 July 1985.

Shulman, Milton. "Horror Unlimited Hits the Aldwych." Rev. Shakespeare Memorial Theatre Company, Aldwych, London, 15 Dec. 1960. Dir. Donald McWhinnie. *Evening Standard* 16 Dec. 1960.

Wardle, Irving. "Clearing the Vital Hurdle Boldly." Rev. Royal Exchange, Manchester, 16 Sept. 1980. Dir. Adrian Noble. *Times* 17 Sept. 1980.

———. "*The Duchess of Malfi*: Stratford-on-Avon." Rev. Shakespeare Memorial Theatre, Stratford-upon-Avon, 15 July 1971. Dir. Clifford Williams. *Times* 16 July 1971.

———. "Much Ado in a Beardsley Garden." Rev. Festival Theatre, Stratford, Ontario, 8 June 1971. Dir. Jean Gascon. *Times* 12 Aug. 1971.

———. "Right to the Heart." Rev. Royal Exchange Theatre Company, Roundhouse, London, 1 April 1981. Dir. Adrian Noble. *Times* 3 April 1981.

———. "An Uninhabited Nightmare." Rev. Royal Court, London, 18 Jan. 1971. Dir. Peter Gill. *Times* 19 Jan. 1971.

"Webster for the Royal Court: Peter Gill on his Production of *The Duchess of Malfi*." Rev. Royal Court, London, 18 Jan. 1971. Dir. Peter Gill. *Plays and Players* 18.6 (1971): 30–31.

"Webster's Play Well Handled." Rev. Shakespeare Memorial Theatre Company, Aldwych, London, 15 Dec. 1960. Dir. Donald McWhinnie. *Times* 16 Dec. 1960.

Whittaker, Herbert. "Splendid Production of *The Duchess of Malfi*." Rev. Festival Theatre, Stratford, Ontario. Dir. Jean Gascon. *Globe and Mail* 10 June 1971.

Worsley, T. C. *"The Duchess of Malfi."* Rev. Shakespeare Memorial Theatre Company, Aldwych, London, 15 Dec. 1960. Dir. Donald McWhinnie. *Financial Times* 16 Dec. 1960.

Young, B. A. *"The Duchess of Malfi."* Rev. Shakespeare Memorial Theatre, Stratford-upon-Avon, 15 July 1971. Dir. Clifford Williams. *Financial Times* 16 July 1971.

Theatrical Promptbooks

The White Devil

Greenwich Theatre. 1 Feb. 1984. Dir. Philip Prowse. Promptbook held by the Greenwich Theatre.

National Theatre, Old Vic. 13 Nov. 1969. Dir. Frank Dunlop. Promptbook held by the National Theatre, London.

The Duchess of Malfi

Festival Theatre, Stratford, Ontario. 8 June 1971. Dir. Jean Gascon. Promptbook held by the Stratford Festival Archives.

Independent Theatre Society, Opera Comique, London. 21 Oct. 1892. Dir. William Poel. Promptbook held by the Victoria and Albert Theatre Museum.

Royal Court, London. 18 Jan. 1971. Dir. Peter Gill. Promptbook held by the Victoria and Albert Theatre Museum.

Royal Exchange, Manchester. 16 Sept. 1980. Dir. Adrian Noble. Promptbook held by the Royal Exchange Theatre.

Shakespeare Memorial Theatre Company, Aldwych, London. 15 Dec. 1960. Dir. Donald McWhinnie. Promptbook held by the Shakespeare Birthplace Trust, Stratford-upon-Avon.

Shakespeare Memorial Theatre, Stratford-upon-Avon. 15 July 1971. Dir. Clifford Williams. Promptbook held by the Shakespeare Birthplace Trust, Stratford-upon-Avon.

Index

Absurdist theatre: Webster linked with, xx, 92
Alexander, Nigel, 140
Analogical probability, 45, 84, 86, 158 (n. 6)
Archer, William, 18, 82, 91
Aristotle, 100–102
Arnold, Matthew, xix
Ashcroft, Peggy: as the Duchess, 138–39
Atkinson, Brooks, 93
Auden, W. H.: adaptation of *The Duchess of Malfi*, 93

Bandello, Matteo, 18, 78
Barber, John, 119
Baroque, xxi, 150–51, 162 (n. 1)
Beckerman, Bernard, xv, xvi, xviii, 1, 23, 29, 51, 55
Belleforest, Francois de, 78
Belsey, Catherine, 39–40
Berlin, Normand, xx, 92
Berry, Ralph, xxi
Bevington, David, xvii
Billington, Michael, 67–68, 77
Bliss, Lee, 9, 40, 63, 65, 70, 112, 120
Boklund, Gunnar, 2, 26, 54, 56, 63, 76, 78, 80, 113

Bradbrook, Muriel Clara, 139
Brecht, Bertolt: adaptation of *The Duchess of Malfi*, 93
Brennan, Elizabeth, 56
Bron, Eleanor: as the Duchess, 77
Brooke, Rupert, xvii
Brown, John Russell, xxi, xxii–xxiii, 17, 40, 82, 91, 98, 108, 112, 149, 150
Brown, Keith, 105
Bryden, Ronald, 95, 115, 153
Burke, Kenneth, xiii, 28

Caricature, 37, 62, 75, 88, 89
Champion, Larry, 54, 66
Coleridge, Samuel Taylor, xviii, 23
Concentric design, 40, 94, 97–98, 105–47
Croll, Morris, 150–51, 162 (n. 1)
Cushman, Robert, 153

Dallby, Anders, 53–54, 55, 109, 112
Dench, Judi: as the Duchess, 77
Dent, Robert, xxii, 121
Devil's Law-Case, The, 148–49
Donaldson, Ann, 68
Doran, Madeleine, xiv, xix, xx, 18, 21–22, 112

Dramatic construction: in classical drama, xvi, xviii, xix; episodic, 21–22; in medieval drama, xvii; in Renaissance drama, xv, xviii, 23, 29, 51, 55, 131, 155 (n. 4); term redefined, xvi; Webster's criticized, xvii–xviii, 17, 21, 49, 54, 91–92, 105, 131. *See also* Analogical probability, Concentric design, *Duchess of Malfi*, Foil, Parody, Repetition, Subplot, *White Devil*

Duchess of Malfi, The: problem of Act V in, 91–93, 131; split structure in, 131–33, 136, 144; structural repetition in Acts I–III, 2, 4, 18–28; Webster's use of sources in, 18, 22, 53, 76, 78, 134, 135, 156 (n. 9) 158 (n. 5); and *The White Devil*, 50, 76, 82, 85, 91, 94, 99, 100, 103–4, 131, 141, 143–44, 146–47, 148, 151–52

Characters discussed: Antonio, 18–19, 41–49 *passim*, 94, 127, 134–35; Bosola, 41–44, 46, 47, 84–85, 87–88, 90, 92, 94–95, 98–100, 132–33, 139–40, 144–46; Cardinal, 41, 80–81, 89, 93, 97–100, 133, 136; Cariola, 76, 89–90, 130, 144; Castruchio, 44, 82, 84; Delio, 19–20, 102; Doctor, 96; Duchess, 23–26, 43, 46–49, 77–93 *passim*, 126–27, 128–30, 137–42, 144–45; Ferdinand, 15–16, 24–25, 44–46, 92, 94–96, 99–100, 127–28, 133, 135–37, 145; Julia, 76–91, 96–97; Madmen, 136–38; Pescara, 85–86; Silvio, 44–45

Scenes discussed: I.i., 20, 24, 39–50, 77, 79, 86, 134–35; II.i., 13–14, 20, 81, 84, 85; II.ii., 20; II.iii., 80, 85; II.iv., 79, 80–84; II.v., 5, 21, 30, 137; III.i., 6, 18–20, 24, 135; III.ii., 15–16, 20–21, 25, 26–27, 126–31, 135; III.iii., 21, 22, 24, 25; III.iv., 4–5, 22–23; III.v., 128–29; IV.ii., 83, 136–45; V.i., 85–86, 94; V.ii., 79, 86–90, 94–97; V.iii., 102; V.iv.–v., 97–100, 102–3, 133, 146

Stage productions discussed: Barrymore (1946), dir. Rylands, 93; Haymarket (1945), dir. Rylands, 22, 93, 138–39; Independent (1892), dir. Poel, 26, 27–28, 45, 47, 76–77, 103, 138; National (1985), dir. Prowse, 26, 77, 79, 103, 136, 157 (n. 13); Royal Court (1971), dir. Gill, 42, 98, 99, 103, 139; Royal Exchange (1980/81), dir. Noble, 25, 26, 45, 77, 95, 138, 153; Shakespeare Memorial/Aldwych (1960), dir. McWhinnie, 4, 25, 41, 45, 47, 79, 89, 92, 97, 99, 103, 139, 157 (n. 15); Shakespeare Memorial (1971), dir. Williams, 25, 77, 91, 95, 98; Stratford Festival, Ontario (1971), dir. Gascon, 4–5, 92, 103

Eliot, T. S., xviii, 4
Ellis-Fermor, Una, xxii
Empson, William, 71, 75, 78, 84
Erasmus, Desiderius, xiv
Ewbank, Inga Stina [Ekeblad], xxi, 63, 124, 138, 139, 142, 149

Foil, 34, 56, 61, 77–78, 86, 111, 152

Forker, Charles, xxii, xxiii, 14, 17, 59, 62, 90, 136, 141
Forster, E. M., xiii, 56

Gill, Roma, xviii, 71
Glier, Ingeborg, 109
Goldman, Michael, xxv
Greg, W. W., 3, 62

Holmes, Martin, 4, 41
Hughes-Hallett, Lucy, 77

Jenkins, Harold, xix, xx, 2, 31, 33, 54
Johnson, Samuel, 25
Jones, Eldred, 59
Jones, Emrys, 131–32, 160

Kerr, Walter, 68
Kirsch, Arthur, xxi, 74

Lamb, Charles, xvii
Landau, Jack, 68, 119
Langer, Suzanne, xiii
Leech, Clifford, xix, 18, 77, 79–80
Levin, Richard, xviii, 51, 54, 55, 80
Lord, Joan, 138
Lucas, F. L., xviii, 33–34, 35, 56, 91, 115, 119

McCarthy, Mary, 93
McElroy, John, xx
McEwan, Geraldine: as Vittoria, 115
Mack, Maynard, xvi, xvii, 31, 80, 85, 134
McLuskie, Kathleen, 90
McWhinnie, Donald, 41, 79, 92
Madness: in *The White Devil*, 67–72, 121–23; in *The Duchess of Malfi*, 133–38

Masters, Anthony, 116
Melodrama, 8, 23, 74, 79, 100–101, 102, 120, 142, 145. *See also* Tragedy
Middleton, Thomas and William Rowley: *The Changeling*, 51
Mirren, Helen: as the Duchess, 26, 77
Mitchell, Ann: as Cornelia, 68
Moral vision: in *The Duchess of Malfi*, 48, 49–50, 77–80, 85, 88–89, 90–91, 92–93, 99–104, 133, 142–47, 152; Webster's condemned, xviii–xx; in *The White Devil*, 14, 17–18, 31–32, 39, 56, 62–76 *passim*, 111–12, 114, 115–17, 119–20, 125–26, 152. *See also* Tragedy
Morality play, 108, 129–30; *Everyman*, 140
Mulryne, J. R., xx
Murphy, Gerald: as Brachiano, 34–35

Noble, Adrian, 153
Nygh, Anna: as Vittoria, 115–16

Ornstein, Robert, xix, xx, 18, 67, 74

Painter, William: *The Palace of Pleasure*, 22, 78, 134, 135, 156 (n. 9)
Parfitt, Judy: as the Duchess, 139
Parody, 61, 78, 86, 113
Pearson, Jacqueline, xx, xxiii, 60, 77, 92, 96, 116, 138
Phillips, Sian: as Julia, 79
Poel, William, 26, 27–28, 76–77, 103
Potter, Lois, xxi–xxii, xxiii, 82, 92
Price, Hereward, xxi, 39, 40, 115

Prowse, Philip, 57, 79
Puttenham, George, xiv

Realism: vs. symbolism, 63, 67,
    128, 140–42, 153
Repetition: aesthetic functions of in
    Webster, 5, 8–9, 17, 19, 23–25,
    28, 29, 39, 51, 74–75, 90–91,
    105, 133, 146–47, 150–52, 153;
    frequency of in Webster, xxii–
    xxiii; and medieval drama, xvii;
    and Renaissance drama, xiv–xv,
    xviii, 1, 23, 29, 51, 131; and
    Renaissance rhetoric, xiv; as
    universal principle of art, xiii. *See
    also* Dramatic construction
Rhetoric: repetition in, xiv;
    influence on Renaissance drama,
    xiv–xv
Rorke, Mary: as the Duchess, 138
Rose, Mark, xv, 29, 114
Rylands, George, 22, 93

Schuman, Samuel, 59
Shakespeare, William, xv–xvii,
    xviii, 29, 109, 114, 158 (n. 6);
    influence on theatre, xxiv;
    oversimplification of by critics,
    xx, 155 (n. 6); *Antony and
    Cleopatra*, 12, 125; *Coriolanus*, 1,
    12; *Hamlet*, xx, 70, 111, 112,
    114, 131–32; *King Lear*, xx, 29,
    41, 51, 68, 70, 74, 112, 114;
    Othello, 1, 80, 81, 87; *Richard II*,
    112, 131; *Romeo and Juliet*, 47;
    Twelfth Night, 29; *The Winter's
    Tale*, 131. *See also* Webster,
    affinities with Shakespeare
Shirley, Frances, 148
Silence: in *The Duchess of Malfi*, 26,
    81, 100, 141; in *The White Devil*,
    3, 12, 36, 57, 61

Smith, A. J., 121, 152–53
Smith, James, 32, 33, 36
Spurling, Hilary, 115, 120
Subplot: aesthetic function in *The
    Duchess of Malfi*, 84–85, 88–89,
    90–91; aesthetic function in *The
    White Devil*, 61–62, 71–72, 74–
    76; in Renaissance drama, 51,
    54–55; Webster's ignored by
    critics, 51, 53–55
Symbolism. *See* Realism

Theatrical evidence: critical use of
    discussed, xxiv–xxv, 152
Thomson, Peter, xxiv, 71, 152
Tomlinson, Thomas Brian, 133
Tragedy: Aristotelian formula for,
    100–103; comedy used to
    heighten, 96–97; *de casibus*, 111–
    12; divided response to
    Webster's, xvii–xx; in *The Duchess
    of Malfi*, 27, 78–79, 88–89, 92–
    93, 95–97, 99, 100–104, 133,
    143, 145, 146–47; group, 74,
    143, 145; Revenge, xx, 2, 6–9,
    17, 31, 68–70, 74–75, 99, 102–
    3, 111–12, 114, 120, 132–33; in
    The White Devil, 17, 31, 67, 70,
    72, 74–76, 111–12, 120. *See also*
    Melodrama, Moral vision,
    Tragicomedy
Tragicomedy, xx–xxi, 92

Waage, Frederick O., 109
Ward, A. W., xvii
Wardle, Irving, 3, 30, 34, 37, 42,
    57, 63, 70–71, 92, 95, 115, 139,
    153
Warren, Roger, xxii
Webster, John: affinities with
    Shakespeare, xviii, xx, xxii, xxiv,
    1, 12, 29, 41, 63, 70, 74, 80, 81,

87, 109, 112, 114, 125, 131–32, 133, 143, 144, 150, 154; comments on own construction, xviii, 48, 131; differences from Shakespeare, 74, 101, 150; literary career, 148–49. See also *Devil's Law-Case*, *Duchess of Malfi*, Repetition, Tragedy, *White Devil*

Whigham, Frank, 42

White Devil, The: and *The Duchess of Malfi*, 2, 4–6, 13–14, 15–16, 30, 53, 55, 74, 76, 112, 117, 119, 125–26, 151–52; "split" structure of, 2–4, 8, 17, 109–10, 112, 113–14; structure of Act III of, 117–18; structure of Act V of, 52–55; Webster's use of sources in, 2, 4, 30, 53, 57, 113, 157 (n. 1)

Characters discussed: Brachiano, 9–16 *passim*, 33–39, 69–72, 108, 110–14, 116; Camillo, 106, 161 (n. 6); Cornelia, 58–59, 65–66, 67–68, 71–72, 106–7; Flamineo, 13–15, 62–75, 106–7, 120–26; Francisco, 6–9, 16–17, 59, 110–14; Gasparo and Antonelli, 30, 31–32, 35–38; Giovanni, 118–20; Isabella, 161 (n. 6); Lodovico, 30–39, 110, 111, 123–25; Marcello, 58–59, 63–64, 65–66; Monticelso, 7, 110, 115; Vittoria, 11–17, 61–62, 73–75,

107–8, 115–17; Zanche, 56–62, 73–75, 159 (n. 6)

Scenes discussed: I.i., 30–39; I.ii., 33–37, 59, 106–8, 159 (n. 5); II.i., xxiii, 7–8, 37–39; II.ii., 110–11; III.i., 117–18, 120–21; III.ii., 3–4, 57, 114–20; III.iii., 5, 64, 120–25; IV.i, 5–9; IV.ii., 3–4, 9–17; IV.iii., 4, 16; V.i., 58–60, 63–64, 65–66; V.ii., 62–63, 66–67, 68; V.iii., 60–61, 62, 65, 69–71, 72, 111, 113; V.iv., 67–69, 71–72; V.vi., 73–74

Stage productions discussed: Bristol Old Vic (1983), dir. Bannerman, 115–16; Cambridge (1920), 56; Greenwich (1984), dir. Prowse, 34–35, 57, 67–68, 119; National (1969), dir. Dunlop, 115, 117, 120; New Phoenix (1935), dir. Wade, 71; Old Vic (1976), dir. Lindsay-Hogg, 3, 30, 37, 63, 70–71; Phoenix Sideshow (1955), dir. Landau, 68; Renaissance, Scala (1925), dir. Craig, 35, 56, 115, 119; York Graduate (1983), dir. Smukler, 6–7, 57

Whittaker, Herbert, 92, 103

Williams, Michael: as Ferdinand, 95

Wilson, Thomas, xiv

Worsley, T. C., 89

Wright, Abraham, 18